THE
TIP OF THE SPEAR

'The Submarine Arm Is The Spearhead Of
The Royal Navy' *(Anon)*

Pamela Mitchell

Richard Netherwood Limited

This Book is Dedicated to the Memory of My Father.

B. L. Broadbent.

'Mr. Brian.'

'Pop'

Late Chairman of Thomas Broadbent & Sons Ltd.
who made four of the X Craft

This is a complete history of the British Midget Submarines during World War II. Told by the participants themselves with all the candour humour and understatement of ordinary people. The Author has undoubtedly put her heart and soul into collecting the material and making this a fascinating book.

First Published in 1993
by
Richard Netherwood Limited
Fulstone Barn
New Mill
Huddersfield
HD7 7DL

ISBN 1 872955 13 4

Cover Picture: Operation 'Source' by Johne Makin

Printed and bound in Slovenia by
Gorenjski tisk p.o.

Contents

BACKGROUND

Born in the 20's in the inland town of Huddersfield, West Yorkshire, Pamela Mitchell (nee Broadbent) was the eldest of three children. Her father was a Director of the family engineering firm Thomas Broadbent & Sons Ltd - a firm which was selected by the Admiralty at the beginning of World War II to manufacture Midget Submarines. Immediately on leaving school, in 1942, she volunteered for the WRNS, rose to rank of Leading Wren and served in Londonderry, Plymouth and Loch Fyne. Her interest in the sea and ships has continued undiminished ever since.

Shortly after the war she met and married Gordon Mitchell. He had been a career deck officer in the Merchant Navy before, during and after the war. On leaving the Service, he settled in Lymington and, for the rest of his life contrived an almost idyllic existence (for a natural sailor), of sailing all summer and working through the winter. Mr. Mitchell died in 1988 but, four years before his death, the couple had visited the R.N. Submarine Museum at Gosport and seen a restored Midget Submarine. Knowing that her father's firm had manufactured some of these little craft 40 years earlier, Pamela Mitchell started to make enquiries; a single advertisement in the Navy News elicited a dozen enthusiastic replies and a treasure-trove of stories. Here was one of war-time's most fascinating sagas just waiting to be written and here was an author uniquely qualified to write the inside story - from the commencement of manufacture, transport from an inland town to the sea, the heroism and daring of the crews, developing an entirely new form of warfare through to the post-war era and the subsequent pathos of the scrap-metal yard or heritage museum.

Chapter One
In The Beginning

At the beginning of the 39/45 war, two retired Submarine Commanders from World War I, went to the Admiralty with the design for a two/three man midget submarine. Construction commenced in July 1940 and a prototype was built in a small boatyard on the Hamble River at Bursledon. This became known as X3 because X1 had been a giant full-sized submarine and X2 a captured Italian midget submarine.

The basis was a conventional submarine in miniature with two large explosive charges which could be released, after the time fuses had been set from inside the boat. Fourteen limpet mines could also be carried. Or a combination of both weapons as at Operation STRUGGLE.

An escape compartment was designed to enable a diver to emerge from and re-enter the boat, when it was submerged, in order to cut nets or fix explosive charges. This was known as the Wet and Dry or W. and D. compartment. The motive power was Diesel engine on the surface (Main Engine or M.E.), and electric motor powered by batteries when submerged (Main Motor, M.M.).

The X Craft were designed to be towed long distances submerged and on the surface, by a conventional submarine. Or occasionally, as at D-Day, when they were towed half way across the Channel by surface ships, the men found it more comfortable to be towed submerged. When on the surface, they were at the mercy of every importunate wave.

Guy Rendel writes:-

My father Commander H. L. Rendel, was appointed by Sir Max Horton (then Admiral Submarines) to liaise on the construction and trials between the Admiralty, H.M. Dockyard Portsmouth, H.M.S. DOLPHIN the Submarine HQ, and the builders.

The trials of X3 commenced in March '42 and went on in the Hamble River and the Solent. The cover/disguise was a high speed motor boat, and a dummy top was used when the prototype was moored in the river on the surface, although nearly all the trials went on after dark. When not in use X3 was moored in an articulated pontoon in the Hamble, off the Varley Marine Works, Sarisbury Green. It was promptly christened the Art-wot-not. The first time they gingerly submerged in the Solent, the atmosphere in the boat must have been tense, for X3 went straight into the mud at the bottom in 30ft of water.

The Admiralty, prompted by my father, soon realised that this rather amateur approach to construction would not get results quickly enough. X4 had been built, for reasons of security, in three widely separate parts of the country; in Hull at Brighams & Cowan at Moody's yard in Burseldon and in Portsmouth Dockyard, where she was assembled, (a time-and-motion-study experts nightmare). It was decided that these craft could well be built in a good engineering works and then transported for trials to the West coast of Scotland.

In 1942, Vickers Armstrong of Barrow were given the contract to build the first six X Craft, but this was the time of huge allied warship losses in the Mediterranean and as Vickers already had the job of building most of the submarine replacements, they became overwhelmed with work.

In the same year, a senior naval officer called at Thomas Broadbent and Sons at Central Ironworks. He wanted midget submarines built inland, under conditions of the utmost secrecy. The result of this visit was that a group of firms was formed under the chairmanship of Mr. W. Hallitt, General Manager and a Director of Broadbent's, with Broadbent's as the Leader Firm.

Three firms were chosen in all:- Broadbent's of Huddersfield, Markham's of Chesterfield and Marshall's of Gainsborough. My father moved to Yorkshire to liaise on the whole project. The urgency was piled on by the Admiralty, as they eagerly wanted to get at the TIRPITZ, holed-up in a Norwegian fjord and an ever-present danger to allied shipping especially the Russian convoys.

A Sketch of X3 at speed, drawn by Donald Cameron

The three firms worked in the closest harmony and competition. Special bays were erected in the Works and sealed off, with everyone directly or indirectly concerned operating under the Official Secrets Act.

Although the Admiralty had already constructed the prototypes X3 and X4, and Vickers Armstrong were building X5 - X10, the whole saga of the X Craft in a Northern Industrial context started one afternoon in May 1942. Thomas Broadbent & Sons Ltd was a well-established engineering manufacturing Company in Huddersfield in the West Riding of Yorkshire. The General Manager, Bill Hallitt was sitting at his desk when the telephone rang. A curt voice on the other end of the phone said 'The Admiralty here, we are considering asking your Company to manufacture some special equipment, and we would like you to come down to London tomorrow to discuss matters; we are arranging to meet you at Kings Cross station at 11 o'clock'.

Everything was in a hurry in those days. It so happened that Bill Hallitt had a very busy schedule the next day, so he called his Chief Design Engineer, Frank Couch, and asked him to catch the breakfast train to London, where he would be met by a representative of the Admiralty. He said ''it's probably something and nothing, but we have to keep in with these chaps''.

Frank duly arrived in London. After suitable identification formalities, he was escorted to an official car, which had been adapted so that the rear seat passenger was unable to see out. After a fairly lengthy journey the car stopped and Frank emerged to find that he was at a Naval establishment 'somewhere in Britain'. He was immediately taken to meet the 'high-ups' who took him into a large shed, in which was Britain's first midget submarine, built as a prototype by Varley Marine. Without further ado, Frank was asked outright if he thought that Broadbent's could manufacture submarines to this design in their Huddersfield factory. Frank asked for 'half an hour to look round' and then gave an emphatic 'Yes'. Within another half an hour he was back in the blacked-out car being returned to Kings Cross station.

In Huddersfield the same evening, Frank rang up Bill Hallitt (known throughout the Works as W.H.) to say that his visit had been 'hush-hush' and he couldn't say anything over the phone but would be round in 20 minutes. W.H. was even more enthusiastic than Frank and the matter was discussed well into the night. The irony of the blacked-out car caused much hilarity because Frank had spotted, at the naval establishment, a motorised bogey platform, used for observing the performance of ship's hulls in a long tank of water, made and installed there by Broadbent's in 1934!

The Admiralty could not have picked a better team. Both W.H. and Frank were brilliant practical engineers. W.H. had completed the conceptual designs of machines as diverse as heavy bridge lifting gear, steelworks furnace loading machines, a jointed electric locomotive for use in underground mines and a spring-suspended centrifuge, the forerunner of many of today's domestic washing machines. It used to be said of W.H. that he could look at an engineering drawing and, within minutes, say which part would break first. Frank, on the other hand, was the person responsible for translating these design concepts into reality.

Since 1939, Broadbent's had been run by the duo of Brian Broadbent and Bill Hallitt, who were first cousins. It was an excellent combination which lasted a further 30 years before being handed over to the next generation. As soon as it became known that two more firms, Marshall's of Gainsborough and Markham's of Chester-field had also been selected by the Admiralty, who believed that inland firms where less likely to be bombed, Brian Broadbent realised the folly of three separate engineering firms all trying to do the same thing and solve the same problems. He brought all three firms together, then persuaded the Admiralty that, although all three would assemble complete submarines, each firm would also specialise in the design and manufacture of selected parts. For instance, Broadbent's made all the conning domes with their periscope assemblies, whilst Markham's made all the bow cones and stern cones.

Construction called for detailed engineering of the highest order combined with conventional 'boiler yard' techniques. A few precision engineering firms were involved but most of the specialised equipment was made by the three firms concerned, to a unique and non-standard specification. The large crescent-shaped explosive charges, or side cargoes, were made at Staveley and filled at the Royal Ordnance Factory.

Some of Broadbent's workpeople record their war-time experiences with pleasure. Nowadays young women think it's something new to want to do a man's job. In war-time it was commonplace and many a keen young girl was waiting to step into a man's shoes.

The overhead crane driver at Broadbent's at this time, was an attractive young woman Doris Wright who says:-

We wore boiler suits in Winter over our slacks and light-coloured bib-and-brace overalls in Summer. Quite sexy they were too! We didn't wear anything over our hair. We had to wear slacks because of climbing the wall-mounted vertical steel ladder that led 25 foot up to the overhead crane. Standing for 12½ hour shifts five days a week (only eight hours on Saturday) in a little carriage/cradle that went from side to side, on a giant girder/crane that went forwards and backwards. Like patting one's head and rubbing one's chest with a circular motion at the same time.

In 1942 at the age of 22 I was employed by Thomas Broadbent's in the X Department. These turned out to be the happiest years of my working life. We worked hard and played hard in those days but it was all worthwhile and very rewarding to watch the wonderful subs taking shape.

When the subs were having the final tests, the Navy officers who were going to sail them came down to make sure everything was up to expectation. They were all young men and mad as hatters. They had to be to take on a job like this.

When everything was passed by the Navy crew we worked through Saturday night from midnight and lifted the sub on to a conveyor inch by inch. A special lifting beam had been constructed in the shape of a cross, to ensure that the sub remained level. Remember this was the first time that a submarine of any kind had been built in the middle of the Pennine range of hills, in the history of mankind.

Finally the sub was in position and sheeted up to look like a coastal motor boat (for security reasons). It was taken to the railway sidings close by in the early hours of Sunday morning.

Perhaps the most outstanding feature of the whole project was that total security was achieved. Until the news broke that the X Craft had seriously damaged the TIRPITZ in late 1943. A great credit to management and workforce.

In fact the writer's brother, Peter Broadbent, who was then an apprentice with the firm and later Chairman, recalls that something very hush-hush was going on at this time, but he had no idea what it was until several years after the war. A high

Construction

A Sketch of the partitioned off workshop at Broadbents of Huddersfield, where admittance was restricted to staff actually working on the X Craft project. Doris Wright the crane driver, top left, has a bird's eye view of the proceedings.

wall separated the X Craft department from the rest of the works.

Frank Butler of Broadbent's spent the whole of his working life with the same firm. In mid-1943 when the X Craft were being built he was working long hours on this most taxing challenge.

Frank Butler:-

I was married on Boxing Day 1942. I cannot recall just when in 1943 I was asked to work in the X Dept. However, I hadn't been in there long when Ernest Shore came over to speak to me. You can imagine my surprise when his opening words were:-'Have you started turning your back on it yet Frank?' My first reaction was, what's the silly old buffer rambling on about. I soon got the gist of things when his next words were:- 'I would like you to start working nights from Next Monday'.

Some time later when I was about to commence welding the W. and D. compartment for the first sub (X20), he came up to me and said 'I'll bet you a shilling you can't weld up this chamber without a leak'.

This wasn't an easy task as it was welded as a sub-assembly before being built into the remainder of the centre section. Not a pleasant job, as much of the welding was inside relatively sealed compartments, whose plates had been painted with bitumen, leaving a band 1" to 1½" free from paint where the welding was undertaken. So, you had the discomfort of a small sealed chamber, with welding fumes made more obnoxious by the addition of melting bitumen.

I thought to myself, I'll show him whether it will leak. When the work was complete and put on test, there was one minute pinhole in a corner. Needless to say, I never saw that shilling.

There was a character whom we called 'Wally'. His forte was to commence work one day, carry on all night and the following day, before staggering home.

However, he came to me one day with several pieces of 1/8" thick plate and he wanted them welded together to make a metal box. This I did for him and asked what they were for and where they fitted into the sub. 'Sub'? said Wally, 'these aren't for t'subs. I'm putting me money in here and I'm digging a deep hole in't garden and burying it! Might even still be there.

Came the time when the accumulators had to be fitted into the first forward section. Suppliers entrusted with this job, came to Broadbent's with the batteries which they then commenced to fit. After fitting. They were put on charge and only when charging was completed was their mission accomplished. The time taken was usually the day and night and the following day.

This cycle of operations had been complete when my friend George Mellor was setting up his welding equipment (electric arc) to the said forward section.

One of the battery workers said to him:- 'What are you going to do in there'? George replies:- 'Weld one or two brackets on for the fitters'. Battery man:- 'Give me enough time to get well clear afore you start. Because there's going to be an almighty bang'. Moral of that tale:- No naked lights for at least 24 hours after completion of charging.

Squire Jones recalls being asked to work a regular night shift too:-

We actually worked six 12 hour shifts. 7.30pm to 7.30am for two years. Saturday nights being the only one we had off.

I remember one Saturday night prior to the X Craft's departure. We had been working all day, putting the final touches to the sub, mainly at the request of the crew. I think the skipper was 'Terry' the South African (Lt. J. V. Terry-Lloyd S.A.N.F.V. (South African Naval Force Volunteer)) and during the evening, he said how hard we had worked and he wanted to take us to the nearest pub for a drink. I shall never forget the look on the barman's face when this young naval officer went up to the bar and asked for twenty-plus pints.

The writer is more indebted to Geoff Crowe than she can ever express. Ever since

1984 he has been doggedly pursuing lines of enquiry, sifting through old papers and photographs, writing voluminous letters to all and sundry, answering silly questions and generally being invaluable.

Commencing at Broadbent's as a 15 year old lad in 1939 he was first employed, as an office boy, then as an apprentice in the workshop. He was called up in 1946 and joined the submarine ALCIDE as an E.R.A. 4th class. He left the Navy in 1948 as a Petty Officer and returned to Broadbents. He finished up as Manager in the Quality Control Shop.

Geoff Crowe:-

Immediately aft of the control room side of the W. and D. bulkhead, was a bilge acting as collection point for various drains. The outboard induction valve was overhead and slightly to port at this point and the rather large bronze 4-spoked handwheel had been removed (to stop heads continually being knocked against it) and was lying in store in the said bilge. Things were in a pretty advanced stage, valves pressure-tested, as also were the manifolds etc.

It came to pass that when the valve handwheel had to be fitted, it could not be removed from the bilge. It was neatly pinned between the spokes by a manifold drain pipe. This required the manifold to be dismantled to remove the offending pipe (it was a very neat fit).

The wrath of the plumber/pipefitter was terrible to hear, when he had to break his beloved joints in order to retrieve the handwheel.

Complete Leak Testing of Pressure Hull

The procedure for ensuring the hull and apertures were watertight before launching, was to pressurise the hull internally to 30lbs per square inch and apply to all joints and flanges a solution of soft soap suds, to observe any bubbles forming. Preparations had been made on Sunday for the test procedure on X21 and the compressor finally began to pump in the air.

As time went on, it was thought that the time was getting overlong, indicating a major leak, but none apparent. The target pressure of 30lbs p.s.i. was finally reached. Then someone thought they saw slight movement of the 7 ton weights on the W. and D. hatch.

Reason began to take over (long time to reach pressure, no apparent leak) and quickly a substitute pressure gauge was sought and fastened to the hull connections. Fairly swift movements followed, releasing of exhaust flanges etc. as the replacement gauge registered 58 lbs p.s.i. This was the equivalent of an upward force on the hatches of approximately 12 tons.

Further Hull Test Incident

Preliminary pressure test to check security of hatch locking dogs to 5lb p.s.i. (no dead weights to contain upward force on hatches). The test was complete and pressure was releasing. Ernest Shore 'Von Bock' (so called because he was rather authoritarian) was adjacent to the pressure valve and he signalled zero pressure, so the hatches could be opened.

Geoff Shaw was standing on top of the after control room hatch and was about to kick the operating release lever ... when a voice behind said quietly 'Get off Geoff' the Voice of Experience.

Geoff Shaw:-

As I moved to the side and was standing down on the summit of the pressure hull, I touched the operating lever with my knuckle. The lever moved to Open position without any further assistance. The hatch lifted suddenly crashing back on the stops, violently shaking the whole structure. A huge guff of air mixed with dust, old cigarette packets etc. shot out. The hatch then as quickly slammed down shut again, and again opened violently on to the stops. Probably all this took place in about one second.

I often ponder just where I could have landed that day. One thing is for certain, I wouldn't be writing about it today.

Hydrostatic Testing of Fuel and Buoyancy Tanks

After completion of welding, these tanks were subjected to a leak test, being pressurised with water to 200lb p.s.i. The senior fabrication foreman, 'Von Bock', had become a trifle obsessed with leaks from welded joints, even small pin holes, to such an extent that he assumed another name of 'Professor Leak'.

Each time a craft was in the completion stages, its captain and crew came to Huddersfield, or Chesterfield or Gainsborough and the craft and the men 'grew up together' whilst the myriad valves, switches, levers, gauges, basket wheels, precision instruments and perfected pumps; were being installed. Probably nobody ever counted how many there were, but people who spent hundreds of hours inside the vessels, guess these ranged from 200 to 350. All these were connected, of course, to pipes, wiring, shafts and spindles. So that the inside of the complete craft had to be a marvel of skill in packing, in order to leave room for the crew.

S/Lt Alan Wilkie formerly of Helensburgh, who was a frequent visitor to Huddersfield in 1943 writes:-

We were flattered to be asked our opinion on where certain fixtures should go. They seemed to know so much more about our X Craft than we, who were to operate them, did.

From a later article in the 'Huddersfield Examiner':-

People who have never seen the inside of a 50ft miniature submarine, will have difficulty in believing what the working conditions were like. The completion stages of one such craft, present a seeming contradiction in terms. There will be a list of jobs to do which may start with:-

> *Fit extra clip to trim line aft.*
> *Adjust seat of No. 1 main ballast valve*
> *Correct needle on helm indicator*
> *Fit tally labels to spit cocks which show when tanks are filled*
> *Make handle on food locker so that it cannot rattle*
> *Replace Mk VI 1a grub screw dropped in bilges*

and have anything up to a hundred items on it. There were twenty men waiting to have a go, each with a few items to attend to.

The only way into the vessel is through two small hatches, which only a contortionist or a very fit young man could negotiate. Providing there isn't a joiner laying corticine (lino) where he wants to put his foot, or wet paint where he proposes placing his hand or recently-sprayed cork where his head is going to be jammed. To say nothing of a chap with an electric welding set, making things very hot in the neighbourhood of a small steel bracket.

The Operation crew of X21 standing on their X Craft just before launching. Left to Right: S/Lt. H. Stern, S/Lt. A. Renouf, ERA Fred Stanton and Lt. J. Terry-Lloyd. (C.O.)

The inside, is hot, stuffy and smelly in spite of ventilation fans. It reeks of oil, electric welding fumes and the funny smells that electricians make with hot insulating compounds.

First he must wriggle into a position lying flat on his back which will cause cramp within two minutes.

Contending with festoons of wiring, he must do some rather accurate work. He must ignore things like the plumber's blow lamp which may easily be scorching the seat of his trousers, or the boot of the joiner who is trying to fix the brand new ship's crest on the bulkhead. Or the ten or a dozen craftsmen with their tackle, who are becoming impatient and blasphemous within a few feet of him.

It was always a very weary yet proud bunch of men, who saw the finished craft handed over to the Navy in complete going order. Even the fresh water in the tanks was topped-up and ready for drinking, or at least boiling for tea.

None of the workmen will forget their feelings when they saw the captain and crew standing on the superstructure and heard the C.O. modestly but sincerely thank them for the ship.

Robert Barclay, the then Managing Director of Markhams, recalls one poignant incident at this time. In the now-deserted bay, when the men had all gone home to snatch a few hours sleep before the Sunday morning's junketing, Cdr. Rendel requested five minutes private meditation, down below and Herbert Stone, a Markhams executive accompanied him.

No doubt they fondly fingered one or two valves, thinking on the 'blood and sweat' if not 'tears' that had gone into her construction and dwelling on what her future would be.

Rendel sat in the C.O.'s position and Stone in the First Lieutenant's, in complete silence for fully five minutes.

Herbert Stone:-

For my part, as I looked round the spotlessly clean interior with the lights shining on the instruments and the burnished brasswork and felt that if I ever saw a better job than this, I should be a lucky man.

In conclusion, Mr. Barclay recollects:-

I had a pretty good idea what Rendel's thoughts were when he was down below there, but I didn't dare interrupt him, to ask him to say an Amen for me too.

The Little Ship Builders Litany

O HAUGHTY and everchanging Admiralty, ruler of all our trades and knowing none.

Have mercy upon us miserable engineers.

REMEMBER not, Lords, our frenzied figures, nor the offences of our auditors; neither take thou vengeance upon us for the sins of not understanding thy manifold commandments : spare us, good Lords, spare thy people whom thou hast distracted with thy orders, and be not angry with us in our confusion.

Spare us, good Lords.

FROM all signals and requirements; from the crafts and wiles of your technicians; from all explanatory memorandum and from everlasting damnation.

Good Lords, deliver us.

FROM all impossible specifications; from W.P.S. Inspectors, A.E.O. Inspectors and Costing Investigators; from misunderstandings, suspicions and all uncharitableness.

Good Lords, deliver us.

FROM headaches and heartaches; and from exasperation and bewilderment and murderous thought.

Good Lords, deliver us.

FROM D.N.E. and their equipment lists; from D.N.C., D.E.E., their dockets, amendments and cancellations.

Good Lords, deliver us.

FROM all inertia, indecision and suspensions; from all delays, procrastinations and hiatus; from the sanctity of thy files, and contempt of thy Word and Commandment.

Good Lords, deliver us.

WE engineers do beseech thee to hear us, O Lords, and that it may please thee to rule and govern us in the right way and to strengthen us and keep us sane and solvent.

We beseech thee to hear us, Good Lords.

Chapter Two
A Launching And It's Aftermath

It was decided that the official launching of the first two vessels X20 and X22, which had arrived on the same train at Faslane, should be performed by the two young ladies most closely associated with the secret work at the two firms. In this case Marjorie Warwick of Broadbents and Marion Ford of Markhams

From:- Marjorie Warwick of Broadbents:-

At the invitation of the Admiralty I launched the first X Craft Submarine built at Thomas Broadbent & Sons Ltd, Huddersfield; H.M.S. EXEMPLAR X20.

At that time it was on the secret list, and it was many years before we were able to divulge to our own local press the happenings during that period. It was a wonderful occasion, 1st November 1943, to see our little craft take to the water at Faslane, where I performed the christening ceremony. I must confess my heart was in my mouth, hoping against hope there would be no mishap, such as her going to the bottom when she should not have submerged.

It was a happy day for all of us after long working hours and anxieties. It was a great moment to successfully crack the bottle of champagne against X20's bows I believe mine was the only boat to be launched with the real thing later ones had 'plonk'. The E.R.A. stepped forward smartly brought back and presented to me the remains of the bottle, decorated in red, white and blue ribbons, which I still have with other X Craft treasures.

I have many happy memories of that day, with the welcome and hospitality extended to us by Captain Banks and his wife, together with his officers and WRNS officers. We travelled in reserved compartments labelled 'Naval Civilians' (at times run into sidings to make way for trains carrying Service personnel).

I know EXEMPLAR played her part magnificently, and as her skipper, Lt Hudspeth, wrote and told me later:- 'She has won her wings, or fins, or whatever else good little mer-angels earn' Ken had designed her crest. He had added wings and a halo turning a 'Mermaid' into a 'Mer-Angel'. Alas, this was the one and only vessel I launched (although I was present at a similar second christening) so it was no good thinking she might be the first of 1000. My beauty fell short of Helen of Troy's!

Seriously, I am still proud to have been able to launch our little ship with the words 'I name this ship EXEMPLAR, may God Bless her and all who sail in her'.

They accompanied a favoured group of representatives on the train up to Faslane. This was a joyful and almost carefree time, for all the hard work was (temporarily) behind them.

Mr. Barclay recalls how each firm supplied a hamper full of goodies including a plentiful supply of beer. When this ran out the railway people and the R.N., who had all been caught up in the party mood, would obligingly stop the train as near as possible to the local pub.

He regularly travelled with the special train and recalls one incident when the beer ran out prematurely:- 'The day being hot, the train had not gone far before the crew urged Sam (Sam Brocksopp was the Charge-hand Fitter at Markhams) to broach the beer and he yielded to pressure. Submariners are a thirsty lot!

As usually happens in these cases, one bottle followed another and presumably a good time was had by all, until, the Border being crossed, Mr. Barclay who had been travelling in another compartment, put his head round the door. Now Sam, what about that beer? The luckless Sam had to confess that the supply had dried up long ago. Mr. Barclay's comments are not available!

On another occasion after the war, the beer lasted somewhat longer, long enough to render the engine driver incapable of driving the train. In high glee, the craft's crew had to take over in the cab of the steam train 'but the driver wasn't keeping a good look-out anyway'! Perhaps it was the same occasion when the train became 'driverless', that it was discovered that it was also 'guardless'. Consternation reigned, for it is apparently very important to have a guard bringing up the rear, however little he seems to have to do. Anyway, search parties went out and the unfortunate guard was eventually found, meandering along the track in an inebriated condition, thinking he was going home.

On arrival, a stirring sight greeted the Launching Party. The two submarines, stripped of their camouflage, lay on the dockside under a heavy crane ready to be lowered into the water. A Naval Guard of Honour was drawn up alongside and as the two ladies were escorted to the dock, sharp commands rang out, the guard sprang to attention and the officers to the salute. The two vessels were launched in alphabetical order, diplomatically! As the crane gently lowered X22 Marion spoke the traditional words:- 'I name this ship EXPLOIT X22. May God bless her and all who sail in her'. She broke the bottle over the bows and Markham's first midget submarine became waterborne. Her diesel engine started at once and away she went out into the sea-loch.

To round off this moving little ceremony, the Navy gave an official launch party aboard the depot ship anchored in the Firth of Clyde. The Captain presenting tiny stainless steel submarine brooches and submariners' cap tallies embroidered in gold thread, to the two young ladies. Which cherished possessions, of course, they still retain.

On another occasion at a launching of a Markham's midget, when placed in the water, there seemed to be so little of its showing above the water compared to what was submerged beneath it, the 2 ft freeboard continued to disappear too. Someone had left the Kingston valves open and the craft was sinking before their eyes! A hasty shout down the raised induction, Sam acted quickly. The Kingston's were shut and the craft came back up to her marks. Robert Barclay grinned with relief. He'd had a bad moment, on seeing £30,000 worth of his Pride and Joy disappearing at his feet.

Submerging in the correct way appealed to the small boy in both Robert Barclay and Bill Hallitt. They were determined to go for a trip and take their own medicine, which was duly arranged by the redoubtable Cdr. Rendel and Captain Banks. Mr. Barclay remembers this outing as vividly as if it happened last month.:-

One day Bill and I arrived at the Kyles of Bute Hydro (H.M.S. VARBEL) at

Port Bannatyne. The next day we travelled up to the head of Loch Striven, Glen Striven Lodge (VARBEL II) and were given an X Craft. The skippers were told to do as we asked, providing that safety was not endangered. So off we went. Bill with John Lorimer and me with another chap whose name I forget.

After cruising around for a bit, diving to periscope depth and trying out the stern optical thing which they had, I asked my chap how deep we could go and he said '100ft' I think. So I said 'Let's do that' and got a kind of old fashioned look. 'Do you really mean that Mr. Barclay? 'Yes' I said 'it's alright isn't it'? 'Oh yes, it's alright. Very well'

Loch Glencoul with Stack of Glencoul behind. Magnetic detector loop instrument hut and transit poles can also be seen. 22nd March 1944.

So down we went. Down and down. Presently, all the little holes, all the grease nipples for the periscope etc., and there were quite a lot, began to piddle at us distinctly vigorously. I cannot really describe it any other way for we were all getting quite wet.

So after a few minutes I said 'Let's go up again'. Honour had been satisfied. I suppose our trip lasted about half to three quarters of an hour. I remember it well.

Sam Brocksopp accompanied each vessel on its journey up to Scotland representing Markham's throughout the acceptance trials, and went to sea on many occasions.

He recalls steering X22 EXPLOIT on her first voyage from Faslane to the base at Rothesay. The following day he went down with her on her first diving trials to a depth of 100ft., when she made so much water through various joints, seals, lubricators etc. that emergency pumping had to be resorted to, in order to regain control. Sam learned a lot from this rather hair-raising experience, which was to help him when fitting out subsequent craft.

Another reminiscence is of sitting, in search of fresh air, on the casing of another of our midget submarines (much of the foregoing is taken from an excellent booklet called just 'Markham Submarines'). She was proceeding on the surface at 8 knots down the Firth of Clyde, and passed close to the Cunarder QUEEN MARY loaded with thousands of troops, who lined the rails and gave Sam a tremendous cheer. It must have appeared to them from the great height of deck level, that Sam was being conveyed down the Clyde at immoderate speed by an invisible vessel, whilst sitting in the water!

These were modest exploits compared to what the young future crews would undergo. They took their lives in their hands every time they set out on an operation, and even on work-ups. As the skilled, incredibly hard working and modest engineers were always the first to acknowledge.

A pre-war picture of the Kyles of Bute Hydro, taken over by the Navy during the war and renamed H. M. S. VARBEL 1. The happy headquarters of the Twelfth Submarine Flotilla.

Chapter Three
The Ladies

The Visual Signaller Wrens had had a signal tower especially constructed for them on the roof of the Hydro.

Ivor Jarvis:

From this vantage point, one had a superb view across Kames Bay to the Cowal Hills and the entrance to Loch Striven. Some of us being friendly with these delightful W.R.N.S. spent many off-duty hours assisting, or more likely distracting these young ladies, as they kept in touch with X Craft five, six and more miles to the north, by signal lamp.

The two bases VARBEL I and II were linked by daily trawler, SOLSTICE by name. It was a delightful, relaxed, scenic run of some eleven miles up the loch from Port Bannatyne to Striven Head where there is now a power station of course.

The experiences of Wren Dorothy Wallace (now Mrs Peter Kern) are recalled by her husband:

As well as keeping watch and watch about on her signalling duties, she had to give signalling instruction to the young Midshipmen joining the X Craft. As they had all been passed out as officers, after a very brief and concentrated training at H.M.S. KING ALFRED at Hove, their standard of signalling left much to be desired.

On one occasion she was required to join in an X Craft training exercise and act as liaison signal officer on the trawler BENACHIE, which formed one of Captain S/m 12's miscellaneous support training fleet. In those days it was quite unheard of for Wrens to sleep aboard the Navy's small ships, so Wren Wallace had to be put ashore at the nearest Wrennery at the end of each day's training and be collected again the next morning.

The programme ended on an afternoon when the Clyde was experiencing one of its worst gales for many years. As she came into Kames Bay, the BENACHIE was ordered from base to secure to a buoy for the night, rather than risk damaging the Kames Bay pier by coming alongside, to land the midget submariners who were on board. That was until it was realised there was a Wren aboard, when countermanding orders were immediately given, insisting that Wren Wallace should be disembarked at the pier straight away. It was a hazardous undertaking for her, in view of the very heavy sea that was running into the bay. But with her heart in her mouth and prompted by several shouts of 'Jump now' from the midget submariners, she safely made it ashore.

It was quite possibly the same 'Clyde Stinker' which Jessie Wilson remembers so clearly:

The craft were being torn from their moorings and it became necessary for men to stand by them throughout the night. One of the ratings was washed into the loch and was in danger of drowning, until a Wren M.T. driver dived in and brought him out. She was certainly the heroine of the hour.

Although Hazel Lloyd-Jones denies that the M.T. drivers were the elite of the

Service, they seemed to be to the rest of the Wrens. She writes:

There were four M.T. drivers at VARBEL on 24-hr watches, starting at midday. Sometimes we were sent to the distant VARBEL II on the M.V. BENACHIE. At other times we were required to drive through the mountains to Dunoon for mail. A marvelously scenic route but one couldn't afford to take one's eyes off the road to marvel at it. Also to deliver the Top Secret crates and passengers to either Ardmaliesh Point, the Hydro or else straight to Port Bannantyne pier. V.I.P.'s arrived by seaplane.

I got my 10 ton lorry license in Gourock, which enabled me to carry live ammunition. Thereby hangs a tale: One freezing day I had to drive the lorry up that notoriously steep and twisting drive to the Hydro, with live ammo. and flying the red flag to denote the fact. It took me nearly an hour to do so, tacking up inch by inch, as sailors threw sacks and ashes on the compacted snow and ice. It was quite hair-raising and I did not realise how much so, until my lorry and I arrived safely at the top, to somewhat unexpected applause from people who had been watching.

We did maintain our own transport but we had a most helpful Marine called 'Mac' who used to come to our rescue very often. He was a super person, looked rather like George Formby and was marvellous to all us M.T.'s.

Of course we drove the staff car as well, usually with the Captain and senior officers and sometimes with their 'Wives and Sweethearts' too, (the famous toast 'to our wives and sweethearts, may they never meet').

I remember the casualties that we took to hospital when the crews returned from operations. Especially the unfortunate E.R.A. Ken Petty, the long sleeve of whose submarine jersey had become caught in the revolving engine shaft aboard the X Craft, which took his arm with it. After the C.O. had severed the few remaining shreds of skin with a dinner knife, he was rowed ashore, quite conscious by the Torpedoman Elijah Whittaker. His arm followed in a cardboard box.

So many people we met and liked. Many lasting relationships were formed and still survive to this day but then we were not Naughty Girls. The one or two 'Pink Ladies' amongst us seemed very shocking. Pink Ladies? Not 'Scarlet Women' just Pink Ladies.

Many times I have said to our young people that I had a very happy time during my war service. They are appalled. How could I say I enjoyed myself? I did not enjoy the war but I did enjoy my Service life. It was only a continuation of boarding school after all, the uniform and obeying rules. Even the smells were the same and being forbidden to use the grand staircase.

The young people were fun and friendly and the older sailors, the 2 and 3 badgers were marvelously helpful to us when were new to our jobs. They tolerated us very well in a male-dominated society and we were, and still are very grateful to them.

The writer must digress here and add her own rider to the above sentiments told quite independently by Lily Robs, endorsed by Angela Cooper and stressed by Hazel. Although she sometimes worked cheek by jowl with an Able Seaman in the bowels of corvettes and sloops; if his oppo accidentally hammered his thumb, he would put a warning finger to lips, point and say: 'Shush, WREN'! That's the way it was and that's the way they all were. I daresay they were 'ad libbing', 'effing' and 'beeing' continually in our absence but never, that I can recall, in our presence. Which is remarkable when you compare it with today.

Although Wren Angela Cooper was 'la creme de la creme' in her category of Boats Crew, her duties were arduous in the extreme, especially in Winter with biting force 8 winds, once even force 9, and freezing sleet ruining the complexion. Oh those short steep esturial seas with wind against tide.

Wherever they were required to go they generally transported the top brass, across to Loch Striven and Ardtaraig (VARBEL II) but sometimes they delivered cargo and people to Largs or Wemyss Bay. It was quite an adventure to cross the Firth of Clyde on a blustery day. Once they had a brush with the QUEEN ELIZABETH I. She was steaming majestically down the Clyde, but they cannot have realised her speed for they were nearly swamped in her mighty wash.

Boats Crew Wrens performed the correct boat drill with vertical oars when coming alongside the depot ships H.M.S. BONAVENTURE and TITANIA. They also did what must have been outside most Wrens' experience such as all the mucky maintenance on the engine.

Although Joyce MacDougall and her friend remember being taken over an X Craft by an unnamed officer, just before the base broke up and Stan Johnson recalls showing his wife round one in secret and after the day's work-ups, it didn't take too long! It was Angela who must have been the only Wren ever to have steered an X Craft.

A Midshipman friend of hers badly wanted to get out to the trot and as his First Lieutenant hadn't turned up, he asked Angela if she would take the 'Jimmy's' place on the controls, whilst he navigated the craft from the casing. She descended gingerly through the control room hatch and, with hands nervously gripping the wheel and eyes glued to the black pointer on the dial (for ship's heading), she correctly repeated the Mid.'s orders and they arrived at the trot without mishap. It wasn't very far and of course they didn't submerge, but she was so thrilled by the experience that she was still bubbling over with it, 42 years later.

Another member of the boats crew seems to have been one of those rare human beings with a permanently sunny disposition. Bill Morrison, one of the XE heroes recalls, in his marvelously soft lilting brogue:

The wee Scottish lassie who never lost her smile for the whole of the war. However long the hours they had to work (and keep the boyfriend waiting!), however cold, wet, miserable and stormy the conditions, she always came up smiling. Attagirl. I hope she featured in the film that Angela helped to make for the Russians, 'English Women at War'.

But the Good Life was drawing to a close and the turmoil of the weeks preceding VE Day was matched by the very mixed feelings that we all had at that time. 'Varbellians' felt it most keenly because their beloved Hydro was closing down.

Some would spend the rest of their lives searching for the camaraderie they had just enjoyed, but for them all it was a time of uncertainty, doubt and sadness. Yes of course they were glad the war was ending and that the few surviving P.O.W.'s in Japanese hands would be released, and some of the boys had jobs to return to, even if they had no wish to go back to them. But for the unmarried Wrens and a lot of the men, Life after VARBEL was a complete vacuum. They would not see 'light at the end of the tunnel' or regain their sense of purpose for several years to come.

For as one Wren wrote, nostalgically, in a 1948 'Dittybox': 'I do so miss the friendliness which comes when people wear the same uniform'.

But for the more opportunistic ones there were 'opportunities' during the closing days of VARBEL I.

Lt. J. McCaughan R.N.R:

I was told that an officer already drafted elsewhere had left his motorbike at Loch Striven Head. I took XE9 up there strapped the bike to the induction pipe and, without being seen got it landed at the slipway. It was loaded as part of the stores Portsmouth bound. We used the bike untaxed and uninsured in and around Gosport. It proved very useful and we were never asked to prove ownership.

Nevertheless the watchkeeper Joyce's VE Day (May 8) began prosaically enough, with her scrubbing out the S.D.O. office with her stockings rolled down. When the laconic signal arrived, ''Hostilities will cease as from midnight'', she duly presented it, to an Admiral clad in dressing gown and slippers.

Jessie enjoyed herself on VE Day:

It was long celebration and the Captain called for 'Splice the Mainbrace'. Which entitled the men to double tots and the Wrens to half a tot, so we may have been the only Wrens to be given that privilege, officially.

With only a week before the final paying-off it was a very busy time, packing up of stores etc. and it was a very sad day when the ferry sailed from Rothesay for the last time. I had had a last walk round the now empty Hydro, thinking of all the happy times and friendships made. The Breton fisherman's prayer sprang to mind then, for it summed up the spirit of the X Craft teams, so beautifully: 'Dear God Be Good to Me' Now that peace has broken out upon uncharted seas.

Chapter Four
H.M.S. VARBEL

Whilst all this was happening, H.M.S. VARBEL, the training headquarters building at Port Bannantyne in Scotland had twice been sent to the bottom by Dr. Goebbels, Nazi Germany's ace propagandist in WWII The building was still standing in 1990, albeit roofless and floorless. For Dr. Goebbels was more eloquent at propaganda than the truth and H.M.S. VARBEL was a shore establishment or 'stone frigate', incapable of being torpedoed.

Petty Officer Jessie Wilson recalls her time aboard VARBEL:-

I wish I could convey to you the atmosphere of VARBEL I, the Kyles of Bute Hydropathic Hotel, during the two and a half years of its commission, 1942-1945. Men and women were accommodated in the Hydro and it gave one the feeling of working together and seeing familiar friendly faces day after day. It does not take much to evoke memories of VARBEL for me and I can say that unfashionable though it may sound today 'I had a lovely war'. 'By that I know you will understand that I was very happy and have some lasting memories'. However cosy it may sound today, 'We were like One Big Happy Family'.

H. M. S. MALAYA, a World War 1 battleship used in Loch Cairnbawn in 1943 as a target in working up exercises before the attack on the TIRPITZ.

Like a refrain, this theme comes over again and again from all the people, men and women, who were attached to VARBEL. It had housed up to 300 people prior to the TIRPITZ operation.

H.M.S. VARBEL had been created as a training centre for X Craft personnel, with close proximity to that best-of-all training grounds, the West Coast of Scotland. Day after day X Craft would leave the floating pontoons (baffles) or Port Bannatyne pier on 'work-ups', exercises on towing or how to penetrate (and leave!) a heavily defended harbour of fjord, on the emergence from and return to the flooded wet and dry (W. and D.) compartment, on net cutting, on the placing of limpet mines on barnacle encrusted ship's bottoms and on deep dives, or attending perhaps, Noise Reduction Trials at the Hydrophone Range in Loch Goil.

Loch Striven made an admirable 'Altenfjord' and the WWI battleship H.M.S. MALAYA an excellent 'TIRPITZ' for practice purposes.

There is a deep hole in the bottom at the seaward end of Loch Goil, where it joins with the Holy Loch, and this is where the Deep Dives experiments took place. The theoretical maximum depth to which an X Craft could submerge was 300 ft but when one was tested to see how deep it could go before caving in, it was found to 525 ft.

At the end of the day or week, the X Craft would return to the baffles or, if there was any fault to be remedied after the initial teething problems (and there were remarkably few with the craft from the Three Industrial Firms) they would return to the workshop at Ardmaliesh Point roughly half a mile away.

Ray Knight has occasion to remember the slipway at Ardmaliesh for it was the first time he had ever seen an X Craft (probably X3):-

I was on the winch and didn't have a clue what we were docking. It was all done in darkness and we weren't told anything until it appeared in the light from the workshops.

The first X Craft came to Rothesay, if I remember rightly, from Vickers Armstrong at Barrow disguised as a Motor Launch in late 1942. It was off-loaded at a place called Faslane on the Gare Loch, having come by rail on a lowloader, and was then sailed across to Rothesay. The first time we docked it we managed to get it on the cradle halfway up the slipway, when the cradle slipped and it broke away with Commander on the casing, hanging on for dear life! He also had his arm in a sling. I'll never forget it.

Although the Hydro was halfway through its demolition when Lily of VARBEL (Lily Robbs the E.R.A.'s Mess Steward) and the writer went round it in 1985, one could see that it had been a fine, long, rambling building with battlemented ramparts and, according to John Bowman 'a wonderful array of sprays and douches'.

Built in 1900 halfway up a hillside above Port Bannatyne, it had a central castellated tower visible from all over Kames Bay.

The interior was dominated, for the writer, by the magnificent first floor ward room with its gracious aspect of Dutch Interiors seen through open doorways. Its great length and its tall windows giving on to the impressive panorama of Kames Bay and in the distance Toward Point and the entrance to Loch Striven.

I'm told that the wardroom was peopled by the ghosts of many a young officer, most of whom had only just left school or University, who had stood by this same window looking pensively down at the returning X Craft.

'Lily of VARBEL' and the writer standing at the entrance to the now derelict Hydro, clutching their presentation roof slates. September 1985. 'Lonely I wander through scenes of my childhood, the old house deserted, no welcome at the door'. From 'The Old House'.

Lily Robbs records her first impressions:-

I was met at the ferry quayside on the Isle of Bute by a Wren lorry driver, waiting to transport new arrivals to the base. I had a marvellous view of all the ships lying at anchor in Rothesay Bay. When we arrived at Port Bannatyne I got my first look at the Kyles Hydro, which looked like a castle. The steep drive up to it would give any would-be invaders second thoughts.

A three day routine was worked and my duties included:- serving meals, dusting and sweeping E.R.A.'s cabins, (they made their own beds), and scrubbing out at least one every day. It will be appreciated what engineers' cabins were like; even after the men had washed the oil and grease off their hands in those little brown cans of tetrachloride, evidence of their working among those smelly substances for a Watch was still most noticeable.

The meals followed their customary form with always porridge and a 'fry-up' for breakfast, and two-course lunch, with fish on Fridays of course. Tea was bread, jam, cheese or 'herrings in' (i.e. in tomato sauce, of which the Navy seemed to have an endless supply). After which most of the ship's company went ashore for supper which left only the duty watch to feed.

After a few days I got into the routine but couldn't get over the fact that the sailors didn't seem to go to sea, instead they went to work at somewhere called 'the slip' at Ardmaliesh Point. You could see the Point from the mess windows, so we knew just how much time we had after they knocked off, before the 'gannets' descended upon us.

There was always an air of excitement about the place which I didn't understand; when people talked about boats and craft I didn't know what they were talking about, I hadn't seen any.

Gradually I began to realise something special was happening. I was learning the language, craft were X Craft or Midget Submarines, otherwise BOATS.

When you first saw these special craft and heard the stories the lads told of happenings and laughs against themselves, it made your realise just how close-knit a community VARBEL had become. You found yourself conversing on the same level and you knew you'd been accepted.

An XE exercising in Rothesay Bay. The Hydro, altough not clearly visible, is on the extreme left half way up hillside.

There wasn't a great deal of entertainment at VARBEL, with Rothesay being so near, but the weekly Tombola kept the lads and lassies amused, a thriving football team kept the men fit and netball did the same for the Wrens.

The town, of course, boasted several public houses, of which the 'Why Not', now known as 'The Brandy', was one of the most popular. The cinema was a big draw, as indeed was the canteen-behind-the-church; also the Pavilion where some of the Wrens took their dancing very seriously indeed.

After Divisions on Sundays, when Scottish licensing laws prevailed, sailors and Wrens took to the water, and the land. Lily has fond memories of rowing out to the M.T.B.'s in Kames Bay and Able Seaman Eli Whittaker recalls crewing the sailing cutter and winning races against the Colintraive ferry. There were cycle rides all over the island, picnics, occasionally swimming in the loch, scrambles up the hillside to Kames Castle and, for the serious walkers, there was that superb view from the top of Canada Hill.

A happy picnic party from VARBEL on the Isle of Bute in 1943. Within barely 12 months of the picture being taken all four young men lost their lives. Front row, left to right: Peggy Ledbury, Ian McFarlane, Louie Rogerson, Bill Whittam. Back row: Paddy Keiron, Chrissie Yates, Margaret Henderson and Jack Marsden.

The main entrance to VARBEL. The area in front formed the quarterdeck where the ship's company was lined up for weekly insepction by the Commanding Officer (Divisions). First Captain Banks, then Captain P. Q. Roberts.

Lily takes up the story again:-

One of the ratings went A.W.O.L. after Christmas leave 1944. He was a Welsh lad named Ivor (or Taff) and he got 'cells' on his return. Cells were about ten yards from the E.R.A.'s mess, his punishment diet was water and ship's biscuits. So with a few of his friends guarding the stairs and corridors and with the help of the guard, I managed to put a lunch aside which was smuggled in for him. That little stunt lasted ten days and I might add I was relieved when it was over.

The Lift Shaft Incident

The infamous lift shaft was a notoriously finger-trapping, glass and wrought iron Victorian monstrosity and an E.R.A. threw a hand grenade down it. The engineers had been indulging in some rather unorthodox horse-play, with live weapons and the grenade had become separated from its pin! Rather than chance injuring someone outside, somebody threw it down the lift shaft. There was a tremendous explosion and glass showered everywhere. Although no-one was hurt, I'm afraid panic stations reigned for some time.

This was, of course, a very serious offence and the perpetrators were not going to be let off with 14 days stoppages or 'number elevens' as the Navy calls this most lenient of punishments.

As a matter of interest the scale of punishment charges ran (in theory) from No. 20 the most lenient, (for Lascars and other Coloured ratings only) deductions from pay, to No.1 the most severe.

From the relevant pages in Kings Regulations and Admiralty Instructions. A few of the more colourful punishments:-

No. 19 (For boys only) 'Birching on the bare breech. 24 cuts.'
No. 15 (Possibly the worst punishment of all). 'Stoppage of grog.'
No. 2 Corporal punishment. '25 lashes'.
No. 1 'Dismissal with disgrace'
No. 11 By far the most common. 'Extra drill and duty'. Maximum 14 days.

Actually the miscreant's identity was never discovered. Bill Morrison describes the incident and its aftermath:-

I was very much involved with the hand grenade incident. My cabin was very close to the lift shaft and I was just entering my cabin at the time of the explosion. I ran to the scene and at the same time observed a person running into another room at the end of the corridor. When we went to this room, all of the occupants (E.R.A.'s) were well tucked up and 'fast asleep'. This was taken at its face value but many years later I was assured that the culprit was in one of the beds, fully dressed! assuming innocent blissful slumber. The captain at the time was still Captain Banks who decided next day to muster all E.R.A.'s and I was asked to inspect them to see if I could identify the culprit. No way could I do so as I had only seen the back of a figure disappearing into a doorway. I was again informed many years later that the E.R.A.'s were convinced that I knew who the culprit was but had refrained from disclosing my knowledge, much to their great appreciation and respect. I have no knowledge of the truth ever being known or revealed but all leave to all male personnel was stopped for several days. Certainly a certain Sub/Lt. with a history of impetuous dare-devilry, was at this time transferred from our flotilla to undertake a disciplinary course aboard a battleship.

Chapter Five
Working Up In Loch Striven - I

In March 1943 the VARBEL Private Fleet comprised of the Mooring Vessel FIDELE, 2 Drifters PRESENT HELP and STARLIGHT RAYS, N.A.B. COLLINETTE, 4 motor boats, 2 motor pinnaces, 1 motor cutter, 6 motor skiffs and 2 dinghies.

To accommodate the X Craft a catamaran was acquired, to conceal the craft when on passage between VARBELS I and II, only later was it used as a two-berth mooring. Additional jetties and two piers were constructed to support all the extra craft.

Officers were billeted in the house, plus the Wrens who looked after them. Other ranks were accommodated in the Nissen huts.

Following initial training at Fort Blockhouse and a 'stand by' period at the works where the craft were being completed, the crews left for Port Bannantyne.

At H.M.S. VARBEL their training would include:- entering, flooding up, emerging, re-entering and flooding down the practice Wet and Dry Tank (W. and D.) which was moored a short distance offshore.

Sid Woollcott one of the original 'guinea pigs' who were deliberately rendered unconscious in a diving tank as a matter of research recalls the laborious business of donning a diving suit with deep feeling:-

The diver struggled into his diving suit thus:- feet first into the bottom half, then a wriggle and a squeeze into the top part, 'Stick your elbows into your sides', 'OK then. Now don't tear my ears off'! Arms into sleeves and cuffs sealed with broad bands of rubber at the wrist, then a pair of cumbersome lead-soled boots were fitted. For the final act in the drama, the rubber apron at the stomach was folded in the correct way and secured with a belly clamp to make the suit watertight. And woe betide the dresser if the job wasn't done properly and some water seeped through.

A.B Elijah Whittaker (Tubby) recalls that they were ordered to walk straight into 10 ft of water from the shore and to stay at the bottom of the loch for a half hour. So, both to amuse himself and to keep warm at the same time, he tried catching crabs.

String gloves were worn at times too, but only to protect the hands when cutting through nets, or when barnacles were likely to be encountered.

Diving techniques developed and net cutting became so skilled that by the end of the war entire operation was reduced to just nine minutes. It was two and a half in chariots! (human torpedoes) but there was no W. and D..

The X5-10 class differed from their practice-prototypes X3 and X4 in many respects but the latter were the real 'work horses'.

In X3 and X4 the control room for'ard contained the periscope, depth-keeping controls, steering and various navigational items. Next came the escape compartment doubling as the heads and known as the Wet and Dry, followed by the battery compartment. Then right aft came the engine and motor spaces.

Chief E.R.A. Vernon 'Ginger' Coles:-

The boats being designed for three persons only. The bunk was port side aft in the control room. It took minutes to climb into it.

However in time as one C.O. said:-

Crawling over the plank in the battery compartment to reach the engine space, in damp clothes, with the cells fizzing merrily away beneath you and high-powered, live terminals within a few inches of one's bare hands was altogether too exciting. So the control room and battery compartments were changed round in the X5-10's.

Ginger remembers:-

When the fourth man was added, in the X5-10's, it necessitated a place for the other character to rest and the only place available was the battery compartment. This was a lonely and unpopular position; it was isolated from the other two by the water-tight W. and D.

With the increasing concern over habitability and to accommodate the fourth man (the diver), six foot was added to the length for X5-10 class making them 51 ft. A later class called X.E.'s were built 2 ft longer still, to allow for the air conditioning plant and small refrigerator, so essential in the Tropics.

Even so this habitability stopped a long way short of comfort. Living in an X Craft was akin to four men working in a space a little bigger than two cubby-holes under the stairs placed end to end. Under the periscope a short man could stand upright, elsewhere there was sitting headroom only.

'Small Boat Types' amongst the 'Hostilities Only' people, and there were many of them, were used to these conditions and moving from one place to another bent double. Oddly enough, large and small submarines in naval jargon are always called 'Boats'. An uncomfortable life of leisure in peacetime aboard one's own 20 ft sloop was quite different from an uncomfortable and enforced routine in war-time, aboard one of His Majesty's Midgets. The crew did not move about anyway, for it upset the trim; they stayed put (and became constipated!).

The small hatch openings were roughly 2 ft in diameter, not over-large for a man clad in several layers of woollens topped with the light waterproof 'Ursula' suit.

When the four members of the crew were at Action Stations, the C.O. could lean over and touch every one of them without moving his feet.

It was worse still in the engine room. Repairs in awkward places, or even in obvious ones, had to be effected by squirming over a foot-wide fuel tank and making one's body conform to the cylindrical shape of the pressure hull, rising to only an inch or two above one's head.

After all, there was a War on and they hadn't expected an 'upholstered tunnel' with a little 'Stuart Turner' motor at the end. So they made the most of a bad job and, in some cases, an almost cosy domesticity ensued. At least in fine weather! on one memorable occasion on X6, they even managed to have a shave, prior to an equally memorable run ashore.

A lot was to happen before then. Walking a 50 ft midget submarine through a very small gap, wasn't as easy as one might think. Guiding the craft through the heavy net without the tell tale jigging of the surface buoys, without stepping off the narrow casing and, most important, not getting hung-up on the net when the midget surged forward. Sometimes this was amusing, as when the diver got left behind. Once when the X Craft chappie 'pressed the accelerator' by mistake and went ahead through the upside-down vee cut in the net, the diver was able to swim after it with his broad rubber swim-fins, catch it up and bang furiously on the casing. All this took place more often than not, in a deep and rather eerie twilight and in freezing water.

To keep warm in the bitterly cold waters of the North of Scotland, a layer of fine silk underwear was followed by one of the consistency of combinations, 'long johns' they were called. Then came a navy-blue quilted cotton 'Tropal' Suit with its thin kapok-like wadding. The 'Sladen Suit' and canvas boots completed the outfit.

An episode which probably happened more than once befell Lt. P. Dawson R.N.V.R. in Loch Striven. The light life-line, which was attached to the divers at all times, caught in his mouthpiece cock. This was the waycock by means of which the diver could choose, on the surface, to breathe fresh air or oxygen. The line flicked it open to 'air'. Unfortunately, being submerged at the time, he found himself sucking back, not on air, but salt water.

The officer in charge, Lt. P. Westmacott R.N. made him go down again the next day with a heavier line round him, to test his nerve.

Stress manifested itself in different ways and the symptoms were not always controllable. Stress was not harped on then, in the same way as it is now. However the symptoms were still recognizable.

Lt. J. N. McCaughan R.N.R.:-

On a net-cutting exercise with the diver pumping-up and flooding the W. and D., the officer at the steering position muttered that the door was leaking. I said 'Yes it does that until the W. and D. is full. It's OK'.

He then went on to talk gibberish and I realised he was not joking. On completion of the exercise I recommended he should see the doctor. I never saw the officer again. He must have been very quickly whisked off somewhere.

S/Lt. Dennis Easom R.N.V.R. who was First Lieutenant of XE7 on a future occasion honestly admits to his fears:-

There were so many things to go wrong. On cutting through the nets, it was a strange feeling when one saw the boat moving away the weight of the cutters would pull you down if the line carried away difficult to know how one would react under the circumstances visibility was so limited. It was dark, cold and lonely down there and I didn't like the business at all.

There were, in fact, two known casualties on net cutting exercises (the second one has a small question mark it still). On the 1st of June 1943, S/Lt. David Locke R.N.V.R. became "Missing presumed drowned" when he failed to return from a net-cutting exercise. What happened is a matter for conjecture. Either he stumbled and slipped off the casing in the darkened water and the weight of the cutters pulled him down into fatal depths where he suffered an attack of oxygen poisoning, or he became hung up on the net as the craft moved away, and, with his cold, numb fingers unable to turn the small wheel of his bypass valve to put a "guff" of oxygen into his breathing bag to blow himself up to the surface, he plunged to the bottom of the Loch where he met his death.

In the case of the second casualty Jim McCaughan remembers that:-

In November 1944 on a net-cutting exercise in Loch Striven, Erik Jaggers (C.O.) observed through the night periscope that the diver had collapsed on the casing. We immediately surfaced but before anyone could get out of the hatch, he had been washed overboard and was not seen again. The diver on this occasion was not one of the crew but one we had picked up at the jetty fully dressed. Until he was needed to cut the net he had remained in the W. and D. compartment. He stayed there so I never saw his face or insignia and don't remember his name. It would have happened on XT4 or X24.

This can only have been L/Stoker Alfred Brammer of Bucknall, Staffordshire. If Alfred Brammer's relatives or descendants would like to be put in touch with Jim McCaughan, this can be arranged. Erik Jaggers died in 1948.

S/Lt. John Tufnell R.N.V.R. one-time 1st. Lieutenant of X20 :-

I used to think it was a bit of a farce when we took VIPs out to watch the net-cutting exercises.

We went out in a launch and moored over the net. I then climbed down to watch the X Craft arrive and cut through the net. When it was through I surfaced and told the VIPs that the boat had done just that. They could see nothing in the murky water and quite happily took my word for it. Goodness knows what they expected to see.

Visibility depended very much on the weather, if it was sunny the underwater visibility at 60ft was fair; at 100ft it was deep twilight and anything below that was as black as 'Newgate's Knocker'. Torches were useless and hardly ever used.

The anti-submarine nets protecting the WWI battleship MALAYA moored at the seaward end of Loch Striven. (She was later moored in Loch Cairnbawn, made excellent practice targets in the TIRPITZ-mould), they were so widely used with a succession of vee cuts and square holes that they must have hung in ribbons by the time the TIRPITZ was irrevocably damaged, after Op. 'Source'.

John Tufnell :-

It was the practice to take new recruits out in a boat to see how they reacted to diving in the small craft. One trick was to 'crack' the main valve, i.e. to open it a crack and allow water into the bilges. When the boat started to flood, it was always the recruits that spotted it and we used to be amused at watching the expression on their faces. There must be something pretty unnerving about a leak in a submerged submarine. At least to a novice.

On another occasion I remember we dived and went head-on into the mud. Nothing on earth would free her and I began to wonder if this was what the end would be like.

Then someone had a brainwave and we all went as far aft as possible. The change in weight did the trick and we shot to the surface like a cork whilst we pumped water into the tanks as fast as we could.

The writer asked John why they hadn't thought of this before, he explained that:-

The X Craft were very small. One did not walk about, everyone had a seat and stayed there. The Captain gave the orders and the rest of us tried whatever plan he ordered. There were five of us and very little room.

The normal crew of an X Craft was four:- C.O., First Lieutenant, Diver and Engineer. Although all members of the crew had undergone a basic diving training, we only carried five on exercise (except on the D-Day Ops when two swimmers were included). On these occasions we did not have a diver and could take out two extra personnel for the experience.

Passage crews to and from operations and the original prototype boats, X3 and X4 carried a crew of three, two men plus a diver. The problem then was that, in emergencies there was too much to do.

John Tufnell:-

I once ran aground as we were surfacing, when I as 1st. Lieut. was coping with the steering, the engines and the pumps, but not, praise be, with the lunch. I started the diesels but forgot to stop the electric motor. Result:- frantic helm orders and yells of 'Full Astern' but the electric motor quietly drove us on to the mudbank. We refloated at high tide with no damage except to our pride.

Lt. Commander Louis Sheppard describes this business of getting stranded rather more forcibly:-

Here's one that will make you chuckle. I was C.O. of X3 and had to carry out a training operation at neighbouring Loch Riddon, in conjunction with the Army.

The plan was to beach X3 and for me to go ashore and meet up with the Army force. It was pointed out to the 1st. Lieut. that the tide was ebbing and that the ballast tanks were full. All that was required was to blow ballast every so often; and follow the tide out. The Rise and Fall thereabouts is 10ft and the entire northern half of Loch Riddon dries out.

After the Army operation, I returned to X3 to find that the ocean was miles away Fortunately she was sitting on her bar keel but without a drop of water in sight! I got aboard to find the crew guzzling tea and had to wait hours for the tide to return.

He had to put the entire crew (both of them) 'in the rattle'; which is navalese for under punishment.

'Shep' Sheppard was out of luck later on in the same boat:-

These craft were fitted with a short snorkel which one had to shut on diving. I dived X3 and clean forgot about it. I was in the helmsman's chair and the inboard end of the snorkel was facing me. As soon as we dived, the water roared in like a steel bar and hit me smack between the eyes. I got wet. I soon pulled the lever.

Neither were the teething troubles of X4's crew over, when the first X Craft casualty occurred during an aptly-named Endurance Trial in Inchmarnock Water in December 1942.

The commencement of the exercise coincided with a ferocious 'Clyde stinker', perhaps the first storm ever experienced by X Craft. Not realising the height of the waves or how low in the water was an X craft's freeboard, S/Lt. Morgan Thomas opened the W. and D. hatch to ditch the gash (rubbish) and was promptly plucked out by a vicious wave, never to be seen again.

The same wave created mayhem and dismay amongst the two remaining occupants, filling the escape compartment and leaving X4 suspended diagonally on the surface. They were, of course, concerned over what had happened to

Morgan Thomas.

Lt. Godfrey Place R.N. for'ard in the control room was isolated from, and totally unable to communicate with E.R.A. Whitley who was aft in the engine room. The flooded W. and D. could be pumped out from for'ard but not with the hatch open.

Whitley's acutely uncomfortable, and potentially dangerous position was caused by the fact that in X3 and X4 the batteries were aft and there was a real danger of salt getting into the battery acids and setting up chlorine gas. This had been known to happen on previous occasions.

Eventually, Lt. Place, soon to win the Victoria Cross, managed to send out distress signals to PRESENT HELP and after the worst two hours either of them had ever experienced, X4 was found, towed into the lee of the land and pumped out. Place and Whitley were released from what might so easily have been their tomb.

As a direct result of the tragic death of Morgan Thomas, the 'Hezlett rail' was fitted to all future X Craft. This was a horizontal bar and leather belt attached to the induction trunk, the belt encircling the waist of the officer on the casing. It must have saved much compulsory bathing in bad weather. Also devised was a gadget for closing the hatch from the control room, dispensing with the use of a wheel spanner.

For it was Murphy's Law which had decreed that this one essential tool in an emergency should drop into the bilges when X3 lay on the bottom of Loch Striven.

The full account of this incident appears later.

Chapter Six
Working Up In Loch Striven - II

What was it like living in someone else's stately home? S/Lt. John Tufnell records his impressions of Ardtaraig in 1944:-

We were all very young. We believed we were invincible. We were free from the discipline of the big ships and shore establishments. Runs ashore were not easy from Loch Striven, we had no transport except once a week when we went in a 3 tonner to Dunoon. The Summer of 1944 was glorious on the West Coast. We swam in the swimming pool, ideally situated between the house and the loch. Most of our parties were sing-songs round the piano in the mess. We were looked after by a good bunch of Wrens and life was very good. I had recently been told I was colour blind and so could not get a watch-keeping certificate. X Craft appeared to me a marvellous solution and seemed the only way for me to get to sea.

It is over 40 years ago now. I was nineteen then and it all seemed a great adventure. We were only training and I had seen virtually nothing of the horrors of war. The 12th Flotilla was a great unit to have been in and we had some marvellous times.

John Tufnell 'says it all' but a more dramatic note was struck when S/Lt. George Wright, a neighbour of the author's in Lymington, was told when volunteering for Special Service in late 1943 just after the TIRPITZ 'do':- There will be no more need for X Craft in the present war.

Admittedly their greatest exploit 'Operation Source' was behind them, but there were still seven more operations to come, including the two vital Normandy expeditions.

This business of being concerned that one was not doing enough for the war effort, surfaced from time to time and S/Lt. Brian Cross remembers that:-

In June '44 I was at VARBEL II probably working up on one of the XT's or perhaps still 'under training'. Officers and ratings were definitively classified as 'Under Training', 'Qualified' of 'Operational'. They could not pass from one grade to the next without passing the test.

When the news of D-Day broke we besieged 'X' office almost demanding transfers to more active services. Perhaps we guessed the flotilla's days in the European theatre were numbered and that there were sufficient fully operational crews to handle foreseeable commitments. Anyway, we got short shift and were told to get about our business.

Ken Briggs who was later to become a famous Cutter of Cables, also enjoyed it at Ardtaraig:-

Sunday afternoons I remember especially. Majority of the matelots on a week-end leave, which only left a few lowly cads on board, mainly out-of-towners.

In fact, Sundays at VARBEL II were great and Sunday evenings mess was informal. Can you imagine one night, when four so-called gentlemen decked out in pusser (correct naval) trousers tucked into half boots, each wearing a colourful

Ardtaraig on the shores of Loch Striven. This fine old shooting lodge was taken over by the Navy in August 1942 and renamed VARBEL 11. Like VARBEL 1, it was the happy home of many of the 12th Flotilla personnel.

pyjama top suitably sashed, tried to pass themselves off as something we picked up from Russia. The moon was also full that evening and crystal clear with frost nipping at the finger ends and a stillness that was almost tangible.

With the moon, plus myriads of tiny glow worms to light his path he would not have needed a torch for illumination (no torches allowed in wartime even in those remote parts). It was all so peaceful that it must have been difficult to remember that there was a war on.

The following day is remembered even more vividly.

A very quiet day with only about four of us on board. I had been away from Australia for three continuous years, and there had been a lull in mail from home, with no friends around me and I was feeling a bit low. I tried a jug of ale but to no avail, even to this day I feel a little cheated, though of what I really don't know. It was my 21st birthday.

S/Lt. Ivor Jarvis recollects that in his particular training group led by Lt. Symonds:-

We used to keep fit by running up to the top of Croc Maroch the hill behind the house (Ardtaraig) before breakfast.

History does not relate whether Jim McCaughan was at his peak of fitness or not but he didn't go much on this at all:-

In June 1944, my friend Erik Jaggers and I were billeted in a Nissen hut at L.S.H. with some thirty other officers to be taught shallow water oxygen diving. In the morning we were awoken very early and rudely for P.T. Jaggers and I concluded it did not include us, as we had not been previously informed, so we turned over and continued sleeping. However, we were told that everyone was required to do P.T.

and next morning Jaggers turned out. I did not and was put on the C.O.'s report.

I explained to the C.O. that I was not against P.T. but to jump out of bed to do it was, I thought, a strain on the heart. Although he seemed amused at my theory, he ruled that I would have to do P.T. Perhaps in the evening would be better in order to satisfy my fears, I agreed. Needless to say I never did P.T. as the Instructor was not there in the evenings.

Ivor Jarvis comments:-

The bulk of our training was on a daily basis. Each boat was allocated an area of the loch in which to practice the day's exercise. They were designated areas A to E, the latter being at the seaward end near Strone Point, close to where MALAYA was moored inshore.

I remember being disconcerted one day, by the whooshing noises alongside us while we were dived, persuading me that another X Craft was wrongly in our area. It turned out to be the noise of a porpoise, probably some way off because noise travels a long way under water.

Jim McCaughan:-

Sometimes we were sent on navigational exercises. i.e. Proceed to point A submerged, thence in darkness on surface to position B etc. These proved very boring and after a few such exercises we would find a nice quiet spot, settle on the bottom and while away the time playing cards, eating and sleeping. The Instructor seemed satisfied, as the charts were nicely made up with courses, bearings and times.

A word here on the extremely thorough and vigorous training would be appropriate. Predictably the accent was on competent self-reliance and all-round adaptability, every member of the crew had to be able to do the other chap's job and be able to stand a watch.

ITX, the Initial Training Exercise comprised:-

Various manoeuvres involving dry diving, static diving between buoys, running dive with instructor on board, submerged manoeuvring in still water, ditto with increased tidal set, ditto with 'defective' instruments including compass.

ANX, the Advanced Navigation Exercise:-

Highly trained crews only would con the X Craft through busy traffic lanes at periscope depth, with the Instructor on the casing (unenviably!) dodging shallow draught boats. They would run through the craft at stated minimum intervals.

APX, the Advanced Penetration Exercise:-

Penetration of narrow entrances to bays, turning inside and coming out again without departing from periscope depth, with the increasing difficulties of current and diminishing light and various instrument 'breakdowns'. A great variety of conditions had to be devised to avoid detection, and to check the 'nerve', ingenuity and adaptability of all three crews, i.e. 2 Passage crews and 1 Operational (or Attack) crew.

The crews were trained to exploit to the full all natural features such as salt and fresh water layers, shadows, broken water and periods of decreased vigilance. All types of targets should be attacked including submerged electric cables, underwater pipelines and of course 'anything that floats'.

The former instruction foreshadows the two successful operations in Far Eastern waters, when no less than three telephone cables were cut. The last one of the war at Hong Kong being extremely hazardous.

The compiler of the List of Miscellaneous and Cleaning Stores must have had a sense of humour:-

  1 black flag for Roger, Jolly
  Fish scares
  300 paper plates
  6 pillow cases!
  2 rolls bumph (Constipation was the order of the day)
  2 Hammock beds
  Housewife (The cloth, rolling-up kind)

Sometimes on the return trip from these taxing exercises, various instruments would be put out of action and everything made as difficult as could be. This was quite apart from the accidental mishaps, which Lt. Meeke (later Commander W. G. Meeke M.B.E., D.S.C., R.N.) on X5 so graphically describes in the following precis:-

March 30, departed Loch Kishorn, main exhaust pipe burst inside, noxious fumes most unpleasant, considered donning D.S.E.A. (Davis Submarine Escape Apparatus) sets, patch effected by asbestos string, canvas from R.T. set, haversack and field dressing (sticking plaster!). Mock attack on BONAVENTURE highly successful, despite heavy seas causing tool locker to fly open, steel drift jammed between flywheel and top of fuel tank, clearing up took 7 hours.

X6's attack in the same exercise under Lt. Cameron was also successful but not 100% so. He only got nine out of ten!

X7 under Lt Place found that both side charges planed and did not drop straight down. Perhaps it was spring tides, or a strong current, or maybe both. Any combination of these factors over 3½ knots, would cause the side charges to fall leaf-like. The magnetic target indicator had been wished on them by an eccentric inventor and was totally impractical. The pointer on the indicator's dial did not begin to register until they were within the shadow of the target and could see it anyway. Again Ivor Jarvis is a fascinating source of domestic trivia:-

We were always given a fair selection of tinned rations for these training runs. Around mid-day we would go down, sit on the sea bed and cook up on our little stove. All very jolly and convivial, but then crew relationships were necessarily very informal under those conditions.

The 'little stove' was an electric double boiler, or 'glue pot' of fond memory which, together with an electric coffee pot made up the only two cooking appliances. Needless to remark, there was only one plate (a pot one) to use for meat course and pudding. So, washing up at all and not merely between courses, became fraught with difficulty. The use of cotton waste was prohibited for in time it blocked outlets. Anyway the first tin that came to hand might be pineapple chunks for a meat course,

X24 on returning from the 1st Bergen expedition. John Britnell on casing.

not that it mattered much, for in practice, one's appetite decreased in direct ratio to the number of claustrophobic days spent aboard. The favourite beverages, on passage, being orange juice, tea and coffee and the favourite food, bread and jam and barley sugar sweets.

I never knew how cordial such sea-bed lunch breaks could be with one Lt. Percy Westmacott R.N. the most pusser of naval officers, known, of course, as 'Pusser Percy'. It was he who always insisted on formal Harbour Stations and believe me, it took an acrobatic crew with magnetic shoes to stand to attention when entering harbour, on a plunging, rolling 3 ft wide deck.

Even R.N. Lieutenants could be human when the occasion arose. Ivor Jarvis is reminded of one riotous time in Dunoon whither a group of wavy-navy (R.N.V.R.) and 'straight-laced' officers had driven, in order to celebrate Lt. Westmacott's successful Norwegian foray. (He had been C.O. of X24 at the second Bergen attempt):-

We had a special 'lash-up' meal in a Dunoon hotel and were all pretty much the worse for wear. I remember wandering, in my daze, down into one of those subterranean women's toilets in the High Street.

In the course of the revelry, a small group led by S/Lt. Ollie Trier R.N.R. made their way into the crowded foyer of a cinema. In the entrance, splendid in its alcove was a large bust of Robbie Burns. This was duly removed by the lads and transported back to base at Striven-head, where it was used later for rifle practice which did not improve the features at all.

One of the men chosen to accompany Lt. Westmacott on Operation 'Heckle' was 'Tubby' Whittaker and if the R.N. Lieut. had known about the following peccadillo he might have had second thoughts.

Birthdays were the excuse for yet another escapade. One evening after much low-voiced discussion, Tubby and his mates managed to liberate a barrel of beer from their local's back yard. Incredibly, they rolled this barrel down the hill and into the back of the 3 tonner with much exaggerated giggling, stealth and suppressed swearing, without waking the landlord and his wife. They then made short work of free-wheeling back to the camp and disposing of the beer. It was poured into every imaginable container, including, of course, their own stomachs. Cups, saucepans, jam jars and even the kettle were called in as beer bottles, in fact it was 'Whisky Galore' long before it appeared on the cinema screen.

A very good time was being had by one and all when it was realised that daylight would bring recognition of the theft plus the incriminating evidence. Therefore with the ebb in Loch Striven having commenced, the barrel was rolled down to the shore and launched upon its waters, never to be seen again, except perhaps by fishermen in the Irish Sea.

Tubby's tales, in his rich broad Yorkshire, with never the necessity for an indefinite article, are an endless source of nostalgic delight to the writer, having been raised in the West Riding herself:-

I was involved with Lt. Westmacott and X24 again on a training exercise when we were betrayed by the tops of our sea boot stockings.

Lt. Westmacott had taken X24 from Port Bannatyne to the rendezvous at Ettrick Bay, the other side of the Isle of Bute. S/Lt. Robinson, Stoker Luck and myself took passage in a trawler. The skipper was a contrary Hull fisherman, who felt strongly about being seconded to the Royal Navy and denied the visits to his favourite 'Silver Pits', where there would be rich pickings in war-time. So he ran her aground.

Eventually, after much bad feeling and language, a member of the trawler's crew swam ashore with a line and brought back the Carley float, enabling them all to get ashore.

The object of the exercise was to return to Port Bannatyne on foot, across the wild and rugged terrain of the island's interior (and in pouring rain), without being seen by the 'enemy' who were out looking for us in force, with fixed bayonets. Dressed in our camouflage outfits of khaki battledress, Navy caps and sea boots, we set out to tramp the 10/12 miles to the opposite coast. We had done very well to get as far as we did, given the sparse cover of dead bracken, and were almost 'home' having just forded the last stream, when a sharp pair of binoculared eyes from the opposite hillside spotted the white flashes of our stocking tops and forthwith we were 'shot'. That was the end of the exercise and I can't say I was sorry.

To round off this 'chapter of accidents'. Another improbable but true story by Ivor Jarvis:-

On one occasion we took XE9 down to 200ft. That evening I was returning to the wardroom, when a somewhat agitated rating darted out from a Nissen hut to inform me that the L/Seaman who had been on the helm at the time, had gone berserk with a knife! He was claiming that I, his Commanding Officer, was carrying on with his wife, a Wren wardroom steward. This untypical reaction to the trauma of submerging to a greater-than-normal depth, was entirely due to delayed shock and was treated by I.J. with his customary 'coolth'. The rating was transferred to another branch of the Service.

Occasionally the stress symptoms were mistakenly attributed. That most fruitful Source of Anecdotes Jim McCaughan:-

I shared a cabin in the depot ship with S/Lt. 'Kiwi' Smith R.N.Z.N.V.R. for a short time. One afternoon I returned to the cabin to find Kiwi lying sobbing on his bunk,

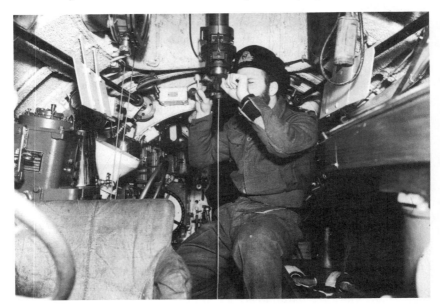

S/Lt. V. St J. Robinson posing at the periscope of an X Craft

with an open airmail letter by his side. I retreated to the wardroom and told the others that Smith must have had bad news from home. I was told that he had had too much to drink and the sobbing was a reaction.

Kiwi shipped out East as No. 1 to Ian Fraser in XE3. The last time I saw his name was on a New Zealand chart, W. J. L. Smith D.S.O., O.B.E., R.N.Z.N. Hydrographer.

Chapter Seven
Working Up In Loch Striven - III

'Luncheon is served' aboard an XT was rather more strenuous than in Lt. Westmacott's case.

S/Lt. Brian Cross:-

I think it was the XT3 I was on. 'Mitch' Matthews in command. We operated out of the Crinan canal basin at Ardrishaig on Loch Fyne. We maintained a set course, depth and speed going South until lunch and the reciprocal course going North after lunch.

The meal was invariably macaroni cheese, cooked in the gluepot by the 1st Lieut. Can you imagine the dexterity required to bring the craft to periscope depth, fire two smoke candles (when exercising in company with surface vessels, the craft fired two smoke candles along the line on which she would surface, warning the former to stay clear), stop main motor, engage engine clutch, start main engine, open exhaust and muffler valves and surface, start a running charge, start an air charge and at the same time, ensure that the macaroni cheese didn't stick to the glue pot and that a plate of the stuff was placed in Mitch's hand when he opened the forward hatch and put a hand down into the W. and D.? Heaven help you if it wasn't ready and properly cooked.

Many years later I asked Mitch why he wanted mac/cheese every day. It's the only thing I could cook. (He didn't cook the -------- stuff.)

Sometimes the Charioteers or Human Torpedo men and the crew of XT3 were rather more enterprising and not only caught lobsters in home-made pots but laid and serviced them, during their exercises in Loch Striven.

The Police cannot have complained of boredom when X Craft people were in town and Brian Cross has a good memory:-

When we left Ardrishaig, the fishmongers sign (a massive wooden fish) travelled in our battery tank. Vandalism was high spirits in those days but, as with the bust of Robbie Burns, it was eventually quietly restored to its rightful perch.

The crew of XT3 became in time, the crew of X20, with Lt. B. G. Clarke R.N. in command.

It was about this time that there was an influx of R.N. Lieutenants as commanding officers, which might have had an adverse effect on morale but which was treated with the 'Wavy Navy's' customary good humour.

However their arrival was not a popular event, especially amongst R.N.V.R.'s who had hoped to command their own craft. These people went through a rapid training and took over from C.O.'s who had moved on to the new XE's.

Until this time an almost family atmosphere prevailed in the flotilla with the C.O.'s being addressed as 'skipper'. This familiarity rapidly came to an end and one became accustomed to 1st. Lieut's trying to stand to attention on a pitching and tossing baffle and reporting a whole series of readiness reports to the C.O. who was now 'Sir'.

Prior to this, the C.O. would jump aboard and the Jimmy (the 1st Lieut.) would report:- 'Everything OK Skipper. Ready for sea', and woe betide him if it wasn't.

Needless to say there was joy in the hearts of certain junior officers when Lt. Clarke R.N. wiped off his attack periscope by raising it under the only buoy within the exercise area!

Prior to the arrival of the 'Pusser Ones', the informality and repartee extended to and from all levels, even from the Lower Deck to the Upper, without affecting their competence. Midget Submarines, like Death and the old-fashioned big ships' Gun Rooms, were a Great Leveller.

Tubby Whittaker:-

At the end of an afternoon's exercise a certain A/B Cook was down below rolling a tickler (It was forbidden to smoke in an X Craft) and desperate to light up:-'Permission to come up for a smoke Sir?' No not for a minute or two Cook, hang on. Right, OPEN ALL VENTS. OK you can come up, blast you.

Brian Cross:-

Lt. Westmacott was an extremely efficient and widely respected officer who had been sent to VARBEL to 'improve' us. This was not an attractive idea and one day when we'd finished exercising off Inchmarnock, he gave the order from the casing to steer 355. The helmsman, by accident or design, repeated the order as 'Dive, dive, dive'. Upon which they executed a very smart crash dive, leaving Westmacott in the water to cool off! (but not for long). Or so the story goes. It is a definite fact that this very gallant gentleman had been serving aboard H.M.S./m UNSHAKEN as her 1st Lieut. a year or two previously in really dreadful weather in the Gulf of Lyons, when the C.O. Lt. Oxborrow and two rating look-outs were washed off the bridge and drowned. Lt. Percy M. Westmacott R.N. promptly took charge and brought her safely back into harbour.

Brian Cross preferred the lighter gastronomic aspects of 'working-up' to the more serious ones:-

Crews carrying out exercises in the vicinity of Loch Striven carried tinned victuals and it was customary to lay alongside Striven Pier and enjoy a stew made by Mrs. Mac, the lady-with-the-heart-of-gold who lived in the house at the end of the pier. She made the stew from our tinned rations and kept the balance in reserve for our return.

For her continual mothering of those hungry, dirty and smelly X Craft men, Mrs. Mac deserves a chapter all to herself. In fact Ken Briggs asks:-

Was it Mrs. Mac who suggested that some of the lamb on the menu was perhaps garnered by a '3 badger' responsible for the canteen messing, on his long walks o'er the heather, seeking out the lambs downed by the inclement weather?

Brian Cross:-

It wasn't all fun and games though. I have personal memories of breaking through a film of ice when I surfaced after a period submerged, observing a craft cutting its way through the anti-submarine nets.

We lost one diver, S/Lt. Locke whilst on a net-cutting exercise. We could only assume that he'd over-exerted himself and gone too deep and met up with the old adversary, 'Oxygen Pete'.

Leave was restricted for crews under training, mainly due to shortage of petrol for transport to Dunoon from VARBEL II. We made our own fun; at one time croquet was the 'in' game until it was realised that a great game of skittles could be played using the croquet balls and empty beer bottles. The C.O. soon put a stop to that.

Brian's naval career seems to have been an occulting one of long periods of escapades alternating with short intervals of routine. 'How I nearly shot George Honour' is one of the former .(Lt. G. Honour, C.O. of X23 was one of the heroes of D-Day):-

Having finished training and there being a surfeit of young R.N.V.R.'s pending the arrival of the XE's, I was appointed No. 1, i.e. 1st Lieut. of PRESENT HELP, the drifter attached to VARBEL for escort and practice towing duties. The C.O. Lt. Brooks R.N. (1914-18 vintage) was a very nervous type. He had been buried alive when Weymouth was bombed.

None of the guns having been fired in many months, I obtained permission to test weapons by firing at the range on Strone Point. We duly sailed and George Honour, recently returned from ops, came along for the ride and went below to have a zizz on Brooks' bunk. We opened fire with the Hotchkiss, which immediately jammed, as was their wont. I asked permission to open fire with the 'strip' Savage.

Permission being granted I opened up on the Point, disturbing some grazing sheep. Brooks shouted at me to fire nearer to the ship, so I lowered the muzzle and produced a glorious display of splashes between ship and shore. Brooks lost his cool and bellowed at me again. I turned to the bridge for clarification of his orders but, like the clot I was, omitted to set the safety catch. The result of this piece of crass tomfoolery was two rounds fired into PRESENT HELP's deck. The steward who was down below, came up on deck more than somewhat agitated and suggested Brooks should come below to see the damage. I was 'invited' to join the inspection party.

Both rounds had entered Brooks' bunk and perforated his writing case with about 1" of paperwork therein. It then went into the drawer below where his civvies were neatly folded and punctured a rather colourful sports blazer and a pair of flannels, 20 holes in the jacket and 18 in the breeks.

Passing into the next drawer below, it had wreaked havoc with Brooks' dirty linen. At this point Brookie gave a despairing wail and, having heaved out the bottom drawer, he grovelled in the bilge below and to his intense relief, produced the ship's stock of duty free gin. This is when I discovered where he stashed it. I was never allowed to be present when he had his duty free sessions with his cronies from the base, Mopsy' Myers & Co. He was, incidentally, drawing my ration of duty free but I was never offered a drink!

The end result of my actions was that the signalman came aboard with the usual pink form, transferring me to BONAVENTURE within minutes of our coming alongside Port Bannatyne Pier.

Luckily for me and more so for George Honour, he had vacated Brookie's bunk just minutes before I peppered it. Had he not come on deck to witness the shoot, he might have had a nasty shock.

Brian and PRESENT HELP were again in trouble on a further occasion with another Lt. Brooks (1939-45 vintage):-

PRESENT HELP had secured to Ardrishaig pier after having escorted a craft for VARBEL I on exercise, PRESENT HELP, had taken a short cut to the pier across a shallow patch, luckily it was on the top of the tide and no damage was done, she was met by the Commander of the base who shouted across a greeting:- 'How's your bottom Brooks'?, 'Fine Sir. How's yours' Brooks replied. The blast he got in return could be heard for miles.

Brooks eventually got a reprimand in green ink on a pink signal form, the strongest type of communication the base commander was in the habit of using. The accommodation ship at Ardrishaig was probably the 170 ton steel schooner the ORIANA.

S/Lt. Ian Clifton, 'George' in the flotilla :-

When I got my Commission in December 1943 I was given a list of choices, none promised of course, and my first three were:- Submarines, Special Service (Human Torpedoes and X Craft) and Coastal Forces. In practise they seemed to merge the first two and I was delighted to join the 12th Flotilla. X Craft.

After training was basically over, I was sent for operational training to X24, Lt. Hayes R.N. in command. I was Passage C.O. - P.C.O. 1 Outward and Fred Ainslie was P.C.O. 2 Return. All operational X Craft had 3 crews, 2 Passage Crews and 1 Operational Crew, i.e. I would be towed underwater with my crew of L.T.O. the torpedo/electrical rating, (the two branches were combined in those days) and Stoker, to a point off the coast. Then the rubber dinghy exchange took place with me handing over a 100% 'ticketty-boo' boat to the Operational Crew. When they got back to the pick-up point, Fred Ainslie would take over with the passage crew for the return to base. All this because the Operational Crew could never survive several days of towing, an operation and a return trip. (Both Passage Crews were combined into one for the shorter trips, making 2 crews instead of 3.)

Be clear. We did not all get on operations by a long chalk, indeed far less than half the flotilla did. At a wild guess at this time (late 1944), there must have been over 100 Sub Lieutenants and midshipmen plus a sprinkling of 2 ringers (Lieutenants) and ratings to match. Operational training was probably nearly completed for everyone. The end of the war was drawing to a close, giving only the senior and/or brightest a chance of attacking the Japs.

This was a continual grouse; the fact that there were not enough operations to go round. The opportunities were there, but the powers-that-be seemed reluctant to take them up. The result of all this was that, given the keenness and competence of their crews, the role of X Craft in WWII was smaller than it should have been.

One of the senior and/or brightest must have been S/Lt. A. M. D. Wilkie R.N.V.R. although he commences his letter with the usual modest disclaimer:-

If I can be of any help I shall be glad to do so but, apart from an enjoyable and paid tour of the world at Admiralty's expense, there is not much that I can tell you.

Previous to going out East:- We were exercising from BONAVENTURE anchored in Loch a Choire (Loch Corrie as it was then called) on the North shore of Loch Linnhe and just North of Lismore Island. My skipper and 1st Lieut. were invited by the R.A.F. at Oban to fly in a Catalina flying boat, to see what X Craft looked like from the air. In the event I think the R.A.F. wanted to show them a thing or two about flying and made the Catalina do things it should not have done. Anyway I think it was X21 that I took out and ran north-eastwards up Loch Linnhe on a prearranged exercise, part of which was to go deep, which I did although not instructed to go to 300ft, and as far as I recall we reached that depth. This was not unintentional and we were ready to blow main ballast if necessary.

Certainly there were some leaks from various glands but nothing serious, so when we returned to BONAVENTURE and reported, the boat was hoisted out and the pressure hull found to be not even dented.

I wasn't unduly worried but maybe that was because I was young and daft. Having seen the craft building and had a very full training in the construction and equipment, I had complete confidence.

Jim McCaughan recalls another untypical and non-serious incident:-

During a deep test dive, there was an explosion like a gunshot. We were hauled up quickly only to find that the glass in the scuttle had cracked. Someone had forgotten to close the deadlight, but there was no damage to the crew.

They must have had nerves of steel.

The Deep Dives were carried out in Loch Long. We were lowered by cable from a Boom Defence Vessel (generally BARFOOT). First, unmanned, with the telephone 'off the hook' and connected to the alarm buzzer so as a dramatic rise in bilge water would warn people on the surface to haul up immediately.

Incidentally in gratitude to the Catalina crew for their 'hospitality', we took two of them out in the boat to give them a demonstration of a crash dive with all lights out. We left the diesel running a moment or two longer with the air induction valve open, thus sucking some water in to replace the air drawn out by the engine. It also affects one's ear drums, then bringing the bow up so that a fair amount of water ran aft over people's feet, still in the dark mind. Being in fairly shallow water, we also lurched off the bottom before coming to rest and then, amidst an impressive selection of grunts, groans, squeals and screeches, finally switched lights on again and pumped out excess water. Thus we reckoned we gave as good as we got.

Several versions of the following brief classic incident have been given to the writer; two venues, two Big Ships, different X Craft and different dates and two alternative endings but the author prefers Alan Wilkie's account:-

On one occasion when Bruce Enzer (later to be lost on a cable-cutting exercise off the Queensland coast) was heading up the Firth of Clyde near Toward Point, he passed the battleship DUKE OF YORK, its great bulk towering majestically above the just-awash casing of the tiny submarine. Bruce craned his neck and his Aldis lamp and flashed, 'Coo, what a Big Bugger'. This, from an X Craft almost invisible against the shore line, brought a sharp reprimand but a lot of amusement to the flotilla.

However, another capital ship did not look down on those capital little ships X-Craft.

Ivor Jarvis:-

There was one most complimentary incident in 1944. Possibly it was the aircraft carrier ILLUSTRIOUS and I remember the X Craft proceeding on the surface past the carrier, with a senior officer on board. Before the midget had a chance to pipe the far more prestigious ship, the carrier saluted the X Craft! A most unusual compliment, indicating the admiration felt by surface ships for the nut cases who served in His Majesty's Midget Submarines.

Clearly an incident of this nature has happened more than once, Jim McCaughan is more candid than most:-

En route from Port Bannantyne to Faslane, to be transported on the special railway carriage for X Craft, we passed a battleship anchored at the Tail o' the Bank. I heard bugles sounding, saw men milling around and lining the rail of the mighty ship. It was not until I heard 'Still' being sounded that I realised this great ship was honouring us with the full salute. Feeling somewhat embarrassed in my greasy tattered battledress and doubtful about how to respond, I managed a salute, and seeing the other ship dip his ensign, called someone on deck to do likewise. Our ensign had to be taken out of its socket and dipped, staff and all.

I had fully intended to just slip by the battleship as we in Submarines really did not pay much attention to naval 'bull', but I realised later that the capital ship was paying tribute to the achievements of X Craft during the war and not to XE9 personally.

Knowing that submariners had also looked down on their midget counterparts. It did take twice as long to train the former than the latter, but, on the other hand, they only received an extra 2/6d a day instead of the 3/6d that the midget submariners received, the writer once asked Brian Cross, a 'towney' of hers, what they had thought of the people on 'boats'. His reply was typical:- We didn't consider the chaps on submarines at all. The only people we looked up to were the Jennie Wrens! The writer purred.

One more charming recollection by S/Lt. Jack Laird who after the war became Chairman of British Ropes. On one glorious June day in Loch Fyne, after a long hot boring night, this genial giant surfaced very early one morning when everything sparkled and all the landing craft were motionless on their trots and even the reflected images of the giants NORTHLANDS and SOUTHLANDS were still. Then he seemed to feel born again as he looked around him in wonderment, at the creation of a new day.

> *Alone, alone to meet this silent day,*
> *We brought to an end the weird strange life*
> *Lived in the busy, keen thrusting knife*
> *With which we had cut through the oily depths.*

Nothing moved upon the glassy surface
The water made a mirror so perfect
Of the shore and all the buildings bedecked
With light-ending the artificial night.

I felt part of this new and gleaming world
Which we had so secretly discovered,
Without confesing- and kept covered
The secret purpose of our mission.

Not breaking the perfect picture then
We slipped quietly into the depths again.

Chapter Eight
The Tragedy Of XE 11

Lily Robbs:-

Up till now I'd never come up against any tragedies, that is until that morning, 6th March 1944. I'd just come out of the E.R.A.'s mess to have a few words with the boyfriend of the moment. I stood at the top of this broad shallow flight of marble steps leading to the ratings messdeck, when 'Scouse' Carroll came out with a big frying pan in his hand. He cracked a joke with me and then as he passed, slapped me across the bottom with the pan, sending me flying down the steps. Whereupon I threatened to murder him when he came back, laughing and shouting curses after him down the corridor.

When news came that XE11 had been sunk with the loss of three men and that Scouse Carroll was one of them I went hot and cold. I felt it was my fault cursing Carroll the way I had; I felt terrible and couldn't put these thoughts out of my head. We all tried to put a brave face on things but we'd find in our quiet moments, we'd be thinking about Lt. Staples, A/B Carroll and Stoker Higgins. Also about the two survivors, S/Lt. Morrison and E.R.A. Swatton trying to help them overcome their ordeal.

What happened was that XE11 left V.I on the morning of March 6, 1945 to calibrate instruments in Loch Striven. Lt. Aubrey Staples S.A.N.F.(V) was in command and the First Lieutenant at the controls was S/Lt. Bill Morrison R.N.V.R.

Unknown to them, but observed from the deck of the Boom Defence Vessel NORINA XE11 had wandered out of her exercise area to where the B.D.V. had just laid out a line of buoys. Thus the bigger vessel was lying with engines stopped and totally inaudible to XE11. The crew of the latter had found a good trim at 100ft. Then moved up 10ft to 90ft, then 80ft and 70ft and so on, calibrating instruments at each step. At 30ft Bill could contain himself no longer and 'Permission to use the heads Sir'? which request undoubtedly saved his life.

Squatting in the W. and D. he heard his C.O. recommending that he stay there a minute or two longer. 'Shouldn't like you to spoil this very good trim that we've just caught at 10ft' he joked (trim was so sensitive on an X Craft that a man could upset it by shifting his weight from one foot to the other). A B.D.V. only draws 9ft and at that moment, with a dreadful suddenness there was a loud jarring crash.

Bill Morrison[1]:-

The first major bump hit us up forward and Staples asked me to open the battery compartment hatch to check for damage. While I was doing this we had been aware of loud scraping noises and of a ship's engine starting up. I think we had come up under her forepart, then slid along her keel, when her screws ripped a hole in our hull.

Although so many things now happened so quickly that there was no time to wonder what had taken place, probably no more than four minutes elapsed between

[1]*Bill Morrison & Les Swatton lost touch after the war for 45 years until the 1990 Re-Union where recognition was instantaneous and emotional.*

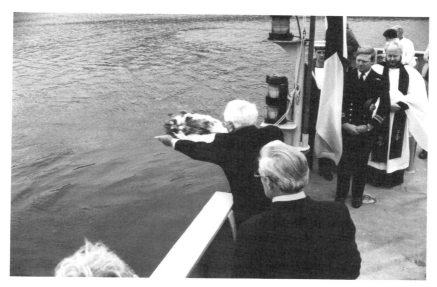

Dickie Kendall casting a wreath on the spot where XE11 foundered in Losh Striven during March 1945, with the loss of C.O. Lt. A. Staples, A/B. Carroll and Stoker Higgins. Bill Morrison, foreground, survived.

The face of a survivor. E.R.A. Les Swatton who, with S/Lt. Bill Morrison, escaped from XE 11.

first impact and escaping. Bill remembers his C.O. continuing to adopt a matter-of-fact and reassuring tone whilst coolly handing round the D.S.E.A. sets, as if this sort of thing was an everyday occurrence. This with the water already trickling, spurting, cascading and roaring into the doomed craft's control room.

As they hit the bottom with a great thud at 180ft, several things must have happened at once. An unnatural hush would have descended on the craft's interior, as the air pressure built up and lessened the inrush of water, the stern-down angle was removed, thereby improving the lot of the men aft and worsening it for those forward. The water reached the fuse box, there was brief display of fireworks and thereafter it was complete darkness.

At last the hatch yielded to the internal pressure and flew open. For which end Bill had been straining every muscle since the first impact. Now that they were on the bottom the internal air pressure had equalled the external sea pressure.

The control room's air was squeezed up into a small cubic capacity in the W. and D. and with a rush, was making its way up to the surface.

Before being carried out by the upward surge, Bill reached back into the control room and found Swatton's battledress top. Whereupon they both stuck in the hatch momentarily, until Bill dropped down and searched with his hand for one last time in the dark swirling water, looking for Carroll. Then oblivion descended and he was carried to the surface by Les Swatton. The man whose life he had just saved, had saved the life-saver. Alas they left behind them three dead men, who were all found to be wearing D.S.E.A. sets when the craft was raised a few days later and must have succumbed to the traditional enemy, oxygen poisoning.

The South African, Lt. Staples, and 'boys' A/B J. J. Carroll and Stoker E. W. Higgins, now lie in Rothesay Cemetery side by side. In March every year flowers are placed upon the graves by Joyce MacDougall, the former VARBEL Wren who still lives in the town.

After the tragedy of XE11, with the loss of three lives, the gloom didn't last long for, as Lily recalls:-

We were always having parties and Bill Morrison's 21st Birthday party, shortly afterwards, was one of the most memorable. It was held at the Royal, Port Bannantyne, on St Patrick's Day (17 March) and Varbelians still speak of it with awe. The unofficial motto was, 'Today we live, tomorrow who knows'. We worked hard and we played hard.

It also helped to erase the memory of the recent tragedy.

Chapter Nine
Sequel To The XE 11 Tragedy

In 1983 there was the Rothesay Reunion which was attended by some of the people from 1939-1945.

A post war picture of lovely Loch Striven in Argyll. This was another well-used training ground for midget submarines. The Royal Navy tender SENTINEL is shown getting up steam to return the former Twelfth Flotilla members to Port Bannatyne in 1990.

Lily Robbs:-

We went back to the Hydro and found a way in by the lower ratings messdeck. For a minute I stood at the top of those marble steps where I'd met Carroll that fateful morning so long ago and a chill ran down my spine; only this time Bill Morrison was with me. When I turned round, he saw the look on my face and he said 'You look as if you've seen a ghost'. So I told him what had occurred when he'd been involved in the XE11 accident. He tried to convince me that it had been a pure accident, and in no way was my cursing Carroll responsible for what happened but even with his assurances I still felt bad about it.

Another version told by one of the Sub Lieutenants, Ivor Jarvis, reads very similarly:-

XE11 had wandered out of her exercise area and come up underneath the screw (actually the bows) of the B.D.V. NORINA, just when she started up her engine so there had been no warning noises. Bill Morrison and the E.R.A. Leslie Swatton escaped together when the pressure equalised, but the other three did not.

Ivor remembers chatting to Bill in the bar at VARBEL the same evening.

I recall he got out when at 180ft, the figure sticks in my memory. He was none the worse for his ordeal.

Alas for appearances ... it was not until thirty-seven years after the event that Bill learnt that he had broken his neck at the time! Their feat of endurance and the depth were listed in the Guinness Book Records for many years and have only recently been superseded. The depth is now 225 ft without a breathing set[1].

Jessie Wilson has vivid memories of the XE11 incident:-

About noon one day the news spread around the Hydro that one of the X-Craft had been in collision with a surface vessel while working out in the bay. Soon we knew that the C.O. and two ratings had not been able to escape before the craft sank. Miraculously a S/Lt. and the E.R.A. had managed to surface, the E.R.A. supporting the by now unconscious S/Lt. The craft was later brought up and put on the stocks at Ardmaliesh Point. The following Sunday I walked with the E.R.A. to the Point. He was very shaken of course and later showed me a gold cigarette case, which had been given to him by the parents of the S/Lt. Inside were inscribed the words 'In gratitude'.

There followed the funeral of the three who had died. A very emotional experience and it was attended by the entire VARBEL ship's company.

Jo Terry-Lloyd (now the widow of Lt. J. Terry-Lloyd) remembers being told by Cdr. 'Mopsy' Myers after it was over, that the poor young bugler was so overcome with grief that he could not blow the Last Post.

As Supply Petty Officer (Clothing) Jessie Wilson recalls:-

I had, in the course of my work, occasion to meet with all personnel, as I issued cash, clothing, tobacco and also the protective clothing worn by the crews and other maintenance staff. Apart from the usual loan clothing, leather seaboots, jerseys etc., there were special kits I remember for X Craft crews. Three layers were involved:- first white silk combinations from neck to ankle, then woollen combinations on top of them and finally a 'Tropal' suit of navy blue padded material. We had a stock of yellow string gloves for protection of the hands, when cutting through anti-submarine nets underwater. After trying them out, it was found that they were visible to a vigilant enemy aircraft, so I had to send off a big box of them to a firm of dyers to have them coloured black.

Obviously those of us who were not in the category of 'need to know', accepted that at some points the crews were 'just away'. One day everyone was told to listen to the 9 o'clock news. That was when we heard that the X Craft had put the TIRPITZ out of action.

Some time later there was a call to clear lower deck, which meant all of the ship's company assembling on the quarterdeck. It was to greet the arrival of the 'Returning Heroes' but before their appearance, we were given the names of those who would not be returning. That news sent an audible sigh around the hall. Soon to be followed by great excitement, as many of us were waiting to see those who were special to us. Parties followed as always and the local at Port Bannatyne was once again filled with celebrating naval personnel.

[1]*Since the introduction of immersion suits where the diver breathes the air in the suit, breathing sets have largely became obsolete. The greatest depth which a man (Lt/Cdr Matthew Todd) has acheived in such a suit is now between 500 - 600ft.*

Chapter Ten
The X3 Incident

Although it did not prove fatal, easily the most terrifying accident during the training on the Clyde, involved a young Scottish officer, John Lorimer.

One of the first volunteers for the X Craft, Lorimer had joined them as a Midshipman fresh from the officers' training establishment, H.M.S. KING ALFRED at Hove.

By November 1942 Lorimer had become a Sub-Lieutenant and was acting as Lt. Don Cameron's 'Number One' on the X3.

With their relatively long experience of X Craft. Cameron and Lorimer were acting as instructors to the latest recruits. Cameron took classes out in the mornings, Lorimer in the afternoons.

The afternoon of November 4 started off like any other afternoon. Indeed it was a remarkably fine afternoon for the time of the year. A bright sun was shining and there wasn't a breath of wind. Lorimer was taking S/Lts. Gay and Laites for a practice dive in X3. They were accompanied by a small motor boat which was in touch with them by telephone. They also towed a small steel buoy to mark their position when submerged.

In due course Lorimer gave the order, 'Shut off for diving'. This meant that the engine exhaust pipe had to be closed and checked (also the hatch and the air induction pipe).

The induction trunk was the forerunner of the 'schnorkel'. It was a tall pipe that could be raised vertically, thus enabling fresh air to be drawn into the submarine without the seawater entering too.

Lorimer then gave the order to dive. The X Craft slowly dipped into the waters of Loch Striven.

Suddenly a startled cry rang out within the narrow confines of the midget submarine.

Water was pouring into her like a miniature Niagara.

Lorimer instantly ordered full pressure of air on the ballast tanks to empty them and bring the craft to the surface.

Slowly the X3 surfaced. A shaft of sunlight came through the observation window. Water was still pouring into the sub. She tilted to an angle of 85 degrees and began to sink again by the stern.

Within four minutes X3 was on the bottom of Loch Striven in 180 ft of water.

To make matters even worse, the battery had been flooded and was giving off thick chlorine fumes. Soon the atmosphere inside X3 was poisoned. Lorimer succeeded in tracing the fault to the air induction pipe, whose valve had jammed.

He was able to close it, but by then X3 was half-flooded.

In a last desperate effort to bring them to the surface, Lorimer decided to blow the main ballast tanks. Impossible. The tilt on the sub had thrown tools all over the place. The wheel spanner, without which the high-pressure air could not be turned on, had been lost. No amount of frantic searching could trace it. The lights flickered, then failed, leaving them in complete darkness.

One final catastrophe. They tried phoning the motor boat on the surface, only to find that their sudden plunge to the bottom had broken the cable.

Their plight was a spine-tingling one. X3 could not rise to the surface under her own power and to be raised by salvage craft would take a matter of hours. The chlorine-polluted air was rapidly becoming unbreathable and their D.S.E.A. only had enough oxygen for three quarters of an hour.

Lorimer made his decision quickly. There was only one thing to do, 'bail out'.

To do that he would have to flood the submarine deliberately, so that the hatch could be opened when the pressure inside equalled that outside.

As the X Craft slowly flooded, they put on D.S.E.A. sets. S/Lt. Laites had trouble with one set. He tried another, and had trouble with that one too.

After forty minutes in their steel potential tomb, S/Lt. Gay managed to push open the hatch and shot up to the surface. Laites was changing from one set to another at the time. Lorimer made another quick decision. Any further delay and Laites might not survive at all. With a sudden effort, Lorimer thrust him through the hatch with no D.S.E.A. set on at all, then Lorimer himself squeezed through the narrow hatch.

All three reached the surface safely, thanks to Lorimer's coolness and exemplary presence of mind. They were numb with cold, the water being in the low fifties.

Without loss of time, they were taken aboard the depot ship, a drifter appropriately named the PRESENT HELP, rubbed down and given hot tea.

Even nowadays Lorimer shudders at the memory of that afternoon. ''The most unpleasant hour of my life'' is how he describes it.

The salvage of X3 was almost as remarkable as the escape of its crew. The salvage ship H.M.S. TEDWORTH raced to the scene, with a team of expert divers aboard.

By 2300 that very night, X3 had been raised. A magnificent exhibition of salvage.

Chapter Eleven
HHZ Loch Cairnbawn Pre-'Source'

'There's the end of the world' said Captain Fell and pointed to a great pinnacle of rock with a white lick of foam at its base; 'The Old Man of Stoer'. The South Western extremity of the entrance to Eddrachillis Bay which led into Loch Cairnbawn, which in turn branched into Lochs Glendu and Glencoul.

The end of the world, and yet the beginning of it. For the wild geese which sight it on their migration from Iceland and for the teal, mallard and goldeneye flying South in the Autumn.

Virtually the only house at Badcall Bay, in the North or Scourie side of Eddrachillis Bay. The deep-water channel through which BONAVENTURE had to pass on the other side of the group of islands.

To them it is a rich and welcome land this barren-looking county of Sutherland in the far North of Scotland, with its treeless purple highlands, its greeny-brown peat bogs and its rust-coloured streams filling the winding silver lochs.

That much loved Leader of Men and keen fisherman Captain Fell, the New Zealand-born Captain of BONAVENTURE, the depot ship for X Craft training, loved the wild and rugged places.
Captain Fell:-

Really to appreciate Cairnbawn you must take a boat and explore, have leave to fish the many rivers and spend the whole year watching the seasons change, see the waterfalls blown vertically upwards, the stags fighting, the salmon leaping and

The new bridge over the Narrows, with a strong flood tide running helped by a brisk Westerly breeze. During their training. X Craft and Chariots went through here underwater.

the rising trout, the basking sharks and the great billows of sea birds, below the slopes of Quinag.

Ivor Jarvis, a S/Lt. who was later on the XE8:-

The location really was very remote. Some of us loved it. Others plainly didn't. Various exercises involving X Craft were carried out from BONAVENTURE. Quite a lot of time was spent on avoidance exercises.

An X Craft would move East from Eddrachillis Bay, submerged of course, and attempt to traverse Loch Cairnbawn without being detected by hydrophones manned by other crews on the South shore.

If you were on shore and believed you had heard the tell-tale sounds of an X Craft's motor you heaved three hand grenades off the rocks into the sea. The local pollack didn't take too kindly to this, but there weren't many of them.

Various ruses were used in these avoidance attempts. Some skippers tried a static trim at periscope depth (9ft) and attempted to move in silently with the incoming tide, and without steerage way. One tried the idea of hand cranking the engine, turning the propeller slowly and silently to get some forward momentum.

In other busier lochs, someone had dreamed up the imaginative ruse whereby the C.O. hung around outside the entrance, waiting for an incoming vessel, then tagged along behind her at periscope depth. A Canadian Officer adopted it from his own name - Johny Ruse! The strategy was used with great success at the forthcoming Operation 'Source'. The resulting kerfuffle heard in the hydrophone operators' ears would have been indistinguishable from that of the vessel's wash alone and the few inches of her periscope that were visible to the naked eye, would have been lost in the commotion. Fishing boat traffic in Loch Cairnbawn at this time, was negligible. In fact the dodge was so popular that Ian Fraser once hung about off the entrance to another loch for an hour and twenty minutes awaiting the scheduled arrival of MacBrayne's steamer, in order to prevent the noise of his engine reaching the hydrophones.

Another 'attack' on BONAVENTURE was made by Lt. Cameron on X6 making a night entrance to Loch Cairnbawn, in the face of 'stiff' opposition from Lt. Terry-Lloyd and party. Trimmed down and sitting on the casing with the sound-powered handset, waist deep in water. (He could speak on an S.P. Handset). He likened this novel experience to surf riding. "Water up to my middle. Damp but good fun.
Ivor Jarvis:-

In June 1943 the loch was also used for sea-bed explosions of experimental charges. The ensuing column of water, which was all being recorded on a movie camera, was measured by the Boffins to calculate the probable effectiveness of the detonations.

Trial charges were dropped, in this case from X7 and fired in Loch Glendhu, where the depth was considerable and the width only half a mile between high mountains. The charges went off punctually and the effect was most spectacular. A wall of solid water rose and came sweeping down the loch like a tidal wave and the sea rose up the rocks where Captain Banks and the V.I.P. onlookers were standing, a distance of 10 to 15ft. (Captain Banks was the Commanding Officer of VARBEL I).

The official report isn't quite so enthusiastic but nevertheless compared to a magnetic mine, the height of splash is unremarkable but the width is much greater. Two peaks of water 400ft apart but smooth water between and on either side. Only half a dozen whiting washed up disappointingly but, according to the locals there was no fish in loch anyway at this time of year.

E.R.A. Ginger Coles and party, who had gone along to see the fun, were even less enthusiastic and, in fact were a wee bit disappointed. Perhaps this had something to do with the fact that an unthinking authority had obliged them to observe this exercise from the steep opposite shore. Where, in the event of a really earth-shaking explosion, the entire hillside might have detached itself and glissaded in to the loch, carrying the unfortunate Ginger and Co. with it.
Ivor Jarvis:-

The Western seaboard South of the Minch was frequently used in 1943/4 for long-distance towing exercises. Big sub. on the surface towing little sub. submerged at 50ft at the end of a nylon tow rope.

The trouble on these runs was that the tow rope stretched so much that the phone cable running through its core became vulnerable and sometimes failed. Inter-sub.

contact then being nil. This could be a problem, as I found once on a future occasion when in XE8 off the Mull of Kintyre, submerged on the end of a tow rope and having to surface without the big sub's knowledge.

A day off a run ashore from Kylesku was across Scotland, driven at high speed by a Marine driver, sometimes in fog, on the switchback single-track road, to Invergordon. A distance of some 70 miles each way, with the inevitable stop for refreshment at the inn at Oykell Bridge. All very enjoyable but I remember that there was very little to do in Invergordon when we got there. Especially on a Sunday. Oh those Scottish Sabbaths. We were quite daft really.

Oykel Bridge Hotel, a favourite watering place on the road between Cairnbawn and Inverness. The single storey part in front has been added since the war

John Bowman also recalls this memorable journey :-

While BONAVENTURE was at Loch Cairnbawn a duty shooting brake, or 'tilly van' as it was called elsewhere, left Kylesku Hotel every day 0830. Drove right across to Invergordon to ferry mail, stores, passengers etc. and returned to Kylesku at about 1800. There were, of course, regular boat connections between Kylesku and BONAVENTURE. At infrequent intervals too, a ferry crossed the quarter-mile-wide Narrows, from Kylesku in the South to Kylestrome in the North.

One of the principal divers on BONAVENTURE was Stan Johnson of London, later of Goole, a Petty Officer. He has fond memories of the former Clan Line

The Kyleku Ferry. June 1981

ex - merchantman:-

    H.M.S. BONAVENTURE was based in the loch very close to the island with the unpronounceable name of Eilean a Ghamhna (island of the blue convolvulus) in the S.E. corner. She was surrounded by nets, patrol craft and guards and used as a 'target ship'. The X Craft had to penetrate the defences and lay dummy charges under her. One of my jobs was to recover these charges, usually from about 21 fathoms. This was rather a contrast to my previous two years diving duties in Alexandria for in May 1942 I had recovered two Italian chariots from Anfouchy Bay near Alex. They had been scuttled by their crews after the successful attack on the battleships QUEEN ELIZABETH and VALIANT.
(The British went to enormous pains to prevent the Italians finding out the success of this operation).

    So my work at Loch Corrie was a lot deeper and colder, but it was great to be part of B. V.'s team.

Former charioteer Sid Woollcott recalls:-

    The human torpedo crews were also trained and carried by this ship. When the chariot ratings first went on board BONAVENTURE, they were split up and allotted to several different messes on the seamen's mess deck. After just leaving TITANIA where they had enjoyed the privacy of their own mess, to be mixed in with strangers, most of whom were working the normal ship's routine, did not please them at all.

Every night about half of them would be in the loch, carrying out chariot exercises, which meant that they would need to get some sleep in the daytime. With the routine of the ship going on all around them. This would make sound sleep hard to come by, so a mess of their own was organised.

Right up in the bows of the ship there was an empty cargo hold. Athwartships across this, about five feet from the deck, two wires were strung with the ends shackled to ringbolts welded on to the ship's sides and at the correct distance apart for slinging a line of hammocks. It was a good idea but it had its disadvantages. The wires were rather springy, so every time someone climbed into or out of his hammock, or even turned over in his sleep, the rest of the hammocks would begin a wild dance and start bobbing up and down like so many steeds on a roundabout.

However, they soon became accustomed to this bizarre way of sleeping and the charioteers had quite a happy time aboard BONAVENTURE.

Peter Smail was a Shipwright Artificer on the 'Bonny', or just B.V. as the depot ship was affectionately known.

Peter Smail:-

We were very busy and it was the accepted thing that often duty called upon us to work all night as well as all day, when X Craft tails had to be changed so that they could operate the next day. The 'tail' or after part had to be removed if an engine required working on.

Prior to the big day of September 5 1943, when live side cargoes had to be fitted to all six X Craft in readiness for Operation 'Source', we seemed to spend all our time chocking down midget submarines and fitting dummy side cargoes for practice runs. The amatol explosive that went into the side cargoes took the form of grey granules, rather like instant gravy.

After fitting and securing 'fit for release', I often had the task of being hoisted up and out with the craft and then when she was waterborne, lying along the top of the charge half in and half out of the water, readjusting the tension of the charge bottle screws to get them 'spot on' for release.

Runs ashore were not that frequent really. Time, opportunity and pay were not that generous at the time. While we were 'way up North', Kylesku Inn was a rather long walk from the 'Bonny'. The NAAFI manager organised his own canvas pub. With very few glasses available, he hit upon the idea of drinks from jam jars, which caused some amusement.

Moreover security was very tight and anywhere beyond a radius of a couple of miles or so was out of bounds, with Army Security personnel to make sure that it was kept that way.

Nevertheless, to prepare the men for 'living rough' in case they had to make their way across the wild terrain of Northern Norway into neutral Sweden, Stan Johnson remembers that:-

Special Service Officers and ratings trained vigorously and were often landed in the most outlandish places with no food, money etc. and had to get back to base.

When this happened at Loch Corrie it did not suit Jim McCaughan at all. S/Lt. J. N. McCaughan R.N.R. remembers one exercise with extreme distaste:-

It consisted in being taken in a closed lorry into the mountains and return undetected to attack the depot ship. We had, of course, no idea of the direction the lorry had taken and we were finally let out in very bleak countryside, God knows where.

Making use of our escape equipment i.e. maps, compass, emergency rations etc. and evading all patrols, we were judged to have made a successful overland attack. I can still recalls the difficulty in keeping together in the thick mountain mist, the cold and the fright we got when we stumbled into a herd of deer. I recall the walk through mist, more mist, bogs and not getting below the tree line until dusk. The sore feet and stiff legs the next day are also remembered.

Sid Woollcott was a charioteer at Loch Cairnbawn at this time and doesn't remember the canvas pub (surprisingly!) he does recall a rough corrugated iron affair half way up the muddy hillside, at the foot of which BONAVENTURE lay:-

There was just a beaten-down track to the 'pub'. The floor inside was like a quagmire most of the time. It is possible that the barman had some duckboards to stand on but the customers didn't fare so well. Seaboots were a necessity. After standing at the bar for a half hour or so, the customer would find that he had apparently shrunk in height about six inches. Either that or the bar had gradually grown higher. At closing time the clientele left, to a chorus of loud sucking noises as they dragged their boots out of the mud.

One of the men who plainly didn't think much of Cairnbawn was A/B Paul Hurrell who later on was to serve aboard X25:-

Well one blade of grass looked much like another and it was all buried under feet of snow anyway!

He must have been there for the bad Winter of 1944/45.

In summer the marsh flies were worse than the midges (called Clegs by the locals).

A/B Stan Pulham on the BONAVENTURE.:-

Loch Cairnbawn was a desolate place. Kylesku Inn was the nearest point to go ashore for a drink of beer that had hops floating about in it. Or the village of Drumbeg about eight miles away. We were moored near to the twin peaks of Quinag.

O Lord above send down a dove
With wings as sharp as razors
To cut the throats
Of them there blokes
What sells bad beer to sailors.

I remember the battleship MALAYA coming to Loch Cairnbawn so that X Craft could practice attacking her.

One afternoon it was decided that several messes have a race round the ship in Carley floats. This was a very impromptu affair. 'Ready - Steady - Go' and we were all paddling like mad in our tippy floats for B.V.'s cliff-like side. One man hung on to the rope ladder and the rest would swarm up the verticals to the boom, chase inboard to the next boom and back down into the float, which the seaman who had remained behind had paddled there. It was pandemonium, but it did give us some exercise and fun.

We also had rowing races in the two whalers. I was in the young seamen's crew and we were up early for training, 0530 or 0600. I believe the Stoker 'B' team eventually won.

We had a cinema on board BONAVENTURE in the forecastle. One night was for officers, next night Chiefs and P.O.'s, then the third night was for lower deck.

There was even a small NAAFI canteen on board where cigarettes, soft drinks, 'goffas' they were called, nutty bars (bars of chocolate), toothpaste and writing materials were for sale. Also a fairly large rest room and library aft.

Alan Kevan, who was a P.O. Writer in BONAVENTURE's Staff Office from 1944 until she paid off in 1952 and is an inexhaustible and inestimable source of information, recalls how they kept the lads from getting bored out of their skins:-

There were a number of other activities aboard BONAVENTURE in order to keep the large crew from getting too bored. Request music was played over the ship's speaker system, there were special talent nights and we did have a magazine called FLUSH. I remember all these because I was directly involved with them.

As a seaman Stan Pulham was sometimes in the part of the watch which did the upper deck work:-

Hoisting in and out of X Craft, manning the steadying lines fore and aft that were attached to her to prevent swinging until we wished them far enough! Painting ship. Hoisting out s/charges on the after well deck. These were to be secured to the sides of the craft, and were released from the inside.

On the fore well deck was the opening to a large hold, into which the X Craft could be lowered by two powerful cranes called Jumbo Derricks. This hold was in fact a well stocked workshop.

I remember another duty we did at Loch Cairnbawn. About five of us were detailed to spend the day at the side of the loch and set up a listening post, to try and detect any noise from an X Craft moving up the loch underwater. I cannot remember whether we heard anything now. I don't think we did.

Perhaps Stan enjoyed his time in Loch Cairnbawn more in retrospect, for when he learnt that B.V. had been broken up in Hong Kong in 1962 and that her plaque was missing, he was quite surprised that someone had not obtained this as a memento or souvenir. (I expect they had, and still have).

Don't you think someone of the Clan Line would have the plaque somewhere? Surely they wouldn't have let that go to Hong Kong. I wish I could have had a last look round the Bonny before she was scrapped. She was my home for three years and she was a Happy Ship.

S.D. Christie of Dartford, a Petty Officer on BONAVENTURE remembers the listening post incident too. Perhaps he and Stan were in the same watch.

We worked up for 'Source' mostly at Kylesku, Lochs Glendhu and Glencoul. I remember putting an Asdic loop across the loch which was manned day and night. The X Craft would come in from Eddrachillis Bay to attack B.V., well protected with nets.

We were top priority then and out on shore walking the sheep trails, you could be confronted by a bloke wanting to know 'who are you and where from'. He would be armed of course.

By early September Loch Cairnbawn was completely sealed off, for security reasons. The only approach road, which led up from the South to Kylesku ferry was blocked to all traffic except our own and the Drumbeg 'road' which led West was just a gravel track. The few people who lived between BONAVENTURE and Cape Wrath had to go North and then half-way across Scotland, before they could turn South towards civilisation.

The popular Drumbeg Hotel.

The road from the South from Lochinver to the Drumbeg Hotel remained open throughout the war, except when it was impassable in Winter. The hotel visitors' book contains the names of non-naval civilians, as well as some famous long gone midget submariners.

In the photo of all the X Craft crews that took part in Operation 'Source' taken on BONAVENTURE's forward well deck 'You can see the drum of a large steam winch in the background' says Stan Pulham. His party had an unenviable task:-

I remember about four of us were given a giant crow bar to endeavour to guide the thick wire on to the drum evenly, when we were hoisting inboard the first X Craft for the first time. Not very successful I'm afraid, too much weight on the wire. An X Craft weighed 35 tons without her cargoes. I believe a device was later installed to do this more effectively.

Peter Smail mentions the big day when the live side cargoes were fitted to all six X Craft. The smoking side cargo probably occurred on the same day but again, as Dick Kendall said:-

I don't blame the men for not waiting to find out.

Nevertheless, Captain Fell thought highly of the craft crews and his ship's company:-

Their lives were bounded by isolation, rigid censorship and a total lack of comfort and they stood the strain with a stoicism and remarkably little grumbling.

Uppermost in everyone's mind at this time was the preparation for an even bigger day; the departure of Op. 'Source' on September 11. When all twelve submarines, six large and six small would set off for Northern Norway. The two spare submarines SEADOG and SATYR (there were no spare X-Craft) were standing by at Scapa Flow in case of need.

Winter arrived prematurely in 1943 and in early September there was already snow half-way down the mountainside in Loch Cairnbawn and when the violent gales didn't stop the X Craft exercises altogether, they made life out in the Atlantic, appalling.

The full story of the working-up for 'Source' and of the operation itself, is told in other chapters. The reader can picture the scene of almost frenetic activity in this normally deserted loch, during the preceding weeks.

The tenders, H.M. Drifters EASTER ROSE and STARLIGHT RAYS, had the task of escorting the submarines up from Rothesay, together with that 'maid of all work' the small fishing vessel REAPER. Liberty boats would commute between ship and shore at regular intervals, visual signallers would be 'clack-clacking' Aldis lamps urgently to their opposite numbers and motor cutters and pinnaces would be dashing around between depot ships. For real emergencies there was a skimming dish or speed boat driven by Able Seaman Pearson.

BONAVENTURE, TITANIA (with towing submarines alongside) and ALECTO in background. HHZ in August 1943.

All stores and equipment arrived by road and sea and had to be transported to the depot ship by boat. Helicopters were in their infancy and some years were to pass before they were large and powerful enough to carry heavy loads.

Sometimes a conventional submarine, often with an unconventional one in tow, would enter or leave the loch, securing alongside or departing from BONAVEN-TURE or TITANIA.

One man who saw it all but whose lips were sealed because of his inclination and remote habitation, was an eccentric but kindly and erudite man of letters who lived in a tiny croft, Rientraid. This was the closest to and the only habitation near B.V. The croft has been well maintained, and extensively enlarged and in recent years has been owned (appropriately) by Earl Jellicoe.

Chapter Twelve
Operation 'Source' 22 September 1943

Have you given up all plans for doing anything to TIRPITZ while she is in Norway?

So came the message from an impatient Winston Churchill early in 1943.

It is a terrible thing to think that this prize should be waiting and no-one able to think of a way of winning it.

Unknown to the great man Operation SOURCE had already been conceived until the Spring of that year, been aborted, and came to fruition again in September.

The 'source' of all this concern was lying in a remote Norwegian fjord and had been there for many months but, unknown to the British, the giant battleship displacing 41,000 tons, had been forbidden to attack our convoys for fear of being sunk. Also Germany's oil fuel supply problem was already acute in 1943 and TIRPITZ could use approximately two tons a minute, when cruising at quite a moderate speed.

This was an ironic decision, when most of Britain's heavy units were employed in preventing her from getting out into the North Sea. The potential of this lurking menace, fifty miles inland, was perhaps even more worrying than if she had emerged.

The German capital ships BISMARCK and TIRPITZ had been laid down in June and October 1936 respectively. TIRPITZ was launched by Admiral von Tirpitz's daughter on April 1st 1939 but was not completed and ready for sea trials for another two years. Except for the Japanese YAMATO class, they were the largest battleships in the world.

The date of her launching, April 1, would have been a 'source' of mirth in Britain and the fact that she seemed reluctant to leave the security of the stocks, a bad omen. The occasion was made into a major propaganda event with even the Fuhrer and the National Socialist hierarchy in attendance.

The roar of approval as TIRPITZ finally entered the water must have been audible a long way outside the dockyard at Wilhelmshaven, and the show of Heil Hitler salutes from thousands of Dockyard workers must have gladdened Hitler's heart, despite his prejudice against his capital ships.

What would Admiral von Tirpitz, the instigator of the WWI German Big Ship Fleet, have thought of the battleship that was named after him, if he had known that she would spend most of her unspectacular career skulking in coastal waters and hiding from the enemy?

Why has so much more been written about the TIRTPITZ than about any other German warship? Her great size didn't necessarily make her the most formidable foe. In some ways it made her more vulnerable. Between her completion in 1941 and the final 'coup de grace' from the R.A.F. in November 1944, her value was in the threat of her existence. The concept of the 'fleet in being'.

This meant that the less powerful maritime nation (Germany) had ships that, although they didn't engage in fighting, represented a threat to the nation which had the greater sea power (Britain) and which had to keep ships at sea ready to counteract any possible threat from a ship or fleet in harbour. TIRPITZ was the classic case.

In 1943 the tide of war was beginning to turn in our favour. Our catastrophic reverses and withdrawals were being turned into modest successes. Still far too many British ships were required to watch the TIRPITZ and prevent her breaking out into the Atlantic.

For want of these ships, merchantmen with valuable cargoes were sunk in the Atlantic, battlecruisers were lost in the Far East and Russian convoys above the Arctic Circle were decimated. If TIRPITZ could cause those sort of losses just by sitting in a remote fjord, what she could have done if allowed to roam free would have been catastrophic. Even Hitler concurred and stated at the time:- The outcome of the war lies in Norway.

Although many miles from the open sea into which she hardly ever ventured, there wasn't a single theatre of war in which TIRPITZ's presence in far-off Norway wasn't noted and her consignment to oblivion devoutly wished. At the end, it was learnt that her big guns had been fired in anger on only one occasion, against a virtually undefended hutted encampment on Spitzbergen, that was the Anglo-Norwegian Weather Reporting Station.

As Mr. Churchill commented in respect of TIRPITZ:-

It exercises a vague general fear and menaces all parts at once. It appears and disappears, causing immediate reactions and perturbation on the other side. If she were only crippled and rendered unseaworthy the entire naval situation throughout the world would be altered and the naval command in the Pacific would be regained.

Very much planning had gone into this difficult and dangerous operation called SOURCE. Conventional submarines could not navigate the narrow twisting fjords and hope to remain undetected. Charioteers, (for whom the fjord was beyond maximum range) canoeists and frogmen could not have carried anything nearly powerful enough to do more than dent the TIRPITZ, even if they could have withstood the cold. Also in narrow Kaafjord, surrounded by high mountains, she was very difficult to hit from the air, so the idea of sending midget submarines was conceived.

At least one Chariot operation had been mounted against TIRPITZ when she was lying in Trondheim fjord but due to a stroke of incredibly bad luck, and when almost within sight of TIRPITZ, the chariot suspension wire eyebolts which were slung beneath the fishing boat ARTHUR, had carried away. Perhaps this most imaginative and ingenious method of getting them there would have been repeated, if the astute Germans had not salvaged the scuttled ARTHUR, discovered the eyebolts on her bottom and put two and two together. For fishing boats can go anywhere, in a way that naval craft cannot.

With the arrival, in late August, of the depot ship TITANIA and the six towing submarines:- THRASHER, TRUCULENT, STUBBORN, SEANYMPH, SYRTIS and SCEPTRE, Loch Cairnbawn (or HHZ as it was known in security language), was becoming crowded. The actual loch was of average size but the sea-facing 'delta' was very large and would have taken the entire Royal Navy's Submarine Fleet. Nowadays it would probably take the German Navy's too. September 5 saw all six X Craft hoisted inboard of BONAVENTURE and their live side-cargoes fitted.

This operation also sparked a controversy. A small fire had been started by a welding torch close to no less than six pairs of charges that were lying on the deck. A General Panic ensued (in the naval sense) and a hose soon put the fire out but a certain sheepishness was evident when it was learnt that only electricity could detonate the primers not heat and there had never been any danger.

X Craft crews aboard BONAVENTURE just prior to Operation 'Source', with Jumbo winch for hoisting X Craft in the background.

When departure time approached. Sir Claud Barry, Rear Admiral Submarines made his final and most encouraging speech and among other compliments he described the men as being like boys on the last day of term, their spirits ran so high. Captain Fell had given the thumbs up sign and there was even a telegram from Churchill wishing them 'God Speed'.

The culmination of weeks of planning and all possible reconnaissance, months of training for men and craft and years of research, was about to pay off. How many would come back? In fact, although all the participating X Craft were lost, only two and a half crews did not return. Nine men. For an operation of that magnitude and daring!

Of these ambitious three targets TIRPITZ, SCHARNHORST and LUTZOW, how many would they sink, or only cripple? or even dent? Perhaps they wouldn't even survive the crossing, with the equinoctial gales of September blowing. This was daunting enough in all conscience. A thousand miles of notorious North Sea then, after slipping the tow and exchanging crews in the pre-arranged position, sixty miles of a navigator's nightmare, traversing every anti-submarine and defensive device that the Germans could devise.

TIRPITZ and SCHARNHORST supposedly lying in Kaafjord, were to be attacked by X5, 6, 7 and X9. 10 respectively and X8 was to have a crack at LUTZOW in neighbouring Langefjord. An ambitious task indeed. Their only armourments the massive side charges.

The X Craft themselves carried no defensive weapons whatsoever, no guns, torpedoes, not even a revolver. Relying on their prior-intelligence and skill to avoid visual detection from sea, land and air, Asdic detection from ships and shore, sonobuoys, thermal detection, submerged magnetic loops, hydrophone listening posts, shortwave radar, search lights, mines and anything else that might be used against them. Even some guard ships had been issued with depth charges, for the Germans knew about the midget submarines. Not how robust they were, nor how they were armed or how they were transported to the vicinity of the target. From being mystified, when X6 and 7 were finally discovered, as to how they had come all the way from Britain to Northern Norway, the seamen of the TIRPITZ were lost in admiration. They thought these tiny submarines had crossed under their own steam a distance of 1500 miles!

In order to obtain really accurate vertical photographs of 'the Beast in its Lair' as Churchill called her, three Spitfires had been transferred to Vaenga in North Russia. The excellent pictures thus obtained, were immediately despatched to London by the Catalina shuttle service, thence to the large and small submarines that were involved in Op 'Source'.

However, the Spitfires which had flown all the way from R.A.F. Benson, only stopping to refuel in the Shetlands did not arrive in Vaenga until eight days before Op. 'Source' was due to sail from Loch Cairnbawn (on September 11).

Previous Russian reconnaissance had shown all three battleships to be in temporary berths but the Spitfires first sortie on September 7, showed only the pocket battleship LUTZOW in hers. The consternation felt at the Admiralty and elsewhere, on receipt of this news, can well be imagined. One of the top priorities with an operation of this nature, was for the targets to be where they were supposed to be!

The Norwegian Resistance, that incredibly brave and unsung body of men and women, was able to report only three days later that both TIRPITZ and SCHARNHORST had returned to their berths in Kaafjord. In the event only TIRPITZ remained, also that the least significant of the three targets LUTZOW was nowhere to be seen. She reappeared soon afterwards.

This information was signalled via London and gratefully received by the six towing submarines and their offspring, who were by then a third of the way across the North Sea.

Flight Lieutenant Mike Hodsman, who was engaged in Photo Interpreting at Vaenga with the Spitfires and Mosquitos at this time recalls:-

To ensure maximum security. One thought security and talked likewise. We had to be especially careful when speaking on the telephone, even resorting to riddles, like 'Tommy hasn't moved yet and Sammy is smoking his pipe'. 'Tommy' was TIRPITZ and 'Sammy' as SCHARNHORST, must have been getting up steam.

Although willy-nilly 'we' the British and 'them' the Russians were allies, the atmosphere between us was distinctly odd, with doubt and mistrust on both sides.

When these six small submarines departed Loch Cairnbawn, TIRPITZ had already survived eight operations of destruction. Bombs, torpedoes, mines, depth charges and Chariot warheads had all been brought against her, to no avail.

So its hardly surprising that BONAVENTURE's Chief Electrical Artificer James Williams, who now lives in a Retirement Home in Chatham, should feel intense pride and sadness, on witnessing the departure of these half dozen X Craft.

He had been with them from the beginning and had helped nurse the crews (wet-nurse, some would say) through their Initial Training Exercises (INX), their Advanced Training Exercises (ANX) and finally the APX, Advanced Penetration Exercises. He seems to have total recall:-

I remember Lt. Cameron coming down on X6 one night at 20.00 hrs in his No. 1 uniform. We were working on a trim pump to get the boat ready for the morning's exercise.

Off came his jacket and, as always, he started work himself. I said 'Look Sir, your good white shirt is getting coated with oil'. He replied 'You worry too much Chief. I've a dozen white shirts but only one X Craft'. Such was the man, such were they all.

After the war I visited the Base HHZ, the loch that holds so many memories for me. I stood there and thought of the day when our six X Craft left in tow. I'm not ashamed to say we had pride in our hearts and a tear in our eye, tough as we were. Then when they had all left we were somehow lost, our 'babies' had gone. It was hard going Sir but I wouldn't have missed it then for any other project.

The date of the operation was September 22, 1943 and this has become the date for subsequent reunions. The time of 0730 was also commemorated at a hilarious rendezvous in New Zealand some years ago.

The reunion was christened Operation SAUCE!

X5

Operational Crew:-
C.O. Lt. H. Henty-Creer R.N.V.R.
S/Lt. A. D. Malcolm M.I.D.,
S/Lt. T. J. Nelson M.I.D.
E.R.A. R. Mortiboys. M.I.D.
(These decorations were awarded posthumously).

Passage Crew:-
C.O. Lt. J. V. Terry-Lloyd M.B.E., S.A.N.F.

L/S Norman Garitty
L/S B. W. Element,

Towing Submarine:- THRASHER:-
C.O. Lt. A. R. Hezlet D.S.O, D.S.C., R.N.

The first of her class, X5 PLATYPUS was launched at Faslane on December 31 1942. The Beginning of an Era had coincided with the opening of a new year. It was a good omen, although not for X5 whose motto 'While I breath I hope', was not a propitious one under the circumstances.

THRASER towing X5 leaving Loch Cairnbawn at the start of Operation 'Source'

As none of X5's operational crew survived the operation, it is left to Lt. Lorimer of X6, to describe their departure for 'Source'. (From the Glasgow Sunday Post 1957.)

On September 11, 1943 an incredible armada put to sea from remote Loch Cairnbawn in Sutherlandshire. It consisted of six full-sized submarines each with an X-Craft trailing along behind the submarine, like cygnets behind swans.

This was it, the climax of 18 months of intensive training. Operation 'Source' was beginning. The midget submarines were going to war for the first time. Over 1,000 miles away across the North Sea lay their targets, three German battleships.

A tremendous responsibility too, for the crews of the X-Craft. If they succeeded in destroying or crippling the TIRPITZ, the British Home Fleet could give it's protection to the U Boat haunted Atlantic convoys and the lives of thousands of Merchant Seamen might be saved.

Tremendous also was the courage of the men who manned the midget submarines. They were proud of their little machines and confident that they were capable of the job in hand.

X5 in tow of THRASHER, had made an uneventful passage from Loch Cairnbawn.

Unfortunately very little is known of the movements of X5, after she arrived at the slipping position, West of Soroy Island on September 20, and been handed over to the Op. crew by the Passage crew, assuredly in good condition.

The Supplement to the London Gazette of February 1948 states:-

The wind had dropped to a S.E. breeze, the sea had gone right down and visibility was good. Enabling all submarines to fix their positions accurately'.

What is known to have happened now, is that :- At 2315 on September 20, X7 sighted another X Craft and exchanged shouts of Good Luck and Good Hunting. Although not definitely identified, the other X Craft was certainly X5, who now passes out of the picture until her sighting and destruction on 22 September.

All four remaining X Craft, X5, 6, 7 and X10 slipped from their towing s/sms between 1845 and 2000 on September 20, all being in good heart and trim, (X8 and X9 had already been lost).

Unfortunately X10 when almost within sight of TIRPITZ, succumbed to her many defects and Ken Hudspeth, her C.O., made the difficult but sensible decision to turn back.

So then there were three.

The intentions of the Commanding Officers were to proceed dived up Stjernsund during daylight on the 21st September in order to reach Altenfjord by dusk; then to proceed southward to charge batteries in the vicinity of the Brattholm Islands, about four miles from the entrance to Kaafjord. All three had intended being at the entrance shortly after daylight on 22nd September. X Craft were forbidden by their orders to attack the TIRPITZ before 0100 G.M.T. 22nd September but were free to do so at any time after that.

As all X Craft Commanding Officers had agreed between themselves not to set their charges to fire in the 0400-0500 period, it was expected that they would carry out their attacks somewhere between 0500 and 0800 G.M.T. laying their charges set to fire about 0830 on 22nd September by which time it was fervently hoped they would have been able to withdraw from the area.

In the unlikely event of all three craft being unavoidably delayed beyond the set firing time, a second attacking time of 0900 was allowed for in the orders.

Regrettably, the next sighting of X5 is also the final one.

Henty-Creer, Tom Nelson, Alistair Malcolm and Ralph Mortiboys came within striking distance of their target and may possibly have laid their charges.

John Lorimer from his position of advantage on the deck of TIRPITZ and facing up the fjord recalls with clarity this periscope approaching, 'And there was far too much of it showing!' There was only one X-Craft which it could have been and that was X5. Unfortunately this fact had not escaped the Jerries either and a destroyer was despatched to drop depth charges on the spot where the periscope had last been seen. John remembers seeing wreckage blown into the air and then an oil slick was visible.

All the crew were awarded a posthumous Mention in Dispatches. People in the know consider that they should have been given a much higher award. The cairn erected by Peter Cornish's second exploratory expedition in 1976, whilst searching for X5, gives firm credit to all the attacking crews.

Hopes were raised too when in 1976, portions of an X Craft were brought to the surface. Alas, and it must have been acutely disappointing for the Henty-Creer family, Godfrey Place's concretion-covered sextant was found in the bow section, proving conclusively that the remains were those of X7 and not X5.

It is doubtful if it will ever be known whether X5 placed her charges under TIRPITZ or not.

X6

Operational Crew:-
C.O. Lt. D. Cameron R.N.R., V.C.
Lt. Lorimer D.S.O., R.N.V.R.
S/Lt. D. Kendal D.S.O., R.N.V.R.
E.R.A. E. Goddard C.G.M.
Passage Crew:-
C.O. Lt. A. Wilson M.B.E., R.N.V.R.,
L/S J. J. McGregor L.T.O.
W. Oxley S.P.O.
Towing Submarine:- TRUCULENT
C.O. Lt. R. L. Alexander D.S.O., R.N.

Prior to Operation 'Source' X6 had had an eventful life.

Although he felt that staff officers were over-optimistic about the projected attack on the TIRPITZ, Lt. Cameron's notes on the final work-ups suggest considerable confidence in X6 which became known as PIKER II. The name is derived from the fact that Lt. Cameron and Lt. Meek had served aboard the submarine STURGEON before joining X3 which they called PIKER 1. (A piker is apparently a baby sturgeon). So their second X-Craft became PIKER 11.

The Pride of the Flotilla as they called her, was first away towed by TRUCULENT but she was very nearly the last too, for on the first night she was almost rammed by one of our own trawlers. Thereafter the passage to the slipping position was uneventful but certainly not dull.

With eight days and nights of vigilance, unrelenting concentration, hard work, cooking, eating, cleaning, occasionally sleeping and coping with the everlasting maintenance there wasn't time even to read a newspaper, assuming one could be found that hadn't become limp and soggy. The charts being canvas backed fared rather better. Most of the discomfort fell on the passage crews, who were the 'workers' in the midgets. The glory went to the operational crews.

Two men out of three had to be on watch for all of the 24 hours and someone had to keep an eye glued to the inclinometer and depth gauge (usually the E.R.A.), all the time that they were submerged, in case of the tow suddenly parting. In which case the craft would have plunged down below the safe depth of 300 ft.

With a passage of this length, the Care and Maintenance (C. and M. as it was always known) must have been almost overwhelming. There was the charging of batteries every six hours, endless mopping up or drying the bilges, testing of equipment and the drying of electrical gear with a ladies' hair dryer (most effective it was too). Cleaning metal and paintwork, clearing the heads, greasing and oiling machinery, checking insulations and chasing innumerable earths. Checking, checking, checking. As the items of 'dry stores' became soaked in the damp conditions, they were replaced by tinned food. There was certainly no time or inclination to toast one's toes in front of the quaintly named non-luminous hot air footwarmer, which was supposed to reduce the clamminess of the interior of the craft.

All these mundane tasks were routine in a normal submarine but were magnified in an X Craft because of the small number of available hands. Although there were still the same basic things to go wrong.

Fortunately, from the earliest stages of the Initial Training Exercise these men had been instructed in how to do each other's jobs. Every man could stand a watch alone, the E.R.A. could navigate and handle the craft, the C.O. could prime and start the engine, and the First Lieutenant could wash-up.

For the first six days of the passage the three men in X6 had encountered bad weather and then it had moderated slightly, fortunately in good time for the crew exchange.

An X Craft's operational crew travelled in the towing submarine as far as the slipping position, enjoying the rest, good food and warmth. In fact 'recharging their batteries' whilst the mother submarines spent most of the hours of darkness ploughing along on the surface, trailing her submerged little sister astern about 50 ft below her.

The exchange was successfully accomplished, after dark and in reasonable weather. John Lorimer gives credit where it was due:-

We transferred at about 1800 hrs paddling across in our rubber dinghies and found that Willie Wilson and his crew of two had left the craft in A1 condition. How they had stood up to eight days of being towed in that confined space in poor weather I have no idea. It must have been grim.

All the X Craft made successful landfalls, due West of Soroy Island and just beyond the Declared Mined Area which stretched right across the entrance to Soroy Sound. This led into Stjernsund and thence into Altenfjord, with Kaafjord tucked away at the very end. Although four X Craft reached the far end of Altenfjord, by the time they had done so only two were in a fit condition to attack the giant battleship.

Now at long last, the operational crews of these four X Craft X5, X6, X7 and X10 had slipped their tows and were on their own, in a craft which was behaving perfectly. Expectations were high, as they crossed the minefield independently and entered Stjernsund. They were determined to accomplish what they had set out to do. Sink the TIRPITZ.

X6 and X7, the two heroes of the future David and Goliath encounter were sailing in company unknown to each other. They did, in fact, keep so strictly together and to the original Target Plan 4, that two days later and after a 1,500 mile crossing from Scotland, they entered TIRPITZ's netted enclosure within five minutes of each other.

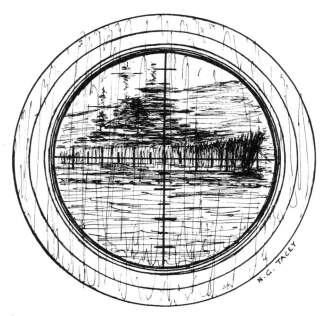

'The Beast In Its Lair'. Tirpitz viewed through the flooded periscope of X6 by Lt. Cameron, 0700 hrs 21st September 1943.

Soon after leaving HHZ X6's starboard charge had become flooded, but the passage crew managed to correct this. It wouldn't do to have their 'modus operandi' out of action at this stage. The periscope had also developed a defect and later on this became serious, so serious that finally Don Cameron was navigating on TIRPITZ's shadow, waiting for it to darken the glass scuttle head in the casing above.

As they entered Altenfjord, the passage had been reasonably straightforward and X6 and X7 spent the last night on the surface, hiding amongst the Brattholm Islands and pushing as much juice into the batteries as they would take. The islands were opposite the entrance to Kaafjord but TIRPITZ herself was still invisible, being around the corner.

Don Cameron describes his feelings at this time:-

The elation of sitting in the middle of the enemy's fleet anchorage, vied with the feelings of a small boy very much alone and wanting to go home and be comforted. I was not conscious of fear, just wanting someone to talk to.

Don had only recently married his Eve, who later became the wife of Commander Richard Compton-Hall, Director of the Submarine Museum.

John Lorimer:-

We had to dive several times that night as we were very close to the main shipping route to Hammerfest. At one point when I was on watch, we were almost rammed as the steering locked. Fortunately it freed in time and we avoided jeopardising the entire operation. It was a close shave.

Although they all kept their thoughts to themselves, nobody in any of the craft had any illusions about the dangers ahead. If things went wrong it would not be a matter of pottering back with a shrug to friendly old BONAVENTURE for a gin in the wardroom.

The periscope was being increasingly troublesome and flooded soon after they'd left their billet. It was taken down, dried and reassembled, but flooded again and again until it was amazing how Cameron managed to navigate at all. 'Might as well have looked through a beer bottle' he grumbled. Steer he did, straight for the gap in the anti-submarine nets which were not quite blocking the entrance to Kaafjord.

With unbelievable coolness they went through on the surface, in broad daylight and in the wake of a small coaster whose crew must have been looking ahead not astern, for they were not spotted. Also with the coming of the daylight at 0500 the German shore listening post had closed down.

The real testing time was now fast approaching, for the icy waters of the fjord were glassily calm and any strange purposeful ripple would be bound to be noticed. Even an X Craft's pencil-slim periscope raised two or three inches, created a wake.

With only two miles to go a blurred and distorted TIRPITZ appeared in the swamped lens, 'Like a great haystack', said Don. Then the periscope hoisting motor brake burnt out. Thereafter steering was by guess, by God, by Direction Indicator and Dead Reckoning.

Eddie Goddard's adrenalin was working overtime at this juncture, for twice they only just avoided collisions by a coat of varnish. Chief E.R.A. Edmund Goddard was on the wheel when, on the first occasion; they slid under the bows of a destroyer, between its stem and its mooring buoy! On the second, Eddie had to make a violent alteration of course when a large tanker buoy suddenly appeared in the sights.

Approaching anti-torpedo nets that surrounded the battleship on three sides, X6 again found the gate obligingly open. It was almost as if they were expecting her. This was to enable a German picket boat to enter. So of course X6 fell in behind her.

Now we have the diminutive David within striking distance of the giant Goliath. The crew were jubilant but their luck would not last much longer and with the gate behind them shut, there was no going back.

Lt. G. Place R.N. and Lt. D. Cameron R.N.R. The two commanding officers who both won the V.C. at Altenfjord.

Unfortunately, on the North shore of the enclosure and almost within the shadow of the looming great presence, X6 failed to prevent herself from breaking the surface. This momentary appearance was observed by TIRPITZ's sentries and had they had fewer false alarms in the past and felt less blase about them, all hell would have broken loose upon the luckless midget. Translated from the German, TIRPITZ's log entry reads:-

Through an Unter Offizier (N.C.O.). Within the net trappings, about 20m from land, an object resembling U-Boat, black with a longish body was reported'.

After about five mins they decided that the object was a porpoise.

As it was, the delay in reporting this porpoise-like object enabled X6 to close inside the range of TIRPITZ's subsidiary guns. Five minutes later, they again hit a submerged rock and were forced to the surface. This time there was no mistaking their presence and intention, but for the Germans it was too late.

Approaching about 60m away on diagonal course for turret A, a small U-Boat was recognised as it emerged, quickly a K-Boat (small launch) lying in the gangway with one officer aboard, approached and threw hand grenades which missed. The action of the anti-aircraft gunners was handicapped because the U-Boat was too close. Also there were other vessels and trawlers alongside.

Reminders

As you know, several of our Officers spent some years in prisoner-of-war camps during the late war. We have pleasure in reproducing a drawing of the German pocket-battleship, 'Von Tirpitz' and cartoons of German Officers which were made by Lieut.-Cdr. D. Cameron, V.C., while he was in Germany.

The German Pocket Battleship "Von Tirpitz" by Lieut.-Cdr. D. Cameron, v.c.

Cartoons of German Officers by Lieut.-Cdr. D. Cameron, v.c.

By now X6 was in a parlous condition. Although still able to submerge, the gyro was 'off the board' since the grounding and the periscope was, of course, useless. So Cameron navigated on to the target's port bow by eye. He surfaced alongside and was promptly greeted by the staccato rattle of machine gun bullets on the hull. As Cameron reflected later.

Not lethal but it made a helluva noise. Like a lone dockyard riveter. Hand grenades were also thrown down from the deck high above but thanks to the overhang, most of them plopped harmlessly into the water and exploded well out of effective range.

Here indeed was an almost comically ironic situation. TIRPITZ, the Lurking Menace, with her massive 16" guns capable of blowing an enemy ship out of the water at 15 miles distance was reduced to firing rifles, revolvers and even hand grenades at her 'bath toy' attacker at point blank range and still do no damage.

Nobody aboard X6 had time to ponder the irony as, realising that escape was hopeless, Cameron ordered the most secret equipment to be destroyed. Scraping along TIRPITZ's side, - there was no need for caution now, he made the craft go astern until she was abreast of the most-favourable position, he then had the supreme satisfaction of feeling the pre-set side cargoes containing four tons of high explosive, disengage and float gently down in the clear water, to rest under the battleship's 'B' turret.

'Abandon ship', ordered Cameron hurriedly for the craft was already rapidly sinking. They had opened the Kingston valves to scuttle her, as soon as Dick Kendall had released the charges. A German motor boat under Lt. Leine tried to take X6 in tow but the line had to be freed, as the submarine was heavier than the launch and would have dragged her down on top of the charges.

John subsequently wrote:-

'We did indeed bail out and we were very sorry to see X6 go. It was like parting from an old and very dear friend'. Cameron himself, of course, with water rising to the top of his boots came, last but as he said, 'I forgot my pipe and baccy'.

It transpired that Don Cameron, John Lorimer, Dick Kendall and Ernie Goddard did not even get their feet wet. They were transferred from the launch to TIRPITZ's accommodation ladder which they mounted, feeling a mixture of tiredness, apprehension as to how the Reception Committee on deck would react to their presence, relief and a certain elation too.

Unsurprisingly no remains of any kind were ever found of the already scuttled X6. She was lying adjacent to six tons of Amatex explosive and not far from a further two. Each side cargo carried two tons of Amatex and as X6 and X7 had both dropped their cargoes underneath or very near TIRPITZ, no wonder she rose 6ft in the air when they all detonated together.

X7

Operational Crew:-
Lt. B. C. G. Place D.S.C., V.M., V.C., R.N.

Lt. L. B. Whittam R.N.V.R.
S/Lt. R. Aitken D.S.O., R.N.V.R.
E.R.A. W.M. Whitley
Passage Crew:-
Lt. P. H. Philip M.B.E., S.A.N.F. (V)
A/B. J. Magennis V.C.
Sto. I. F. Luck
Towing Submarine:- STUBBORN
C.O. Lt. Anthony Duff D.S.O., R.N.

PDINICHTHYS was the strange name chosen by Lt. Godfrey Place for X7. It means 'A prehistoric fearsome fish' which laid two eggs (side cargoes) but her motto explained it all 'Not to our friends, only fearsome to our enemies'.

When on September 11 H.M.S. STUBBORN under Lt. A. Duff took up the tow, Lt. P. Philip the Passage C.O. was going slowly ahead in X7. He had already brought X7 up alongside the planes of his towing submarine, seen that the tow bar was correctly inserted into the bellmouth at the craft's bow and that the locking device had gone home. Once the tow was connected, the parent sub. slowly went ahead paying out the tow rope. The main concern of everybody was to ensure that the tow rope didn't wrap itself round the propellers. There was no sudden jerk when the bight of the 600ft tow line began to emerge from the water and straighten out; just a slight and steady increase in the X Craft's forward motion. Before that the Passage C.O. would have made sure that the helm was amidships and that his eyes were glued to the periscope, awaiting the expected signal to come from STUBBORN's stern. This announced that, (as Godfrey Place termed it), they were starting out on the Great Adventure at last.

Launched early in 1943 with scant ceremony she had taken part in the experimental sea bed explosion of side charges in Loch Glendhu, so X7 had her fair share of incidents even before Op. 'Source'.

All went well until the fifth day of the passage when the weather started to deteriorate and a log-entry at noon read, ominously:- 'Sea rough to very rough'. It was about this time that X7 suffered her first mishap and STUBBORN's report reads as follows:-

      1213 S/m sighted believe to be U-Boat. STUBBORN dived
      1325 Surfaced
      1550 Tow parted. X7 surfaced and auxiliary tow passed
      1700 Proceeded together
      1718 Closed and joined by midget s/m X8 (Who had also had a
             parted tow but who had lost her parent SEANYMPH).
             All three proceeded in company to look for SEANYMPH.
      1900 Dusk. Resumed course for Altenfjord (without having
             found SEANYMPH)
      1954 Signal made to Admiral Submarines in London to be

passed to SEANYMPH
2358 Contact lost with X8. (She had gone off at a tangent
having misheard the course, shouted above the noise
of wind and waves).

It was not for another 37 hrs that SEANYMPH and X8 made contact, by which
time STUBBORN and X7 were pressing on with the tow rope bar taut endeavouring
to make up for lost time. Bob Aitken recalls the procedure for passing the auxilary
tow in more detail:-

*The auxiliary tow was passed by putting me in an inflatable dinghy and floating
me down to X7 on a line attached to the auxiliary tow on STUBBORN. Once alongside
X7 the auxiliary tow was hauled over and secured to X7's bows. I nearly exhausted
myself attempting to return to STUBBORN by hauling on the auxiliary tow before
finding out the light line, still attached to the dinghy had become attached to X7 and
I was attempting to haul X7 as well as the dinghy and myself. When the rope was
released the return journey was made without incident and greatly relieved that I
did not have to finish the tow in X7, I climbed aboard STUBBORN.*

Despite the delay they arrived at the slipping position on schedule and as the
sea had gone down a little, Lt. Place, S/Lt. Aitken, Lt. Whittam and E.R.A. W. M.
Whitley (of whom only the first two would ever see Loch Cairnbawn again) crossed
over to X7 in two trips.

There was a certain pecking order to this. Sensibly, the C.O. and First Lieut. of
the relieving crew went first, floating down on to the craft, drawing a grass line
behind the inflatable dinghy. This would give the C.O. and P.C.O. a few minutes
hand-over time. Then the relieved or Passage crewmen would be hauled back to the
'parent'. The E.R.A. and diver would cross over to the X Craft and the P.C.O. would
return.

The Passage Crew were in high spirits as they scrambled down the vertical
ladder into STUBBORN's familiar smells, warmth, and mouth-watering aroma of
frying bacon.

Commenting on this exchange some years later Peter Philip wrote:-

*When we changed over outside Soroy Sound, Godfrey borrowed my boots,
enormous fleece-lined jobs, five guineas at Gieves and the apple of my eye.*

Alas this was the last that Peter Philip ever saw of his most treasured possession.
A letter written to him by the writer in 1987 enquiring as to their whereabouts,
elicited the reply:- 'John Lorimer says that, when Godfrey came aboard TIRPITZ
he was wearing some very large boots'. Peter Philip continues:-

*I presumed that these were mine and that they did not survive the P.O.W. camp.
I keep meaning to ask Godfrey but I keep forgetting.*

Alas Peter Philip died before he got around to asking.

He is remembered with affection for, amongst other things enjoying gargantuan
feasts when on passage. The short and lightly-built South African's favourite repast
was:- tomato soup, lamb's tongues with green peas and tinned new potatoes. These
were all heated together in one saucepan with loganberries and tinned milk to

follow. Given the restrictions, Mick Magennis was an excellent chef (he was later to win the Victoria Cross in the Johore Strait) but there was no way in which even he could improve the barley sugar, which very soon palled. It had been provided by a generous Government, even at a time of strict sweet rationing, as a convenient stand-by, and energy supplier.

Normally, slipping the tow coincided with the crew exchange but as X7 had exchanged her crews early during a lull in the weather, the tow had had to be retained. It was most unfortunate that STUBBORN, on going ahead after changing-over, parted her tow again. With the main tow having already parted three days before and with the auxiliary tow also having to be jettisoned, it was necessary to use a 2½" wire spring. Great difficulty was experienced in passing this, in the dark and with still a big sea still running. Eventually when STUBBORN was cautiously able to go ahead, X7 remained stationary. It was soon found that the shackle pin at the X Craft's end had come adrift and the whole procedure had to be gone through again, this took two hours. Lt. Anthony Duff's exasperation (and language) at this further delay, can well be imagined. It was not until 2225 on 19 September, four hours after the first parting of the tow, that both submarines were able to proceed together and close the mainland of Norway. The casing parties must have looked and indeed felt like drowned rats.

Before X7 reached the minefield at the entrance to the fjords, she had an uncomfortable encounter with a loose mine. STUBBORN saw it first and managed to avoid it but the mine's parted mooring wire caught in the tow-line and it slid gently and inexorably down towards X7. Five pairs of horrified eyes watched fascinated as this obscene object slowly impaled itself on X7's bows. This brought Godfrey Place up on the casing and forrard in a rush. Thence by his deft footwork, he persuaded the mine to disengage and seek another target. As the huge metal ball bobbed slowly and still menacingly astern, five breaths were exhaled and five pairs of eyes swivelled back to their original positions as Godfrey remarked:-

'You know, this is the first time I've kicked a mine away by its horns!' (The lethal bits).

The last incident of this unforgettable day, occurred just before midnight at 2315, when X7 spotted and spoke to what can only have been X5. This was the last sighting; all that happened afterwards was, and still remains to this day, informed guesswork.

X7 was still remarkably free of defects and, apart from having to dive with annoying frequency to avoid enemy vessels, she proceeded up Altenfjord virtually unhindered. A startled shout escaped Lt. Place's lips as he spotted a large warship in the lee of Aaroy Island.

'I'm pretty sure that is SCHARNHORST'.

Frustratingly, he had to press on to his rightful target, the TIRPITZ.

That night, X7 charged her batteries on the surface alongside one of the Brattholm Islands and taking advantage of the intervals between interruptions caused by small surface craft, E.R.A. William Whitley (so soon to lose his life) commenced fixing the spare exhaust pipe. Only to find that it did not fit. Luckily and thanks to his unremitting efforts, a repair was accomplished by means of chewing gum, canvas and vast amounts of electricians tape.

Long before dawn, X7 left her billet and set out on what was to be her final journey. Still lucky at 0400, she found the gate in the anti-submarine net open to admit a German trawler and following the trawler entered Kaafjord submerged and unobserved. Then things started to go wrong. First she was forced deep by a patrolling launch and got caught in LUTZOW's nets.

Bob Aitken:-

After wriggling for some time, forward - astern - light trim - heavy trim, Godfrey decided the boat was well and truly caught and told me to get into my diving suit and cut the net off our bows. When I was nearly dressed Godfrey found we had drifted off the net and thankfully I was able to take the suit off. Then her defects began to mount up for, as with her 'chummy' X6, her gyro was off the board and her trim pump defunct. Thus making her trim at periscope depth somewhat unstable.

Up to this point no suspicions had been aroused in TIRPITZ and normal harbour routine was in progress. The everyday life of this enormous ship with the population of a small town had begun. The Post Office alone required an organisation equal to that of a small urban Post Office, handling letters and parcels to and from 2,000 men, in addition to the mass of routine official correspondence. Mail was an important feature in maintaining morale at such a remote place. The cooks were preparing food in the ratings' and officers' galleys, yawning stewards were setting cutlery in the wardroom, cleaners were sweeping along the brightly-lit passageways, magazines were being opened and ammunition checked. The hands had been called at 0500 and sentries were being allocated duties, the pre-breakfast cleaning party was cheerfully dismantling the smaller guns and deep down in the bowels of TIRPITZ the operators of the hydrophone watch had (luckily for X6 and X7) switched off their sets to start the daily maintenance.

An almost leisurely 'peacetime' and certainly peaceful atmosphere existed, with not the slightest hint of the devastation, damage and death which would occur in a few short hours time, when the tranquil ambience of austere and lovely Kaafjord would be riven by two enormous explosions and several less violent ones and the mighty TIRPITZ rendered forever unseaworthy.

X7's position became increasingly precarious. Having extricated herself with difficulty from LUTZOW's net square Godfrey Place decided, at 0710, just five minutes after X6 had passed through the boat gate, to try to get underneath TIRPITZ's anti-torpedo nets rather than wait for the gate to be opened.

X7 was in and out of those nets for the next hour as, contrary to what they'd been told, one of the three nets extended all the way down to the fjord bottom at 120ft. Strangely they were still unobserved, for the net buoys on the surface must have been performing a dance. Backing and filling, to-ing and fro-ing, wriggling and blowing and with the compressed air in the remaining bottle becoming dangerously low they emerged at last, the motor was stopped and X7 was allowed to come up to periscope depth with very little way on, Lt. Place wrote in his report:-

By some extraordinary lucky chance we must have either slipped through the boat passage or, less likely, through a gap where the anti-torpedo nets did not overlap, for on breaking surface the TIRPITZ with no intervening nets was sighted right ahead not more than 30 yds away.

'Forty foot' was ordered and X7 at full speed struck the TIRPITZ a glancing blow on the port side below 'B' turret and slid gently under the keel where the starboard charge was released. Going slowly astern X7 dropped her port charge approximately under 'C' turret ('X' turret in British ships).

After PDINICHTHYS the Fearsome Fish had lain her eggs under the TIRPITZ, and the charges had been set to fire in an hour's time, she endeavoured to make their escape but became caught in the nets again. As they were only 170ft from TIRPITZ and in an uninterrupted line to the charges with the time for the explosion drawing ever nearer, the feelings of those on board while they were struggling to extricate themselves, can well be imagined.

In an attempt to crawl through the very small space between the bottom of the net and the bottom of the fjord, X7's bow was caught under the bottom wire and was ensnared. Although she eventually freed herself, she suffered irrevocable damage and became uncontrollable. Godfrey found he could only get her to the surface or the bottom.

On breaking surface she came under small arms fire and immediately went deep and into another net at 60ft. Whereupon, at 0830, two gigantic and almost simultaneous explosions shook her free and she found herself on the seaward side of the nets with the open fjord beckoning, but unfortunately she was doomed.

The pressure hull was still intact but the internal shambles was such as to make escape impossible. Having decided to abandon ship Godfrey took X7 to the surface, opened the forward hatch and clambered out waving a rather dirty white submarine jersey muttering 'here go the last of the Places'. He had decided to bail out first because every time X7 came to the surface, it was raked with small arms fire. Robert Aitken recalls that:-

As soon as Godfrey got out of the Hatch he realised that X7 was heading directly for a practice target moored in the centre of the fjord. Realising that with so little buoyancy X7's bow would be dipped under when it hit the target, Godfrey pushed the hatch shut. Not knowing this, I, coming up behind Godfrey, tried to push the hatch open. As X7 hit the target some water entered the hatch, X7 lost her buoyancy and went to the bottom, the hatch being slammed shut by the pressure of water and a helping foot from Godfrey.

Godfrey was quickly picked up and transferred to TIRPITZ's upper deck more or less dry-shod, where X6's 4 man crew were very pleased to see him. 'Godfrey was wearing an enormous pair of boots' wrote John Lorimer later (not knowing of Uncle Peter's loan) also a submarine sweater and thick woollen longjohn's, with no trousers. He was a cheering sight standing shivering underneath the guns of 'Y' turret.

Only one of the remaining crew who went down with her, would ever see daylight again. That clear, brilliant, diamond-sharp light that, up in those latitudes and at that time of year, lasts for most of the twenty-four hours.

For Bob Aitken, Bill Whittam and Bill Whitley it was a bitterly cold and painfully slow wait of two hours before the pressure equalised in their flooded, gaseous and pitch dark submarine and Bob Aitken was able to raise the hatch, come to the surface and feel the frosty taste of glorious early morning air. He had already ascertained that his two companions had died.

The oxygen of the two friends had given out shortly before Bob Aitken had made his way to the surface, so he had very nearly been entombed under 120ft of water with two lifeless bodies.

Although chilled to the bone and suffering from shock, he was taken aboard TIRPITZ and revived with hot coffee and schnapps. It happened that he did not see the five other survivors on board TIRPITZ, (who had been hustled below after the explosions), until a few days later in the Tromso Police cells.

Determined to learn more about these uniquely robust secret weapons the Midget Submarines, the Germans scoured the bottom of Kaafjord with chains and soon discovered X7. She was hauled up on the beach, minus her bows and these were not discovered for another thirty-two years. X7's battered bows and the heads are now squeezed in amongst WW11 aircraft at the Imperial War Museum's Outstation at Duxford, Cambridgeshire.

The recognising of Place's sextant in the bows after being inundated for such a length of time, was a revelation and prompted the original manufacturers Kelvin Hughes, to reclaim and refurbish it. On completion, they presented it to a delighted Rear Admiral Place in token of his supreme bravery. He had been awarded the Victoria Cross for this operation, as had his fellow Commanding Officer, Lt. Donald Cameron R.N.R.

When the Germans brought X7 to the surface in October 1943, they only discovered and interred one body. Bill Whittam, who had cut down and handed round the breathing sets with nonchalant sang-froid when the craft was plunging out of control, was buried with full military honours and his plain naval headstone still stands today in Tromso Cemetery.

Along with the seven other 'Source' casualties, Engine Room Artificer Bill Whitley whose dexterity had saved the day when the exhaust pipe failed to fit, has no known grave but the sea.

X10

Operation Crew:-
C.O. Lt. K. Hudspeth D.S.C. and 2 bars, R.A.N.V.R.
Lt. B. Enzer R.N.V.R.
S/Lt. G. Harding R.N.V.R.
E.R.A. Leslie Tilley
First Passage Crew:-
P.C.O. S/Lt. E. V. Page M.B.E., R.N.V.R.
E.R.A. H. J. Fishleigh D.S.M.
P.O. A. Brookes
Second Passage Crew:-

Lt. Peter Philip M.B.E., S.A.N.F.(V)
A/B J. J. Magennis V.C.
Sto. Luck
Towing Submarine:- SCEPTRE C.O. Lt. McIntosh (I.S.) M.B.E., D.S.C., R.N.

X10 had also led an eventful life pre-Source, having been sunk in Kames Bay in the summer. Her induction pipe shut off valve had been inadvertently left open, when her crew departed ashore.

As the pipe was housed in the horizontal position dribbles of water entered, gradually become a continuous stream until X10 lost buoyancy and sank.

At her subsequent refit in Barrow the Perspex observation dome was removed. X10 was the only craft to be so fitted. It had never been popular.

In tow of H.M.S/m. SCEPTRE, X10 left Loch Cairnbawn two hours after her predecessor and roughly two hours before her successor. The passage to the Slipping Position was uneventful.

Temporary Acting Sub Lieutenant Geoff Harding was relishing his first trip in a big submarine. Although SCEPTRE's passage across the North Sea had not been over-exciting, he'd enjoyed every minute. The change over in the rubber dinghy, even the night's run on the surface over the minefield had been a new and exciting experience. This was 'messing about in boats' par excellence.

They were still in the minefield when they dived and Geoff was still enthusiastic about the following hair-raising experience ten years after the war had ended.

I was sleeping in the battery compartment and awoke to hear a wire scraping the hull. I looked aft and saw three white faces, looking just as anxious as I felt. We all held our breath. The noise stopped. We all breathed again. It started and stopped several times during the next hour, until we felt this particular minefield must have the density of a Portuguese man-of-war's tentacles.

There was nothing we could do about it until it was time to surface. Whereupon we discovered that the auxiliary towing pennant had come adrift and it was this, scraping along the craft's side from time to time, that had made the noise. It was a piece of wire rope about ¾" diameter and was permanently secured to a towing point on the craft. .It was also made fast to the edge of the deck with clips. It wasn't very long and it was there to provide a means of towing an X-Craft if all else failed. It could only have been intended to be just better than nothing at all.

Secret Service agents in Norway were very Anti-Nazi and pro-British. Obviously the 'grape-vine' operated in war-time too, especially where one's mates were concerned. The fact of A/B Bob Evans having been shot as a spy in Norway the previous year, despite being a member of H.M. Armed Forces, had not escaped them. Chief E.R.A. Ginger Coles at the first Bergen do had been persuaded to put up the crossed anchors of a Petty Officer on his sleeve, and remove the Chief's three gold buttons on his cuff for the same reason. In the event of capture, he might have been taken for a postman or other civilian, and shot as a spy.

A/B Evans had been wounded in a brief exchange with German guards, after a party of Charioteers had 'walked across Norway', and had been left for dead.

He had not been quite dead, but had been rushed to hospital, operated on and saved. Subsequently he was interrogated, his story not believed and was taken out and shot.

The essential facts were known at this time but the whole story was not learnt until after the war.

Incidentally, and in this context, it seems relevant to point out that after the war when the Henty-Creer family were researching into the death of Henty, the C.O. of X5, they went to the lengths of consulting a medium. They were told, so the story goes, that a party of men could be seen 'walking across Norway' and one member had a bandaged head. With respect to the clairvoyant, this must have been the party of Charioteers who had arrived by fishing boat, (it happened about the same time of the year), and not Midget Submariners at all.

Unfortunately several defects had manifested themselves during this time, including one major one, the tail clutch, so Ken Hudspeth prudently decided that they hole-up in a deserted fjord, not too far off their route, and have a lengthy make-and-mend.

There not being much for Geoff to do, he spent most of the day sitting on the casing, fishing and looking at a giant jelly-fish:-

I remember there was a Jerry camp not far away, just over the hills. It was a strange feeling to be sitting in such tranquil surroundings, in glorious sunshine and in complete idleness! The sun was almost hot and I shall always think of Smalfjord as being a beautiful place. In a way I was sorry to leave.

They departed at 1800 with most of the defects cured but on the run-in up Altenfjord, one of the side cargoes flooded, this was serious and incurable.

With a partially flooded side cargo, progress was either like a bird with a broken wing or a porpoise gone berserk, depending on which plane (or creature) one preferred. Geoff still found it all jolly good fun:-

On one occasion we had to blow main ballast to avoid going down too far, then a few seconds later we were on the surface doing everything possible to get down again. We were close to the shore and near a guard-post at the time. It was still more or less daylight and my sentiments at that time were a combination of feeling cross and scared alternately. Mostly the latter I expect.

The boat was leaking above the main switchboard and when we were approaching the target all the fuses blew. It was my job to replace them, by the handful, as they continued to blow. There was a real firework display with sparks shooting all over the place. We had to use the fire extinguisher at one point, only to find that the label on it read 'Not to be used in confined spaces'! We found this hilarious.

At this stage of the proceedings, there was so much loose electricity about that we could probably have boiled the kettle by touching the plug against any bit of metal in the craft. I expect Bruce (Enzer) would have tried if he hadn't been so busy.

It was about this time that the gyro compass failed too but the magnetic compass flooded later.

At 0200 the following morning periscope depth was ordered, only for the periscope hoisting motor to burn out immediately the switch was pressed. The craft filled with smoke and had to be surfaced. Luckily there was no sign of life anywhere and in a few minutes they were able to submerge again.

The best that could be done in the circumstances was for the hoisting wires to be cut and the periscope manhandled to a suitable height then firmly lashed in the fixed position with codline. Near to it was hung a sharp knife and a notice saying:- 'To lower cut the line and stand clear'.

This impressive list of major defects was not getting any less, in fact the tally was mounting and they were not really in a fit state to go anywhere, let alone into a major attack.

Nevertheless at 0215 when the craft had bottomed in 195 ft just four and a half miles from the entrance to Kaafjord.

Geoff Harding:-

Ken Hudspeth asked each of us whether we wanted to go in. Of course we all said Yes, but after due consideration Ken said that it wasn't really practicable, which we already knew, and that if seen on the surface we might jeopardise the others' chances and what fun it would be to lie on the bottom and listen for the bangs. If there weren't any, well we'd think again and maybe 'have a bash' ourselves. At least if they did go off, we were far enough away to remain undamaged.

We continued to toil away, at the long list of repairs.

We felt like kids at a Punch and Judy Show, knowing that Punch was about to clout Judy and enjoying the fact that Judy didn't know. At exactly the right time, 0815, the bangs happened. They were a lovely sound. Soon afterwards, there were lots more bangs but we didn't know whether they were more side cargoes or depth charges.

Conditions were such as to make it imperative to stay on the bottom, so that's what we did, all day. I think we were all feeling a bit churned-up inside. We were glad about the bangs, but sorry that they weren't ours. We were pleased that we didn't have to take our wreck of a boat into Kaafjord, but sad that we'd had such an appalling run of bad luck.

By 1800, just twenty-four hours after we had left Smalfjord in high spirits, we had been on the bottom nearly sixteen hours. The air was becoming increasingly foul, making us disinclined to continue with the repairs, in fact we were just lying still and waiting for a good time to get away. It was not a happy party. We were desperately disappointed that, despite all our efforts, we had been unable to fulfil our task.

Nobody said much, but I think each of us knew what the others were thinking. I looked at Ken and Bruce and Tilley, on different occasions, but conversation was obviously pointless.

So Hudspeth decided it was time to go home.

Admiral Barry's report stated:-

I consider Lt. Hudspeth's decision to abandon the attack was in every way correct. To have made the attempt without a compass and with an immobile periscope, would have made any chance of success remote indeed. It would have been doomed to failure from the outset and would merely have been an unnecessary loss of valuable lives Lt. Hudspeth showed good judgment in his decision, thereby enabling him to bring back valuable information.

His crew was the only one out of the six to return to the U.K., bringing back the welcome report of the partial success of the operation. Although they had only heard and not seen the attack, being too far away from it, they would have had a good idea if TIRPITZ had sunk.

The C.O. continues the report expressing the highest opinion of all his crew throughout the whole time they were on board.

They worked long and arduously in the face of ever growing disappointment, and at no time did their zeal or enthusiasm fail.

Geoff Harding was the youngest officer taking part in the whole operation. He was just past his 19th Birthday. Prior to leaving HHZ he had still been a Midshipman and had been wearing an Army battledress top dyed navy blue, with the 'Snottie's' Midshipman maroon patches on the lapels. In the event of capture, this 'fancy-dress' effect would not have been very convincing, so the rules were bent and Geoff was instructed to put up a single wavy-navy ring promoting him to Temporary Acting Sub Lieutenant, four months prematurely. Again it would not do for the Germans to take him for a railway porter and have him shot as a spy.

I do in fact always feel sad about missing the SCHARNHORST, particularly when some other people sank 'my' boat! We were in such a terrible state inside, that it would have been suicidal madness to have continued.

Especially as SCHARNHORST had left her berth anyway. Consider the disappointment, after having gone through all that, then to learn that she wasn't there.

At 1800 they surfaced into the anonymous darkness and commenced the homeward journey.

Geoff Harding:-

We went flat out down Altenfjord with the skipper on deck. We dived once or twice under patrol boats, and at these times Ken would come below caked solid with ice and refusing all offers to take over from him up top, when we surfaced again. He had to 'con' us all the way out on the surface, as we had no compass. Once we tried running on the Directional Indicator. This was when Ken was down for a spell but when he got back up top, he found we had turned through 180 degrees and were running up the fjord again.

Down below we all got cross with the Directional Indicator and, being somewhat temperamental, it didn't work again after that.

By this time we had ditched the side-cargoes as they were both flooded and were reducing our speed considerably. Knowing how temperamental they could be, especially in deep water, we had an anxious time after releasing them. Nothing happened, nothing at all. We were, of course, busily leaving the dropping zone but 'hell for leather' was only about six knots so we would not have got very far clear.

0215 the next day (23 September) found them once again at Smalfjord. As the little bay was completely deserted and snow squalls frequent, Ken Hudspeth remained on the surface and secured to the shore with his grapnel, (the risk of detection being slight with both ship and shore covered in snow) and enjoyed some much-needed sleep.

Crossing the minefield that night presented no problems and 2300 found X10 at the first of several alternative Recovery Positions. A complete absence of enemy and allied, shipping in the area, enabled her to remain on the surface all day and signal with R.G. gear at night, hoping that she would be either seen or heard by one of our towing submarines. This went on for five whole nights. Harding found it a dreary business:-

The days were the longest I have ever known. None of us seemed particularly worried though and we spent the time making ever more far-fetched plans for escape routes, should no-one ever turn up to claim us.

They had a serious discussion concerning the two options open to them:- Either they could stand out to sea to avoid the offshore islands, whilst making the dangerous 500 mile passage to the small British Submarine base at Polyarno in North Russia or they could ditch the craft and walk across Norway into neutral Sweden, which was much nearer. The Germans were not particularly thick on the ground that far North, but the snow was, and neither proposition was very attractive.

Ken gave it two more nights. The first 'planned recovery position' not having produced a rescuer they moved on to the second, on the northern shore of Soroy Island where they again made fast to the beach of a deserted and scenically perfect little bay called Ytre Reppafjord. Geoff the 'Youngster' records his impressions:-

A waterfall emptied into it on one side and we had great plans to swim ashore and get some fresh water. The sea was practically ice and it would have been a pretty chilly swim.

As we were considering this, we suddenly heard an aircraft. The last man had landed below and the plugs pulled out in about five seconds flat. Our periscope was still showing above the surface, when we hit the bottom at nine feet. The chart had showed a lot of water there too. It was a funny feeling doing a spectacular dive and then promptly landing on the bottom only nine feet lower down.

To brush the cobwebs away we decided to have a wash on deck. It took us about half an hour to get undressed. We tried the special issue salt-water soap but found it produced much more scum than lather and we produced enough of the former ourselves. So we used Chemico instead, and followed this with a wonderful meal:-

> *Tinned tomato soup*
> *Tinned chicken*
> *Tinned peas*
> *Tinned spuds*
> *Tinned fruit*
> *and a Bruce Enzer cocktail consisting of malted milk*
> *made as thick as porridge*
> *Bon Appetit.*

The second alternative position having proved unsuccessful, Ken motored gently down the S.W. coast to Ofjord, where a towing submarine was expected that night. Down below on X10 the feeling of expectation was very high for they had decided amongst themselves that if no-one turned up by 0100, they would put their Emergency Plans into effect. An unnatural quietness descended on the control room and there was much surreptitious glancing at watches, as the minutes ticked by.

'Bruce, there she is'! rang out an excited voice from the casing where Ken and Bruce Enzer were keeping an extra sharp look-out. Sure enough an Infra-red beam was sighted and closed. It was STUBBORN and how glad they were to see her; it didn't matter one little bit that she wasn't 'their' submarine, anything would have sufficed. Tow-passing in the open (cold) sea was always a hairy business because the bit of the tow that was attached to the X Craft, was a 6ft long round bar of about 1¾" diameter with loops formed in each end and with the tow attached to one end.

The sea was getting up and it took some fifty minutes before the tow was passed. Engrossed in this operation, they hadn't noticed how fast the iron-bound coast was approaching. Before the tow could be rigged, Geoff was summoned on to the casing:-

I saw that we were very close to the rocks ashore. I was rather ill protected in battledress and gym shoes. Bruce tied a line around my waist and threw the other end to the submarine. Having come up out of the light into the dark night, I hadn't got my night vision, so that when someone shouted 'Jump', I had to leap across almost blind. Anyway I landed safely on the side of the conning tower and had kept my feet dry.

Down below', a voice instructed me. I had no idea that I had landed on STUBBORN. I leapt over the side of the conning tower and missed the ladder. I dropped straight down and landed on the hatch below, rather shaken and a bit bruised.

Apart from his final trip to X10, that was the end of Geoff Harding's part in Op. 'Source' and a fine part it had been. The weather became so bad that it was not until 2200 the next day, forty-four hours later, that the rest of the operational crew could transfer. They had been aboard their craft for almost exactly ten days which was then, and still is, a record. Despite the acute discomfort and profound disappointment, they were none the worse for their experience.

STUBBORN had lost her towing gear on the outward passage but an extempore tow was passed and having withdrawn to seaward, STUBBORN with X10 in tow and with X7's Passage Crew under Lt. Peter Philip S.A.N.F. aboard, set forth on her 1,000 mile passage to Lerwick in the Shetlands.

The homeward passage was not destined to be as uneventful as the outward. Much later Peter Philip described what happened next:-

At 1240 on the 3rd of October the tow parted and X10 dropped rapidly to 140 feet. We were getting so used to this caper that we went through the drill with almost casual nonchalance, shutting main vents blowing main ballast, engaging the tail clutch and motoring up to the surface. As soon as we arrived there, I went out on the casing to contact STUBBORN. Although it was broad daylight, there were no signs of STUBBORN of any other ship. We were completely alone on the ocean and about 300 miles from land in any direction. I have felt lonely from time to time but never as lonely as I did at that moment. Fortunately the magnetic compass was having one of its good spells, so we started the engine and set off across the ocean in the general direction of the Shetlands. Our solitary state, in fact, lasted for a 'long' fifteen minutes! At 1245 I saw a small speck on the horizon and as it grew larger I was delighted to recognise STUBBORN returning to seek her errant charge.

At 1330 STUBBORN informed us that her end of the towing wire had wrapped itself around her screw, so we steamed round in circles while she disentangled herself. It was at this stage that I became careless. I thought that STUBBORN was still stationary and that it would be safe to cross her bows but she was, in fact, moving ahead slowly, and I suddenly realised with alarm that we were going to collide.

From water level, where I was, her bow plunging up and down looked menacing and enormous. She struck X10 amidships on the port side, just abaft where I was standing. It drove the craft down into the water, so that I found myself still standing on the casing but submerged up to my chest. It was a nasty moment. Fortunately the impact had not been sufficient to penetrate our pressure hull. X10 slid out from under and slowly rose to the surface, bringing me up with her. I shouted down the voice-pipe to discover whether I still had a crew, and was relieved to find that all was well except that the hydroplanes and rudder seemed to have jammed. At first I ascribed this to the collision. Then discovered that it was, in fact, caused by our half of the wire tow, which was leading aft from the bullring and over the planes and rudder, whence it hung straight down. We had been so extravagant with tows that STUB-BORN was finding it difficult to keep up with us. At that stage, we were reduced to using her spare periscope wire, which was not as heavy as a 2½" spring (mooring wire) but was nevertheless much too heavy for me to haul up single-handed.

At that moment, Ken Hudspeth and Bruce Enzer arrived alongside in the inflatable, bringing STUBBORN's half of the tow with them. We rove it through the bullring, shackled the two ends together and then, as the submarine went ahead, she slowly hauled the wire up and out of the water. When we saw our end appearing we quickly secured it to the bullring with a round turn and two half-hitches, in real seaman-like style. The chances of such a primitive device remaining intact for long were very small but it was the best we could do.

The original tow had been shackled to the tow-bar when we sailed from Loch Cairnbawn but that was the last time that we in X7 and X10 used it. It was very much easier and just as effective, to secure the various makeshift tows to the bullring.

Ken decided that, as he and Bruce had four days in STUBBORN they were fully rested and would prefer to man X10 for the remainder of the voyage home. Much to their disgust, we sent my Passage Crew, Magennis and Luck, back in the dinghy and the three of us then prepared to take the X Craft the rest of the way. We had come 800 miles from Altenfjord by then and had about 400 still to go to Lerwick. All these complicated manoeuvres took time to accomplish, and it was not until 1745 that we were ready to proceed. I use the word 'ready' in a purely relative sense because X10 was, by then, in a dreadful state of disrepair, and seemed to be held together with 'string and stamp paper'.

Hardly anything worked. The periscope had jammed in the raised position and sprouted incongruously from the casing. The gyro compass was out of order and the magnetic compass only worked spasmodically. The automatic helmsman had expired, and so had the W. and D. pump. The glue pot only cooked after the most complicated evolutions. Half the lighting circuit had ceased to function and there were leaks in the air compressor and the airline. The first main line valve I tried broke in half, while No. 1 main vent had jammed open and it had taken much time and effort to get it shut again[1]*. The last straw was the demise of the heads pump, that 'diabolical heads' again, which was a serious matter in that confined space. We had to put a bucket in the W. and D. to replace the heads. I issued strict instructions that the ships' company was to do everything possible to become constipated.*

STUBBORN began to move ahead, the bight of the tow rose slowly out of the water and became taut and we were under way once more. Ken opened the hatch and leaped lightly into the W. and D. I really should have told him, indeed I would have had I not had other things on my mind. He landed right in the bucket and knocked it flying. Poor old Ken. After all those vicissitudes, he really deserved better than that. He spent the next half-hour cleaning-up himself and the W. and D., a responsibility which he manfully accepted. Then Ken always did have a highly developed sense of duty, which explains why he finished the war with three Distinguished Service Crosses.

However, it was, in fact, the end of our voyage. At 1915 STUBBORN began flashing. She told us that a full gale was predicted, and that she had received instructions from London to disembark the Passage Crew and for them to scuttle their craft. At 2030 on the 3rd of October X10 was scuttled and we were back aboard STUBBORN.

When we received the order to scuttle our feelings were mixed. On the one hand, it was frustrating not to be allowed to finish the job, particularly since two thirds of the voyage had been accomplished already. On the other hand living conditions inside the boat had become very bad indeed, since practically nothing worked and the stores and foodstuffs were running out; the water had done so already.

There was also a very large question mark over the tow, which was so makeshift that its chances of survival for more than an hour or two, were slight indeed. In a rough sea they were nil.

I suppose, to be honest, it was these factors which took precedence over the frustration I have mentioned. The factors enabled us to feel extremely relieved at the prospect of finishing the voyage in the relative luxury aboard STUBBORN, without feeling too guilty about leaving the job only half-done.

Geoff Harding obtained permission to make a last trip over to X10 to pick up some things:-

Although the sea was pretty bad, I went over in the rubber dinghy. Got aboard the craft and collected a pair of shoes I wanted but I had to leave all the other odds and ends that one collects, aboard. Just before we abandoned ship someone threw me up the ship's crest. This was a thick, heavy wooden affair and I remember someone cracking a joke about 'weighting me with the crest and sending me down with the

[1]*With the words Open and Closed having the same vowel and to avoid confusion in an emergency, the word 'closed' is taboo in the Submarine Service. It is always SHUT. Only the pub closed!*

craft. This very nearly happened for, as I jumped for the dinghy, I slipped and landed half on the rubber rim and half in the water. With the weight of the crest inside my battledress, I jolly nearly scuttled myself.

It was a sad business sinking the boat. She had been our home for nearly two weeks of momentous hours and never to be forgotten living and we felt it pretty badly. Nevertheless we sang lustily, 'Three Men in a Boat', until we reached STUBBORN, when we all went in the drink getting aboard.

And so ended Operation 'Source', the X Craft first, biggest and best op. but it was by no means the last. After TIRPITZ had been crippled, and could never put to sea again and harry the convoys and there had been two operations into Bergen, the emphasis of the war shifted away from Norway. First into Normandy, where there were two highly successful ops., and then the war in the Pacific drew them into Japanese held waters and there were three more, making eight operations altogether.

If only the X Craft potential had been fully realised by the authorities during the remainder of the war, it might have shortened it by several weeks and many lives would have been saved.

Chapter Thirteen
The Aftermath Of Operation 'Source'

When the charges went off, the explosion was simply colossal, the sound of it echoing and re-echoing amongst the hills surrounding Kaafjord. TIRPITZ leapt six foot out of the water, like some great wounded animal. Vast fountains of water were thrown up and crashed down onto her decks. All the lights failed and oil started to leak from her side and spread over the surface of the fjord. TIRPITZ's crew panicked, there's no other word for it, and started shooting at anything that moved. Seagulls, their own machinery, ships, shore batteries, and at each other but not, praise be, at the Four Brave Men from X6.

Dick Kendall from the deck of the TIRPITZ:-

As we went up the ladder John was ahead of me, Eddie (Goddard) and Don (Cameron) behind. As we reached the Quarter Deck John turned to me, conscious as ever of protocol, and said, 'Do we salute the Quarter Deck'? It was the last thought that crossed my mind and besides, I wasn't wearing a cap. I think John 'cut off a smart one'.

We were just for'ard of the quarter deck and kept within close contact of each other. Don walked over to me and said 'Sorry about this'.

The feeling was one of resigned expectation, what would happen when the cargoes blew. Would we be blown up too, after all we'd been through, would we be blown up by our own charges? This wasn't in the Manual at all. The overriding sensation was one of relief that we'd done what we came to do.

Don and John were moved away to be interrogated. Eddie and I were moved to a compartment on the port side, with a couple of guards. Ten minutes later the cargo side charges blew.

We ended up on the deck, shocked but unhurt, and were hustled back to the quarter deck.

There was consternation. We were more or less left to ourselves while German officers and men rushed about, putting into practice Damage Control measures. Some were injured (one was killed), others spat in our direction. TIRPITZ developed a list to starboard.

A German officer pulled out his Mauser and snarled at me, 'How many submarines? If you don't tell us, we'll shoot your friend'', pointing at John'.

A swarm of infuriated German sailors surrounded them. Fists were shaken and the mood was ugly.

At this point the Germans' attention was drawn to X7 which had just surfaced and they opened fire with small calibre guns. 'If it hadn't been for the distraction' John remembers grimly, 'I think we would have had it'.

Ten minutes later, Godfrey Place appeared on deck from X7. He was wearing massive 'dung hampers', (longjohns), and heavy boots. Which belonged, of course to Peter Philip.

Then they opened fire with medium armament and appeared to hit something close to the S.E. shore. I assumed it was X5 (which it must have been). Then we were taken down to cells and were transferred to Tromso Police Station the following day, by a minesweeper.

Dick had assumed there was only one survivor from X7 and he was delighted to meet Bob Aitken in the Tromso Police cells, the next day. Next they were all taken aboard another minesweeper down to Trondheim where they were transferred to a train, with the luxury of a third class carriage all to themselves, in which they awakened to the P.O.W. camp at Westertimke near Bremen.

The Interrogation

Dick Kendall:-

Remember we were very well briefed:- If you're captured, you'll be told you'll be shot unless you tell them what they want to know. If they're going to shoot you, they'll do it whether you tell them anything or not. So don't say anything.

At the interrogation on TIRPITZ, I don't imagine any of X6 said a thing. The only thing the Huns wanted to know was how many X Craft there were.

There was the business about shooting us and some fiddling about with pistols but the interrogators were not brutal to me.

We had a couple of months in solitary. Mainly contriving to contact each other whilst being interrogated in the Dulag, which was where the P.O.W. camp was, Marlag Milag Nord. Much use was made of the heads as a Post Office Box.

The interrogation at Dulag outside Bremen, was much more professional and subtle.

The proper thing was to say absolutely nothing, but that's not so easy. They talk for half an hour about this and that, London, close relations, sports, books. I had a small bible and some photos in my pocket and these were discussed, in a kindly way.

They kept us very short of food for two months and continued the threats, but I would not call the treatment brutal.

I think we all talked a bit. Don, I know, had common acquaintances in New York with the interrogator. I can't imagine anybody blabbed about the operation. I know somebody, Bob Aitken I expect, asked about Bill Whittam and Bill Whitley's bodies (the two who were lost when X7 sank) and was told that they'd been buried with full military honours. (Nobody has been able to find their graves.) Bill Whittam's grave has since been found in the Tromso Cemetary. The Germans were sticklers for form so, the reason that Bill Whitley's is still unknown may be because, when they wrenched off the bows of X7 with their dragging chains in October 1943 his body may have floated out. Anyway, as far as is known, it was never found.

So then we were moved to the main camp, Marlag 'O'. Life was what we made it.

A lot of the time we started tunnels. We had surreptitious news on illegal radios. The theatre was a very busy occupation to many. We played games to keep fit, soccer and rugby. We learned languages, and navigation. We had a good supply of records and books from the Red Cross. Several people took an interest in religion. We made fast friends.

There were culinary efforts at Birthdays and Christmas. We had a flourishing black market with cigarettes as currency (of which the Germans were desperately short themselves. In fact the whole country was in dire straits in this, the last year of the war). And of course there were letters. Glorious letters from home. It brought the best out of a lot of us.

The following recipe is taken verbatim from Guy Morgan's book on P.O.W. life 'Only Ghosts can Live':-

Take 5 Canadian Biscuits and grind them into a powder, personally I wrap them in my face towel and bash them with a boot. Mix a little Klim (skimmed milk), about one tot of whisky, some sugar a handful of raisins and a knob of butter about the size of a golf ball. Stir the muck up till its the consistency of bran mash and bung it into a well greased Klim tin. If you want almonds on top, use the kernels of prune stones; if your room mates object to hammering I know where you can get them ready sucked and cracked for 10 cigarettes a hundred. Bung the tin in the oven and there's your Birthday Cake. When its baked cover it with good thick Klim and leave it outside the window to freeze.

The feelings of Robert Aitken on mounting TIRPITZ's ladder differed very little from Dick Kendall's. Naturally they were all disappointed at seeing TIRPITZ still afloat. Nevertheless all experienced a quiet elation, but couldn't help feeling a little apprehensive about their reception.

Bob Aitken:-

This proved to be very formal and correct. Surprisingly I had always been confident of escaping from X7. I was the sixth person to be interrogated. They had run out of cells and placed me in a large steel cabinet used for storing hammocks.

By the time I arrived at Marlag 'O', it was well-established and all Red Cross parcels were pooled.

The arrival of parcels was a highlight for the camp rather than individuals. Their receipt was not all that regular but during the eighteen months that I was a prisoner, we never ran out and a small buffer stock had been built up. Of course those who had been caught during the first eighteen months of the war, tell a very different story.

The writer had asked Bob about any highlights of their drab Camp existence:-

A P.O.W. Camp is not the place for 'highlights' but one I can recall is my 21st Birthday on 1 January, 1944. I hadn't been in the camp very long but, bearing in mind how precious everyone's limited possessions were and had often been saved up over the months and years, my room mates made real sacrifices to give me half cakes of soap, razor blades and some cigarettes and chocolates. All of which had been received in Red Cross parcels.

John Lorimer from the deck of the TIRPITZ after 'capture' recalls:-

The periscope approached some 500 yards outside the nets, and with far too much of it showing.

It can only have been X5 for there was no other X Craft in the area. X6, of which John had been the First Lieutenant, and X7 had already been sunk and X10 was still bottomed among the Brattholm Islands, desperately trying to make good her defects

and waiting for the commotion to die down before slipping away unobserved.
London Gazette:-

It remains to be recorded that at 0843 a third X Craft was sighted. TIRPITZ opened fire and claims to have hit and sunk this 'kleine U-boat'. Depth charges were also dropped in the position in which the craft disappeared.

John recalls seeing wreckage blown into the air and an oil slick was observed shortly afterwards.

This must have been X5 under Lt. H. Henty-Creer R.N.V.R. which had last been seen off Soroy by X7, two days before.
London Gazette:-

No bodies or personal gear have been found and there is no knowledge of any survivors from X5.

Nothing has ever been found of the craft or the 4 man crew who were aboard her, lending credence to the accuracy of eye-witness accounts now widely accepted, that she and all aboard her were blown to smithereens.

Some people maintain that the reason that nothing was ever found of X5 was that, although badly damaged, she managed to limp away from Kaafjord into Altenfjord. Whereupon she succumbed to her manifold defects and may still lie on the bottom, in water far too deep for a diver to penetrate.

The other, much more likely alternative, is that X5's remains and all four bodies still lie on the bottom of Kaafjord, but under tons of rock. For the Germans detonated all the shore-line rocks adjacent to where she was last seen. In a successful attempt to obliterate all traces of their mortification.

Little did they know that the crew of X10 had survived, and lived to tell their tale.

For TIRPITZ the aftermath of SOURCE was short and inglorious. The Germans had no alternative but to try and get her back to a dry dock in Germany in a last attempt to get her fit for sea again. She was irreparable and a heavy-duty floating crane that had been sent from Germany, still hadn't arrived in November of the following year, when TIRPITZ turned turtle.

Her ignominious capsizing sealed her fate for she could no longer fulfil her planned function as a floating gun platform or 'Die schwimmende Batterie'. Six months after the X Craft operation and several R.A.F. bombing raids later, the Germans realised that TIRPITZ would never be able to traverse the North Sea and reach the Fatherland again. So a defensive berth was prepared for her off Haakoy Island, three miles N.W. of Tromso.

One dark night, after feverish patching-up preparations, and escorted by a small convoy of protective ships, the beast left its lair for good. Making her ungainly way to the open sea, she was then towed with weighted-down hawsers, so that they were invisible to the Norwegian Intelligence ashore and were also invisible from above, to suggest to the ever-vigilant R.A.F. that she was capable of travelling under her own steam. Hugging the coast she survived two more bombing raids, but the R.A.F. were not going to let this prize slip out of their fingers, as when the SCHARNHORST and PRINZ EUGEN made their now famous Channel dash. She finally succumbed to the five-ton 'Tallboy' bombs of the great Lancaster bombers. The 'coup de grace' was delivered shortly after she had reached her pre-arranged berth. She capsized completely with her top hamper resting on the bottom and the loss of many more German lives.

It took several years before she was completely dismantled and cut up for scrap. In fact, a deep-sea fisherman friend recalls seeing her vast smooth nether regions visible above the water, like a great stranded whale, and surrounded by a ring of small symbiotic craft, for many years after the war. It is believed that rusting remnants still litter the shores of Haakoy Island and many a TIRPITZ souvenir or small piece of her hull probably adorn the mantelpieces of sentimental German and British families.

Chapter Fourteen
Loch Cairnbawn Post 'Source'

John Bowman has a prodigious memory. This is undoubtedly aided by his job as Degaussing Officer with special responsibility for X Craft and the notes which he took. John shared a cabin on BONAVENTURE at this time with Lt. Robert Aitken R.N.V.R. who three weeks later was barely to escape with his life after being entombed for two hours under 120ft of water, in X7. They met 46 years later at DOLPHIN - and didn't recognize each other.

The actual Degaussing HQ was a lovely old 700-ton schooner, CREOLE, normally based in Scapa Flow and re-named the MAGIC CIRCLE.

THE STAYSAIL SCHOONER Creole, 697 tons. Lent by Mr. Stavros Niarchos, she is manned by British cadets from the Royal Naval College, Dartmouth, Worcester, Conway and Pangbourne.

This lovely schooner was based in Scapa Flow in W.W. 2 as the mobile Degaussing H.Q. She was re-named MAGIC CIRCLE!

John Bowman:-

The official designation of Loch Cairnbawn was 'Port HHZ' but in view of the almost total absence of the usual facilities, 'Port' was very much a courtesy title and it was really more of a sheltered anchorage. In the same way Port HHX was Loch Corrie, Port ZD was Loch Erisort, Port ZH was Loch Eriboll and VARBELS I and II were, for some reason, code-named Bravo I and II. At HHZ a number of heavy mooring buoys were laid at various positions, and that was about it. BONAVENTURE was moored roughly 1,000 yards due West of Eilean a Ghamhna and only fifty yards from the shore.

Port HHZ was 'closed' and all leave was stopped on September 1. This meant that no movement of any sort was permitted, either inwards or outwards.

As a civilian, of course, I had to leave before HHZ was 'closed' and in fact I cut it rather fine, as I was working on the craft until late afternoon on the 30th August and left BONAVENTURE at 0800 on the 31st. I was, in fact, running two of the craft over the detector loop in Loch Glendhu all day on the 30th. and completed my programme at about 1700, just in time.

The next morning I was able to catch a fleeting glimpse of TITANIA which had arrived overnight to act as depot ship for the towing subs. As we know they all left on September 11, but of course I was not there to see them go. I should imagine that it was indeed a very moving spectacle.

The port was re-opened to traffic after Op. 'Source' and for the rest of the year and well into 1944, as X Craft and Chariot crews shared BONAVENTURE and continued to train. At first for the Norwegian forays and then for the Far East, until BONAVENTURE finally left for Australia on the 21st February 1945, taking the first six XE's with her. The 'E' stood for Eastern waters. H.M.S. Wolfe had already left with most of the chariots and their crews on board.

BONAVENTURE also carried the Spare Crews that were attached to these craft, in the ratio of one spare crew to four XE's.

A very different but still exciting form of spare crew activity took the form of serving aboard Lt. Peter Kern's ML.235. This was a Fairmile B-Type Motor Launch attached to the BONAVENTURE as a permanent tender. With her twin 635h.p. petrol engines, she was an exceedingly handsome vessel and the apple of Peter Kern's eye.

One of her many jobs was to take part in depth charge trials, with an X Craft steaming in parallel. She would drop a single charge, wait for the craft to surface and compare notes, then repeat the exercise at shorter and shorter distances. When the odd light bulb began to pop in the craft and an occasional pointer fall off inside the gauge glass, it was considered time to call a Stand Easy.
Peter Kern:-

Another chore was to drop a depth charge near, but not too near, to an X Craft submerged to periscope depth. A hair-raising judgment to have to make. This was done at decreasing distances, so that midget submarine crews would gain some experience of the sound and feel of explosive shock waves if ever they came up against the real thing. In practice and after 'Source', they never suffered the frightening experience of having 'ash cans' rain down upon them.

On passage X Craft were towed by the Navy's normal submarines. In our own coastal waters, while travelling on the surface, these large subs had themselves to be escorted by a surface vessel as a protection against air attacks from both foe and friend. The provision of this escort was one of 235's duties.

Another was to act as a harbour defence vessel when, as a training exercise, the X Craft mounted simulated attacks on an 'enemy' battleship. On these occasions HMML 235's Asdics were brought into use, together with the eyes and ears of her two officers and sixteen crew. As often as not the X Craft managed the inward and outward journeys without being detected and the 'attack' was a success.

Peter Kern's experiences were many and varies; he must also have been a very good officer as the following incident shows. It relates to the manifest desire of everyone, both servicemen and civilian, to ensure that X Craft were as efficient a fighting unit as possible.

Peter Kern:-

I had to take some civilians with Captain S/12 (S/12 referred to the Twelfth Submarine Flotilla (the Navy is so small nowadays that the word Flotilla has died out and even its Small Ships are grouped into a squadron), up to the Hydrophone Range in Loch Long. The midgets were undergoing trials to locate and eliminate any extraneous or unnecessary noise, however small. I remember delivering my passengers to the particular midget under trial and scarcely being able to believe my eyes when I saw one of the civilians solemnly boarding the midget with a stethoscope round his neck.

As a doctor listens for the tiniest unwanted heart murmur, so this man was obviously determined to identify and deal with the tiniest of unwanted noises which might give a listening enemy the hint of an approaching attacker.

These tests and trials were so successful that by the time the XE's were launched propulsion was three times as quiet and the pumps ten times more silent than the original X5-10's.

Stan Pulham recalls:-

We had a bad gale in Sutherland once and the hawsers keeping us in position parted, damaging the fairleads and the guard rails and twisting one of the drums of the winch on the forecastle. We had to abandon the forecastle hurriedly because of the danger and BONAVENTURE left immediately for repairs in Greenock.

The wires had been specially made up and secured to the shore on our port side and to the bed of the loch on the starboard side. The remains of former were found in 1989 when preparations were being made for a cairn to be built overlooking this spot.

Unknown to Stan Pulham BONAVENTURE was making a dramatic mercy dash to Greenock.

Alan Kevan (Leading Writer):-

At the height of an exercise I was taken ill with acute Appendicitis. In fact it took nearly twenty-four hours for the diagnosis to be agreed and then BONAVENTURE sailed at full speed, the fastest she ever did in fact steam, down to Greenock where I was taken ashore in great pain and rushed into the Canadian Naval Hospital. I was operated on within two hours of entry into hospital and the surgeon admitted that any more delay and I might not have survived. What does remain firmly in my memory is that I was conscious during the whole of the operation, the hospital preferred a spinal injection to gas as an anaesthetic, something I had not even heard of. I was forever grateful to Captain Fell for his very humane gesture in steaming down to Greenock.

There was in fact a spin-off because my illness showed up a weakness in the medical cover on board the BONAVENTURE, Captain Fell did thank me later for enabling him to spot the weakness and to strengthen the medical side before we sailed to the Far East as the 14th Submarine Flotilla.

'The Battle of the Minches' from August 6-12, 1944, wasn't really a battle at all, not even against the wind and weather, unless it was a battle of wills. It was much more like hide-and-seek conceived on a giant scale, with BONAVENTURE endeavouring to look invisible and blend her great bulk into the background of many a tiny loch and the X Craft seeking her out.

Captain Fell describes the scene:-

All ships of the flotilla sailed for a five day exercise. We carried out every permutation we could think of involving attacks by X Craft and Chariots. Each night, we in the BONAVENTURE hid in some deserted loch in the Outer Hebrides having dropped our X's far out to sea. The X's then had to seek, find and attack us.

X20, under her C.O. Lt. Ian Fraser took part in this 'battle' and an excerpt from her log describes it in even more detail:-

Sunday, August 6 1944

> 1100 Slipped boom at HHZ for BARBARA ROBB (tender) to carry out Phase 1, PBX14 (PBX14 was the code name of the exercise that became known as the Battle of the Minches).
>
> 1130 Proceeded in tow of BARBARA ROBB manned by PC2 (PC2 was the second passage crew. PC1 must have brought her from Rothesay and have been weary)
>
> 1937 Surfaced towed to Stornoway
>
> 2102 Secured to BARBARA ROBB. Exchanged Operational and 2nd Passage Crew. (Except on operations, X Craft never went any distance without their tenders and depot ship)
>
> 2153 Air charge (It was compressed air that forced the water out of the tanks when they wanted to surface. Obviously these c.a. bottles had to be kept topped up.)

Monday, August 7 1944

> 0538 Slipped from BARBARA ROBB for Loch Grimshader (Leaving PC2 with BARBARA ROBB. Lucky so-and-sos)
>
> 0645 Entered and anchored in Loch Grimshader
>
> 0810 Proceeded from Loch Grimshader, dived (having breakfasted on the surface)
>
> 0845 Entered Loch Erisort surfaced
>
> 0920 Proceeded from Loch Erisort (disappointed. B.V. cannot have been there.)
>
> 1454 Sighted B.V. in Loch Shell. Course and speed as required to carry out attack
>
> 1555 Under B.V.
>
> 1610 Secured to port forward boom
>
> 1640 Battery charge
>
> 1130 Slipped boom as required for EASTER ROSE (tender)

       to carry out Phase II, PBX14.
   2105 Slipped and proceeded in tow of EASTER ROSE
Wednesday, August 9 1944
      0635 Dived for Loch Boisdale to carry out attack having
          spotted B. V.
      1012 Under B. V. released cargoes
      1030 Surfaced and secured to port lower boom
Thursday, August 10 1944
      1200 Slipped boom for H.M.S./m SCEPTRE to carry out Phase III
Friday, August 11 1944
      0825 Surfaced towed. On surface for shallows
      0948 Dived, for Loch Corrie
      1011 Running on engine at 6ft
      1030 Stopped engine, proceeded on motor
      1500 Under B. V.
      1530 Surfaced
Saturday, August 12 1944
      0530 Slipped boom as required for Crinan Canal
      2210 Arrived Kames Bay. Secured to BONAVENTURE (who must
          have done some steaming, for she was too big to go through the
          canal and had to proceed round the Mull of Kintyre)
      2350 Craft shut down
Stan Johnson:-

The following may sound like a matelot's tall story but it's the truth, barring an odd bit of naval language.

As you will have gathered, Special Service Lads had hard training programmes but on the night we got news of the TIRPITZ action, they were given a free evening.

Well, our canteen (Wet) was a few barrels set up in a tin hut on the hillside of the loch. I was duty R.P.O. (Regulating Petty Officer or the 'Crusher') that night and my hobby was playing the accordion. Well the lads approached me about going ashore. It appears they had bought the entire beer stock, got the NAAFI manager hooked, and as this was all illegal, roped me in.

So I transferred about thirty of them ashore, six at a time in our little motor dinghy. A good evening of wine and song was going well into late evening and beer was getting low, so I started to ferry them back to the ship some few hundred yards off shore. It started well, until about twelve were left and the engine of the boat was running hot. A gale started to blow. With six in the boat we shoved off, then the engine failed. If you can visualise pitch black rain blowing like stink with us pulling along the boom nets and drifting under the bows of the guard ship, with armed sentry. And we were spotted.

The sentry challenged me and by chance his light caught my cap badge. I replied that we were a Special Service Exercise Party and had broken down. He called away the boats crew and they took us in tow.

I asked the Coxswain to call at the jetty, just a plank sticking out of the hillside and balancing on some rocks, and pick up the rest of the lads. As they stepped aboard I told all of them, don't forget we've been on night ops. All went well until the last one, a very well-oiled Scot told the truth in real naval language.

I promised the Coxswain my tot next day, which he duly claimed. Got them all safely aboard and then did my job of quietening them down and retired to my bunk.

On duty the following week, my chummy M.A.A. (Master at Arms, the 'Jaunty') gave me a detailed report on the happenings of that night. Even though we were good pals I never did reveal my part in it to him. Until now.

A popular naval ditty of the time ran and probably still runs:-

> *Oh I wonder, yes I wonder,*
> *Did the Jaunty make a blunder*
> *When he made this draft chit out for me.*

> *Oh I've been a Barrack Stanchion*
> *And I've lived in Jago's mansion*
> *And I never want to go to sea*

> *Oh I likes my bar of nutty*
> *And I Likes my weekend leave*
> *And I always says good morning to the Chief:-*

> *'GOOD MORNING, CHIEF'*
> *(Said loudly without music by all the company).*

There are many more verses but these are the most impolite.

Ivor Jarvis must echo the feelings of many when he concludes:-

With fond memories of Sutherland, I had long entertained the thought of returning to Loch Cairnbawn even though I realised that as we humans tend to idealise the distant past, such a return could be fraught with disappointment. I had hoped to climb Quinag on whose summit long ago, in the company of S/Lt. Brian Cross, I had flushed a pair of white ptarmigan. The return in 1986 was by no means a disappointment but the weather closed in and the cloud-wreathed summit of Sail Gorm is no place for a lone rambler in his sixties.

Captain Fell would certainly have agreed with those sentiments. At least the ones expressed at the beginning of I.J.'s paragraph. I'm not so sure about the ones at the end for, as an intrepid sailor, he was still sailing his 40 ft schooner over vast tracts of the Pacific in his seventies. Alas, since 1982 he is no longer with us. Life owes him nothing, after the adventure and excitement that he experienced in the course of a long and eventful life.

He also recalled after a time lapse of forty-odd years:-

Little of the wet and cold and hardship the crews suffered and the dangers they ran is remembered. What do stand out are the nights in the warm smoke-filled wardroom, choruses sung and shop talked, and the feeling of satisfaction as defects in the X Craft were surmounted.

In a rapidly changing world where some people fear to 'go back' because of what they might find, Loch A Chairn Bhain, as it's now called in the gaelic tongue, is still a remote, lonely and quite beautiful place. When the sun chases the shadows at speed over the moutain slopes, one is reminded of the lighter moments of forty-five years ago, the gaiety and party goings-on, 'Today we live, tomorrow who knows'. When the sky is overcast and sombre and the rain comes slashing in from seaward almost horizontally the two peaks of Quinag seem to glower down upon the spot where BONAVENTURE once lay, now marked by incongruous fish traps, and one thinks of the Charioteers who lost their lives in this very deep and dark loch.

As one former Charioteer remarked:-

It was worth fighting for!

Chapter Fifteen
Operation 'Guidance' April 1944

X24

Operation Crew:-
Lt. M. H. Shean D.S.O. and Bar, R.A.N.V.R
S/Lt. J. Brooks, .S.C., R.N
S/Lt. Frank Ogden M.B.E., R.N.V.R.
E.R.A. V. Coles D.S.M
Passage Crew:-
S/Lt. J. Britnell R.N.V.R
L.T.O. (Lofty) Ellement M.I.D.
Stoker William Gillard.
Towing Submarine:- SCEPTRE
C.O. Lt. Ian McIntosh D.S.O., M.B.E., D.S.C., R.N.

Some of the Operation and Passage crew of X24 at 'Guidance' 46 years later. Standing in front of their old X Craft at the R.N. Submarine Museum H. M. S. DOLPHIN at Gosport. Left to right are: Joe Brooks, John Britnell, Frank Ogden, Ginger Coles, Syd Rudkin and Max Shean.

Operation Guidance was the first attempt by the Midget Submarines to destroy the Laksevaag floating dock at Bergen.

The attack on the floating dock was conceived when it was learned that it was being widely used by the German U-Boats and that the dock was also supplying power to two other docks and also just capable of taking the damaged TIRPITZ.

All this information had been supplied by a Norwegian who had worked for the floating dock company before the German occupation and through the Norwegian Underground.

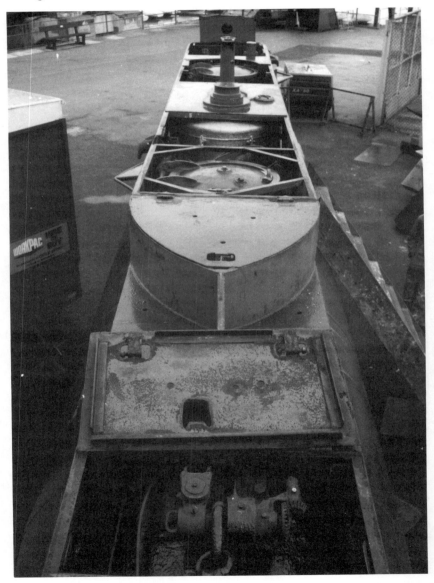

X24 now on permanent display at H.M.S. DOLPHIN, showing her innards whilst opened up for routine inspection and maintenance.

The tortuous approaches were heavily fortified because the port was a main supply base for German U-Boats in Southern Norway. Nevertheless it was also important that the craving of the highly trained midget submarine crews for action should be satisfied.

Max Shean:-

X24 which is now displayed for all time at H.M.S. DOLPHIN the Submarine Base at Gosport, travelled to Bergen in Southern Norway on two separate occasions, both times in tow of H.M.S. SCEPTRE:- Bring-em-back-alive-SCEPTRE as she was known forever afterwards.

H.M.S/m. SCEPTRE under the command of Lt. I. McIntosh R.N. comes alongside the depot ship ALECTO in Balta Sound after the succesful attack on the floating dock in Bergan. The weary members of X24's Operation crew enjoy the fresh air and the luxury of some elbow room.

Although intending to sink the floating dock, widely used by the Germans to service their U-Boats, they in fact sank a German merchant ship BAHRENFELS, a second priority target. So there had to be a return trip in order to sink the primary target.

There had been complications from the outset. In early 1944, X24, under Lt. McFarlane was scheduled to leave the Clyde for important defence - proving exercises at Scapa Flow, which would then have been a convenient jumping-off point for Bergen.

Max Shean:-

X24 had so many defects that sailing was postponed. My X22 was in very good shape, ready for sea in all respects so Captain S ordered a change of craft and crew.

The exercise was to prove fatal for McFarlane, Marsden, Ludbrooke and Pretty, the crew of the X22.

Lt. Max Shean R.A.N.V.R. C.O. of X22, must have hated having to relinquish his X-Craft, little knowing that the exercise was to prove fatal.

Max Shean:-

Joe Brooks, Ginger Coles and I then took over X24, and worked and worked and worked until we had a reliable submarine. Then we took her safely through the Pentland Firth and through the Scapa flow defences. The experience indicated that, with care and with certain techniques, we would have a good chance of penetrating similar defences, providing we were not expected.

The feelings of almost tangible anti-climax after 'Source' had dissipated by the time X24 sailed from HHZ at 10.00 hrs on April 9th 1944 on what was to be the first of the Bergen sorties. She and BONAVENTURE had returned from the highly successful Scapa Flow Penetration Exercises in late March, in readiness for the final work-ups before Operation Guidance.

Operation Guidance commenced with an uneventful trip across the North Sea. We had slipped our tow from SCEPTRE and were proceeding South inside the outer islands towards Bergen, having successfully negotiated the first minefield, but as it was night and because we were in enemy-held waters we were proceeding on the surface at full speed. I was keeping watch on the casing, when the engine stopped. Ginger promptly reported that the high pressure air compressor was leaking air into the cooling water system, which was connected to that of the engine. Water was being blown out of the engine into the engine compartment. He quickly isolated the compressor and restarted the engine. We resumed our progress towards Bergen at top speed.

The strain on the face of a chap who has been on watch for 19 hours. Operation 'Guidance', April 1944. Chief E.R.A. Ginger Coles has put up the crossed anchors of a Petty Officer.

Without the compressor we had limited H.P. air storage, enough to surface the submarine at least once, which should suffice until after the attack. This wasn't good enough for Ginger who squeezed back aft into the very small space between the engine, which was thundering away and roasting him somewhat and the hull. There he achieved a near miracle in removing an intermediate stage bush, refitting and replacing the seals. Then he re- commissioned the compressor and all systems were GO once more.

Shortly after this contretemps, they had to pass through a half mile wide gap between two islands, across which no less than five searchlights were playing. Max tackled this further inconvenience by navigating from a prone position on the casing and having the tell-tale induction trunk in the horizontal position, thereby gliding unnoticed beneath the searchlight beams. They had done this a few times before on entering the Narrows of Loch Cairnbawn on exercise, but it was still a nerve-wracking and damp experience.

Before entering West Byfjord, the main channel leading to Bergen from Hjeltefjord, they dived to periscope depth and promptly encountered the fresh-water layers which they had expected. Being used to Scottish lochs and the burns which fed them, Joe Brooks glued his eye to the depth gauge even more firmly, but they hadn't expected shipping of all kinds travelling in both directions. At least not in such volume.

Apart from the waterborne traffic and the searchlights and the pockets of fresh water, the main hazards were the minefields as well as the anti-submarine patrol boats hoping to catch just such an intruder proceeding with infinite caution a few feet beneath their keels. Indeed on one occasion when they had to increase depth very quickly as a German E-Boat went roaring past overhead, the gap could only have been measured in inches.

The sub-chasers actually made Asdic contact with the X Craft on two occasions and this regular and rather sinister 'ping' rebounding off the hull, akin to the Chinese water torture in its repetition, must have produced a convulsive twitch on the strained faces of the four men inside. By skilful zig-zagging and exemplary navigation Max gradually eluded the a/s boats finally to encounter the inner and last minefield.

On one occasion when Max cautiously poked the stick up a few inches he was so near the stern of the assault craft ahead that the coxswain's seaboots obstructed his view.

West Byfjord and the entrance to Bergen harbour were narrow enough but the passage through the minefield was even more slender and alive with shipping. Only by superb seamanship and razor-sharp reflexes, did they avoid being rammed and sunk-without-trace.

This hectic lifestyle kept them on full alert, right into Bergen harbour.

The object of the operation was to sink the floating dock but, unknown to Max, an additional berth had been constructed near and parallel to the floating dock. In this berth was BAHRENFELS with the same length and the same square-ended silhouette. It was impossible to differentiate between the two shapes from underwater, so it was BAHRENFELS which became the victim of the attack.

An intense Max and his team, made two dummy runs into the target, coolly judging their distance and positioning with complete accuracy. The four-hour time-setting was made with measured clicks and the side charges were released, one for'ard and one aft, then X24 turned around and went steadily down the fjord with her jubilant crew. Her motto was Make Haste after all. The relief was overwhelming for they'd achieved their purpose, or so they thought!

X24 with skull and crossbones. John Britnell is attempting to display it correctly in a fickle breeze. Note the white bar sewn on indicating the sinking of a merchant ship.

She traversed the thirty-five miles to her waiting consort, the faithful SCEP-TRE, in double-quick time, despite equally heavy traffic on the way out and the knowledge that there could be no relaxation in navigation and evasion techniques.

Nineteen hours later they still hadn't been able to surface for a change of air and the atmosphere had become extremely foul.

On the first surfacing a patrol vessel was sighted and X24 dived immediately. Fortunately the second attempt was successful, for they could not have lasted much longer. They also suffered violent headaches, acute nausea and retching. In fact it must have been sheer willpower that kept them going at all.

When Max eventually saw that all was clear he surfaced and ordered Half Ahead on main engine, a thick white mist of exhaust gas emerged and formed a cloud which would have been visible miles away. As it was, the gradual purging of the craft with fresh air did not immediately bring blessed relief for, as often happens sickness visited at least two of the crew. Neither would the engine start for several minutes. It wasn't until some time later that they recovered their composure and high spirits enough to appreciate the pure, cold Norwegian air and entertain thoughts of tow-passing. The big 'nosh-up' that awaited them on board SCEPTRE also exercised their anticipation.

Thereafter it was plain sailing back to Loch Cairnbawn, where the customary joyful naval reception was awaiting them in that magnificent and lonely loch, accompanied by a broadcast of popular tunes of the day over BONAVENTURE's tannoy system and loud hailers.

This silver lining had a cloud and it must have been gall to Max Shean's soul to learn, upon boarding BONAVENTURE and reporting to Captain Fell, that aerial reconnaissance showed that they had indeed sunk the secondary target the merchant vessel BAHRENFELS. A corner of the wharf containing a gun emplacement had also disappeared.

The operation did not end with the safe homecoming, nor the honours that were bestowed upon the crew. For X24 would have to return and go through it all again. A task for which Max promptly volunteered.

Max Sheen:-

It might seem to the casual observer that this operation was of only moderate success. H.M.S/m. SCEPTRE on patrol alone for the same period could have sunk the equivalent of the five thousand ton BARENFELS. Why, then, did Flag Officer Submarines declare it a singular success.

The previous operation (SOURCE) in which TIRPITZ was damaged had resulted in the loss of all six X Craft, two with their full crews and morale had suffered accordingly. On the other hand X24 had penetrated similar defences, sunk a target and returned in seaworthy condition with her crew, thus showing that it could be done.

The two X Craft which attacked TIRPITZ had been seen, allowing some evasive action to be taken, reducing the effect of the explosion. The third craft which approached her was sighted and sunk by gunfire. By comparison, X24 was not seen or detected at any stage, demonstrating for the first time in action that with careful and sparing use of the periscope in a well maintained craft, all detection could be avoided, though the need for up to date and accurate intelligence was essential.

X24 had previously been withdrawn from service and despite several emergency repairs, she had never been completely seaworthy. Her new crew, who had successfully commissioned X22, set about restoring and in some cases rebuilding her until she was in all respects ready for sea and continued to work to keep her that way, even to the extent of carrying out a compressor refit while approaching the target.

X24's success was a turning point in the morale and history of the 12th S/M Flotilla.

It was unfortunate that X24's crew had all dispersed by the time His Majesty King George VI visited Scapa Flow in the Summer of the same year to inspect BONAVENTURE and her associated craft. Max was recalled from leave to rejoin her and to receive the King aboard X24, which had been freshly painted for the occasion.

He was quite inspired by the King's interest and curiosity in his 'not-quite-the-smallest craft of the Royal Navy'. It was fortunate too that they chose the starboard side to mount the wooden staging set up for the King's convenience for, according to Stan Pulham, due to the short notice of H.M.'s visit, it was the only side they'd had time to paint!

X24, now with 2 bars on her Jolly Roger returns to Balta Sound, Shetlands. September 1944.

As we know, X24 executed a successful operation, except that she sank the target of secondary importance instead of the one of primary significance. The Navy wasn't aware of this when it gave her crew such a rousing reception on its return.

Loch Cairnbawn can never have looked so gay and welcoming before or since. 'Above us the Waves' describes it as being like 'Hampstead Heath on Bank Holiday Monday'. Ships were be-flagged, sirens hooted and a fleet of small boats came out to greet the returning heroes. SCEPTRE and X24 entered the Sound to the strains of Harry Roy playing 'In the Mood' on an amplified gramophone.

The second Bergen sortie Op. 'Heckle' commenced and finished at Balta Sound in the Shetlands and did not touch Cairnbawn. One imagines that aboard BON-AVENTURE the operation was given the same rousing acclaim.

Chapter Sixteen
The Loss Of X22

The 26th of February 1944 was a sad day for the Submarine Service. The newly commissioned X22, under the command of Lt. R. M. McFarlane R.A.N. sailed from Loch Cairnbawn to Scapa Flow in tow of HM Submarine SYRTIS. The passage through the Pentland Firth, the treacherous stretch of water between the north of Scotland and the Orkneys was regarded with a certain amount of dread by sailors, as it could be so unpredictable, good weather being followed closely by stormy conditions.

SYRTIS in 1943. In dreadful weather in the Pentland Firth, Lt. Blythe (with beard) was washed off the bridge and never seen again.

And so it proved when SYRTIS started on let passage through the Firth. Conditions in the larger submarine were uncomfortable enough, the bird bath having to be rigged to catch the seas which came tumbling down the conning tower, but conditions in the midget submarine astern must have been miserable in the extreme, being tugged in all directions as the SYRTIS yawed and plunged her way eastwards. The bridge watch, unable to use their binoculars, clung to the brass rail or to any object handy, to save themselves from being knocked over. The safety belts fitted in the German U Boats were not fitted in British boats which tended to be higher in the water and much safer for that reason.

Suddenly a huge wave smashed down from astern on the SYRTIS with such speed and fury that Lt. C. Blythe R.N.R. had only time to shout 'Hold on' before the bridge was engulfed in a mountain of freezing water. When it drained away, there was no sign of Lt. Blythe and he was never seen alive again. Ordinary Seaman Shields on the bridge calculated that he was underwater for at least twenty seconds when the submarine was 'pooped' and remembers that the tow line went slack.

Able Seaman Gammons:-

Lt. Blythe shouts 'Hold on', the wave engulfs us then he's gone. What we thought was him in the water proved to be the X Craft.

Able Seaman W. Harris:-

Saw Lt. Blythe in the water on the starboard quarter.

And according to P.O./TGM Hugh Fowler:-

Answered call for volunteers up on the bridge. Saw the shape of a man, then realised it was the X Craft. Wave smashes her right under the bows of SYRTIS, crunch, crunch, crunch. She is hit three times and the Captain smells oil fuel and SYRTIS rides on over X22.

Nothing was ever found either of Lt. Blythe or the craft of the four galant men who were on board.

The names of the crew of X22 who so tragically lost their lives, are shown in the 'In Memorium'.

Chapter Seventeen
Operation 'Heckle'
September 1944

Operation Crew:-
Lt. H. P. Westmacott D.S.C. and Bar,
S/Lt. Beadon Dening R.N.V.R.
S/Lt. D. N. Purdy R.N.Z.N.V.R.
E.R.A. Bryce Davison
Passage Crew:-
S/Lt. K. St. J. V. Robinson D.S.C., R.N.V.R.
A/B E. Whittaker
Stoker Luck
Towing Submarine:- SCEPTRE
C.O. Lt. Ian McIntosh D.S.O., M.B.E., D.S.C., R.N.

Why Operation 'Heckle' I do not know, the selection of these names just happens, and I suppose that this operation is so relatively small that there were no two thoughts about it. It certainly 'heckled' the enemy.

The writer is particularly indebted for this report of Lt. H. P. Westmacott R.N. (later Commander):-

If my memory serves, it was about 11 on the first Sunday in September 1944 that 'X24' sailed from Loch Striven in tow astern of SCEPTRE. At about 0900 S/Lt. J. Robinson took the craft from alongside ALECTO up to where SCEPTRE lay waiting to pass the tow. We had all been quietly dined by Captain Banks in ALECTO the night before and I recall that I was packed off to get some sleep at a very early hour. The Operation Crew and myself followed up the loch an hour or so later. All was ready by the appointed hour, and SCEPTRE cast off. X24 dived, and all that could be seen was a solitary 'S' class submarine dieseling off down the Clyde.

The passage to Balta Sound in the Shetlands took about fifty-six hours if I recall. I fancy we got in about the late afternoon, after a very rough passage indeed, but Lt. Robinson and his boys had maintained the boat in good shape, despite every temptation of seasickness to prostration. ALECTO was packed with talent from every department, who on arrival slid down to the boat and took over in a big way. Paul Dawson and his boys smacked on a charge and topped up the stores, they were absolutely marvellous, for they got very little credit officially for their work, yet to them had fallen the mighty task of storing and maintaining. On this occasion they put in all night on the job, and when we came to leave later that next afternoon, everything possible was in tip-top condition. There had been some ominous bangs from the side-cargoes on the passage to Balta, which we feared might indicate a loose charge, but these had been inspected and in point of fact there was no trouble on this score.

Beadon and I went for a long walk after tea in the evening twilight, and after a good night's sleep, we embarked together with Davison and Diver Purdy. It was arranged that this being only a short, 2/300 mile, trip, the Operational Crew was to perform the outward passage. At about 1000 we sailed on the last leg astern of SCEPTRE.

We quickly settled down with a first class trim, and high spirits. The afternoon of the first day was calm and sunny, but when we surfaced at 2200 for our routine nightly two hour charge there was a growing swell, the forerunner of a full gale which ultimately delayed us twenty-four hours.

Our routine was as follows:- At 0600, noon, and 1800 we surfaced for ten minutes ventilation, and at 2200 we came up for two hours or so to top up the battery. For each of these routine surfaces all hands were called to take a meal, which had been cooked by the watch.

On diving the two previously on watch turned in, and the other two took on for the next six hours. Life, apart from surfacing for ventilation, was very easy. The planes and helm needed absolutely no watching, so that the planesman was free to read a book or cook, while the other fellow sorted out stores, topped up R.U. stowages, and mopped and mopped and mopped. The condensation and sweating were incredible. We had sorted out the doubtful electrical circuits and practically every one was tested for short circuits with a megger after each six hour watch, and the gyro and periscope circuits were checked every three hours or even more often. We could watch a circuit insulation drop to perhaps 2-300,000 ohms, then put an electric hairdryer over it and bring it up to about two megs. These things we had to do or the machinery would not be available when we really needed it, and just in case the spare hand was idle for a moment there was the never ending mopping of deck and bulkheads. With four of us we could keep pace easily enough. Then we would surface and just the ten minutes up there would cause Beadon and Davison and Purdy to have a bout of seasickness. Even I was sick one night.

However, it transpired that the trip was to take about four days as SCEPTRE was to do the passage dived and finally spend one day on the coast reconnoitring. By the third day, we had accumulated so much garbage, having been unable to ditch it due to the seas being too rough to allow us to get onto the casing, that I had put all hands to work flattening tins to reduce the bulk. I was getting rather desperate about it, and thinking that the weather was easing I dressed Purdy up for the worst, put him in the W & D, warning him that he would probably get a lot of water in with him, told him to get rid of the garbage. Ye Gods! The first wave filled the W & D and the craft sank to about twenty feet, and when she came back, Purdy had gone. SCEPTRE circled round for him, but it must have been hopeless in the darkness and the storm.

It was paramount that morale should not be lowered and that we should press on regardless. Therefore McIntosh and I agreed to postpone our entry into Bergen twenty-four hours, and to send Lt. Robinson over from SCEPTRE to make up numbers in the operational crew. Meanwhile for the next twenty-eight hours with only three of us, we were a very subdued and weary party. There was much work to do, which fortunately left no time to dwell on the tragedy which had just occurred. We were *unable to keep up with the insulation routines and mopping and I had to watch the material efficiency of the craft deteriorate before my eyes.*

Next night, thank heavens, the gale had eased and I got onto the casing myself to embark Lt. Robinson (Robby) who got over by dinghy without difficulty, though the seas were still quite impressive. As soon as he was inboard the three of us more or less collapsed into a stupor, but Robby, fresh, rested and keen as mustard at this quite unexpected chance, went to work like ten men. At the end of that watch, I sat as planesman in mute amazement and admiration, the transformation was miraculous.

Next day, the weather was calm, though there was still a big swell, and the sky was overcast. Life slumped back to its rut of sleeping, eating, mopping and meggering.

Meanwhile, McIntosh quizzed the coast and studied tidal drifts, as he would have to run in after dark by dead reckoning only, with no light to guide him and nothing visible through his periscope. At one stage, just after surfacing, I stayed at periscope depth myself, and peeked a bit. This was my only view by daylight, as ours were the habits of a cat burglar, everything by night. It was a bare and rocky coast with an occasional white house, and in the distance the tops of high mountains.

Able Seaman Eli (Tubby) Whittaker, one of the passage crew of X24 on Operation Heckle, renews acquaintance with his old boat at the Submarine Museum, Gosport.

About six p.m. all hands turned to and we cooked a mighty meal, devoured it, then washed dishes and mopped as best we could. Next we ran up the gyro, and generally prepared, so that by 2000 all was ready. We surfaced alone and in a long and oily swell, beneath a starry sky, with the black shadow of the coast unbroken ahead of us, we slipped the tow, and got under way. I knew by heart every course and distance when we saw them and the characteristic of every light. So at about five knots I ran towards the coast. Shortly, I could see the gap between the two islands through which we were to pass, looking quite ridiculously narrow. The gyro repeater system chose this moment to malfunction, but ace Beadon got it right in a couple of hours, not incidentally, till we were half way through the first minefield. What with the noise of the engine, and Robby and Beadon shouting compass bearings at each other at every alteration of course, there was a fair commotion going on below. The essentials were alright. On the whole we were off to a flying start, except that the compressor was not working and I had only enough air as things stood for about two surfaces. However, I was only looking as far as the next one.

As I approached the coast a flashing light shone out in our direction, and I wondered in horror whether we were spotted thus early; but for want of something else to do, I pretended not to notice and after about five minutes it stopped.

I was dressed in a Ursula suit, with a pair of binoculars round my neck, and seaboots (full of water) on my feet. My throat was as dry as dust, so I had a dozen cans of orange juice sent up and ranged them on the casing, puncturing one every few minutes and drinking it off.

We slid through Fejeosen, with Feje light flashing on the port beam, and came round to the south down the lead of Bergen, still about thirty miles away. Inside the leads the lights were wonderful, a system of coloured sectors pointing the way down the fjord. You ran on in the red sector of a light until it turned white, thence down that beam until in the white sector of another light and so on.

I had a thermos of soup sent up, but after a couple of mouthfuls sent it back, as I did not feel I could spare the time from my binoculars.

We had quickly found that the atmosphere in the craft made smoking impossible, it was normally, in most craft (and certainly in mine) forbidden for that reason and also for the risk of battery explosions; however, after about twenty-four hours on passage, I had permitted 'one all-round', but none of us finished them; now, after about three hours in the open air I was feeling fit enough, being in a broad part of the fjord, and safely through the first minefield, I sent for Beadon, and went down below. Even now a cigarette was so foul that I took two puffs and was nearly sick. So I changed my socks, and came on deck again.

The Hjelte Fjord, down which we were now running took us fifteen miles on our way, before narrowing to about a mile as you turn into the West Byfjord. For most of its length the Hjelte Fjord is anything up to five miles wide, but by the time we got down to the narrows (about one a.m.) the moon which was about half grown, was shining like a street lamp, and I could see cottages ashore without glasses. As the easy swell which had pushed us on our way from the north had ceased, the water was glass calm, and I felt rather like a fly in the middle of a large window. Though there was a large German garrison on the Eastern side of these narrows, nobody saw us, and in another hour I was coasting fifty yards off an uninhabited island, in the shadow, with myself in the W & D, finger on klaxon ready to dive.

So far so good. Realising that there a was corner about seven miles on, which I must go around underwater and which would require daylight to negotiate through a periscope, being well ahead of schedule, with the batteries bubbling merrily at full charge, I dived about 3.30 a.m. We settled down about forty feet, rumbling on at about three knots. Absolutely at crack of dawn's first light we were nosing up to the turn, and rounded it into the full stream of early morning departure. Fishing smacks and trawlers, small motor boats, a German patrol boat, etc.; this was about 0530. It took some doing to get across the lane.

This stretch of the West Byfjord is mined, and my route was a dog leg, so I wanted to keep in the channel if possible but the traffic, which was considerable, rather jostled me up to the north side of my route. Altogether about forty ships and boats passed me bound outward, some very close indeed. I refused to go deep until I absolutely had to because the strain of getting back to periscope depth was something to avoid if possible; with only two second peeps every few seconds, I would hang on till the last minute, then go deep, if necessary, listen to the beat of propellers grow and fade, while my people looked at me with positive pain for the first few, until they grew blase, then back quick for a peep at the next menace. The German patrol vessel passed about fifty yards off and I stayed up for him; he positively blanked my view, but looking back at him after he had passed, it gave me a bad moment to see him signalling to the shore.

Despite this wonderful time, at about 0845, the Puddefjord opened out in front of us and we began to identify things like the Observatory and cathedral and other spires. About 0900 I sighted the floating dock, and once more as we closed it the water became restricted and the traffic denser. The surface was glassy and I was cruising around just below the surface, poking the periscope about like a billiard cue, prohibited by the very necessary caution from showing more than two inches and that for only about ten seconds at a time. This was of course, the moment ordained by Practical Jokes Co-ordination Limited, for the periscope to jam up, and smoke to start from its works. 'Screwdriver, but quickly', and we settled that. I was pretty near the dock now, no nets in sight, and shame, nothing in the dock. However, two small ships were tied up alongside.

There was the mast of Maxie Shean's 'Bahrenfels', with a notice hanging from it, 'Langsam Fahren' (Go Slow). That's alright, I'm only doing two and a half knots. One last quick tussle as I square up to go under the dock, now about a hundred yards away with a small motor boat, which I'm sure went right over the stern and we're under. Phew!

It was about 0930 when we went astern under the north end of the dock, and I let her settle on the bottom while we released one charge, then manoeuvred up two hundred feet under the other end to let go the other. All this was done by 1015 and with the boat feeling like a whippet in my hands, I let her go for a thousand yards clear, took one fix, tucked her head down, and ran like a race horse to the entrance of Byfjord. After the way in and the knowledge that at least we'd done our stuff the outward journey was a picnic; either there was less traffic, or I was getting used to it. We were clear of the Byfjord about 1300, and about 1530 I could see our way clear up Hjelte Fjord. I went deep, and broke down to two watches. Then it hit us. 'My God - Am I hungry?' We had eaten nothing but benzedrine and a couple of toffees since six o'clock the night before. We cooked the most enormous meal and hogged it back before turning in.

We had arranged our benzedrine so that the effect had faded by now, and everyone was pretty tired. The endurance of Beadon, eleven hours on the planes, and E.R.A. Davison, nineteen hours on the wheel solid, is terrific. Beadon's knee, where he'd rested his elbow on it was nearly raw.

After we had eaten Davison and I turned in, leaving word to be called at five p.m. when we came up to the Hjelte minefield. I got about an hour, but it was so deep and I so dead, that when called I awoke as fresh as if I had had a whole night's sleep. Meanwhile, we had been cracking on at about three and a half knots, regardless of battery, and we were well up on time. We slipped through the minefield. With the air quite fresh down below, about 2000 I surfaced, and 2200 found us, wallowing at the rendezvous.[1] SCEPTRE was a bit late and I began to get a bit worried, but about 2300 she turned up, having withdrawn to bury a man who had been killed that day on board.[2] She led us five miles to seaward, and we hooked on the tow, then changed crews, except for Robby, who pressed on to complete his work and finish the passage.

A quick and easy run back in calm weather returned us to Balta about two and a half days later.

Twenty-four hours there, and ALECTO towed us back to Rothesay.

Aerial reconnaissance subsequently showed the dock completely destroyed and one of the ships alongside it sunk, the other damaged. The Germans never knew what hit them; they suspected sabotage, as it happened that ten minutes before the explosions the last Norwegian had stepped off it leaving seventeen Germans, all of whom were killed.

Both Beadon and Robby got well deserved D.S.C.'s and Davison, a D.S.M. Also Luck, the senior passage crew hand, who had taken part in the 'Tirpitz' tow as well, got a B.E.M.

On return to Rothesay, we turned the boat over to another crew, and all went on six weeks leave, before going to Barrow to collect XE5.

Although he declines to mention it, by the end of the war Lt. H. P. Westmacott R.N. had been awarded a richly deserved D.S.O. (Bergen) and Bar and D.S.C. (Hong Kong) and Bar. 'He knew his stuff' did 'Pusser Percy'.

[1] *X24 carried 12 canisters of Oxygen and could propably remain dived for 34/36 hours providing 'Protosorb' changes were made regularly.*
[2] *Able Seaman Douglas of Coleraine County Derry had suffered a fatal accident that morning. Until darkness fell Sceptre had been unable to surface and commit his body to the deep.*

Chapter Eighteen
The Beach Reconnaissance For
The Invasion Of Europe.
Operation 'Postage Able' January 1944

X20

The Crew:-
Lt. Commander Nigel Willmott D.S.O., D.S.C., R.N.
Major Logan Scott-Bowden D.S.O., M.C.
Sergeant Bruce Ogden-Smith D.C.M., M.M.
Lt. Ken Hudspeth D.S.C. and two bars, R.A.N.V.R.
S/Lt. Bruce Enzer R.N.V.R.

In preparation for the invasion that was to take place in five months time, it was vital for the authorities to know every smallest detail of this stretch of the Normandy coast. The composition and contours of the beaches, whether they were mined or not, the presence or otherwise of underwater obstacles, the nature of beach exits and backdrop and the number of gun emplacements above were all significant factors. It was essential to know what to expect if heavy armoured vehicles were to rumble through the shallows and pounding feet go charging up the beach.

The 1st party of reconnoitring sappers had arrived by Motor Gun Boats and Landing Craft in mid-January 1944 and the second party came by X Craft two weeks later, because submarines can submerge and remove themselves from prying eyes.

The Dark of the Moon was fast approaching as Lt. Cdr Wilmott let go X20's mooring chain inside the Portsmouth boom. She was to join her towing ship in the Channel, the trawler DARTHEMA.

For Lt/Cdr. Wilmott, the Founder of COPP (Combined Operation Pilotage Parties) and his long-suffering crew as they contorted themselves into the steel tube which was to be their home for the next seven days, the experience gained from weeks and months of practice was about to pay off. They had developed stamina by crawling up windswept beaches in February, not to mention rushing naked into Chichester harbour in that month! They also became used to spending long hours in 'super slum conditions with its distasteful sewage system', (the diabolical heads) surrounded by freezing Winter seas.

On picking up the tow off the Isle of Wight the 'phone cable laid-up spirally inside the towing wire broke down at once and took a precious hour to repair.

Crawling on all fours from the hatch to the raised induction trunk which, in the absence of a conning tower, was the only vertical support was a feat, in itself in anything of a sea. Hanging on with one hand to the slender trunk and fastening the leather belt under one's armpits was a greater feat.

As she dipped her nose into the trough of the mid-Channel swell, the X Craft was 'shipping it green', and slipping the tow from the large and comforting DARTHEMA brought mixed feelings, especially as there had been trouble with a jammed towbar

The trawler DARTHEMA towing X20, to carry out the reconnaisance of the invasion beaches 5 months before D-Day.

which had taken a further hour to slip. The offshore trawler with her deep draught was unable to cross the minefield. The watch-keeper on X20, embracing his horizontal perch with fervour (with the ocean having submerged the rest of the craft beneath him), had his legs periodically swept from under him and found himself floating out behind like a Japanese paper streamer at a carnival. On returning to their normal position his legs knocked painfully against the periscope guard. 'There is a vacancy in complement for an intelligent merman to fill this role' was suggested later.

There was no protective bridge or conning tower on the tiny submarine, in fact no protection of any sort for the chap on watch who had to occupy this position at night especially in waves over 6 feet in height when the periscope was blind.

They were running late because of the heavy seas but had to reduce speed because of the increasingly violent motion and so that 'The naval officer on the casing should be able to lift his head above the water, for breathing purposes', as Willmott dryly remarked in his report.

They saw the loom of the Pointe de Ver light before they saw the actual beam, just before 0500, and the thin, dark, totally featureless smudge that was the coast of Normandy. The sight of this smudge brought a surge of feeling for this was to become the Promised Land.

They crossed the minefield without mishap. The sky was beginning to pale and a new day dawned, overcast, with drizzle. So, with visibility being poor, they decided to chance it on the surface a little while longer. It was time- and energy-expensive to keep on submerging and surfacing.

Breakfast-time (hard boiled eggs and 'train smash') found them with the sky clearing and a shy sun appearing. They dived and bottomed on the 4 or 5 fathom contour line off the beach and enjoyed an uncomfortable sleep leaving two men on watch.

Rest was a major factor while reconnoitring. The poorer the quality of rest, the more they needed. Twelve to fourteen hours out of twenty-four was a reasonable average. It was usual for four persons out of five to be on watch at any one time; 'under way' three were ON and even when bottomed two were ON. Preparing meals, such as they were, and washing up took time with no galley of any sort. In contrast to some small boats, cotton waste was not used for the latter chore. In time, remnants would have choked the outlets, and become a potential source of danger.

Underway again after lunch and they were slithering gingerly over a sand bank to stop within five hundred yards of the shore. 'That's far enough, let's have a look-see', and Willmott cautiously raised the pencil slim viewer. There, with startling clarity was the village of Moulins St. Laurent, a row of gaunt, shuttered and eyeless houses. Probably evacuated on the orders of the Germans, to give an unobstructed line of fire from the sinister row of gun barrels poking out of the hillside behind.

The beach was hardly ideal for the purpose for which it was being scanned. There was no cover whatsoever from the gun emplacements above (they would have to be dealt with separately) and the main exit was made impassable with the spoil from all the construction work that the Germans were undertaking.

That was 'their' problem. Willmott suddenly had problems of his own when small arms fire commenced. There was a pinging and a plopping all round them. This unnerving display continued for some minutes. 'They can't have seen us?' was the unspoken thought. And in fact they hadn't, for gradually the shooting moved away, leaving the party white and shaken. Tense and aghast they looked at each other. 'I expect they were just keeping their eye in and shooting at anything that moved not realising it was us.'. With that they consoled themselves and exhaled deeply.

'Slowly and silently they stole away', out into deeper water. The day wore on with no outward signs that their presence had been rumbled. No hostile aircraft or darting E-Boats. It was time for the swimmers, Scott-Bowden the Major, very correct, and Ogden-Smith the humorist, to commence the two hour-long and tedious process of donning their frogmen's outfits (but the term Frogman had not been perpetrated then).

Ken Hudspeth:-

Drying the suits and a mass of thick woollen salt water damp underclothing was a problem in X Craft.

(In fact the longjohns must invariably have been 'warm damp' rather than dry.)

The W. and D. hatch was only just wide enough to take the swimmers. Festooned as they were with:- shingle bag, emergency rations, brandy flask, (against all medical advice) sounding lead, underwater writing tablet and pencil, compass, watch, beach gradient reel and stake, .45 automatic, trowel, auger, torch and bandolier and they still had a way to swim and then collect their samples for the return journey.

'Into the drink with you', Willmott ordered and they were over the side with hardly a ripple, looking, and indeed feeling, like encumbered seals. 'And mind you're back before closing time' he admonished, fondly. So he was human after all. They had sometimes wondered, for he had flogged them nearly to death during their intensive training.

They swam, crawled and wriggled to the water's edge then suddenly the wavering torch of an alert German sentry strolling along the sand covered road above the beach stopped and held them transfixed like butterflies pinned to a board. Perhaps the act they were putting on was more convincing than they dared hope, for after a taut and unnerving sixty seconds, the torch bearer recommenced his pacing.

Their luck wouldn't have held a second time so they slithered back into the sea, swimming over to where the dark groynes led down, picking up sand samples in their augers on the way.

The sea goes out a long way off the Normandy coast and they had timed their visit to coincide with the young flood, so that the water would wash away any suspicious footprints. Suddenly staring them in the face and below the tideline, were the marks of a stranger's boots. At least it proved that the beach wasn't mined. Ogden-Smith indicated to his partner that they had better try a little further along, when he felt rather than heard, the soft movement of boots on sand.

Once again they froze. Two vague shapes were stumbling through the soft sand at the back of the beach and when they came abreast of the swimmers, one of them struck something that sent him sprawling. At the same instant Ogden-Smith was horrified to feel the line in his hand go suddenly rigid, then slack. One of the sentries had tripped over the steel sounding stake. Fortunately the sentry did not investigate the object, merely picking himself up with a curse and stomping off to rejoin his mate.

The swimmers were pleased with their investigation after all. The sand was firm enough, even in the pools, to take any number of armoured vehicles. It was now high time to be away from this inhospitable beach with its treacherous stillness and to rejoin X20.

The X Craft had anchored to maintain position in the tidal stream. When Willmott spotted the pin-point torch-signals from the shore, the CQR (See-cu-are, secure) anchor lived up to its name and wouldn't come clear. So they had to steam it out and thereby expend more time, noise and expletives before the exhausted swimmers could reach them, (weighed down as they were), and be hauled aboard by willing hands.

The swimmers were recovered in 16ft of water, 550 yards out. They had a successful, though not entirely carefree time!

Partly recovered the shivering 'seals' sipped some brandy, stripped off their suits, checked and greased their gear, wrote up their notes and consumed a hot meal of sorts. The crew of X20 then withdrew offshore, bottomed and slept.

The afternoon of the second day found them off the adjacent beach of Colleville. Ken Hudspeth had an unfortunate experience on entering this sector:-

I looked through the night periscope (a fixed periscope rising only 6" above the casing), which we used for underwater observations of divers, nets, etc. and found the water polluted by what seemed to be thousands of pieces of toilet paper. We thought the entire German and French navies must be at sea! Until closer inspection revealed them as vast numbers of jellyfish.

Later on and while still heading for the shore, I raised the day (or attack) periscope and found myself looking straight at a couple of French fishermen. In near flat calm, we were surrounded by quite a fleet of fishing boats sailing in company and trailing lines, which fortunately we didn't snag. Needless to say we went deeper very quickly.

Then followed another periscope reconnaissance, sketching any landmarks and mapping it generally. This was not achieved without much underwater manoeuvring and trimming. The River Orne was pouring fresh water into the Baie de la Seine, and once a tortured grinding made them grimace, when the craft sidled across an uncharted sandbank, but the tide was making again and they soon slid off into deeper water.

The short winter's day couldn't end soon enough for the five men cooped up inside their tiny submarine. It was only meant for four. The air gradually turned more poisonous as the Protosorb crystals became saturated with carbon dioxide, and there was still half an hour to endure before it was dark enough to surface and 'guff through' with clean air.

High spots appeared on cheeks and breath came in gasps. Concentration with anything like intensity became a hoped-for triumph over feelings of nausea, violent headaches, stomach cramps and indeed vomiting. 'Scottie' the Army man, was the principal sufferer when the hatch was first opened but this didn't prevent his being ready and prepared on the casing. This was their second foray into enemy territory in twenty-four hours, where a solitary footprint in the wrong place, even a sneeze, might alert the Germans to the fact that something was going on; so they had to be extra vigilant. Barely three hundred yards off the shore, they slipped into the dark and icy sea once more and made their way to the back of the beach without mishap.

They were resting among the banked-up shingle just below the road, when the bombing started. The R.A.F. was busy over the Caen docks. Even thirty miles away the crumps made the ground tremble like a succession of earthquakes. The two military men were glad to be on their particular God-forsaken stretch of coast.

Then Ogden-Smith happened to glance back and saw their X Craft indelibly, unmistakably and mesmerisingly etched on the pale sea. Horror-struck, he gestured wordlessly to his companion, as for the fraction of a second at a time, the reflection of the Caen bomb flashes illuminated this incriminating tableau. One tiny submarine on a vast empty sea. If they could see it, so could the Jerries.

So with the beach continuing to vibrate sporadically like a dying animal, Ogden-Smith gave the thumbs-up sign, meaning 'let's get away now'. They slid cautiously backwards into the sea, methodically collecting samples as they went. These were then decanted into rubber sheaths. Such a use for them the makers had surely not envisaged!

After having had their bodies chilled by the January breeze on the beach, the water seemed almost warm by comparison and the exertion of swimming helped to restore the circulation. Even so, it took the tired swimmers half an hour to swim out, before X20 found them. They lay across her casing like deflating lilos, heaving and gasping. Had X20 not been there the official distress signal to be used was 4 seal barks plus 2 red flares.

In conversation the following afternoon Ken Hudspeth concluded that they could thank God that there were no underwater obstacles, even though they had quartered Seine Bay during the two and a half days that they had been there. Ken, the unflappable and serious-minded Australian, always on his dignity, was now relaxing ever so slightly.

Through the prism, the same tide-line of wrack with the road beyond and the same deserted beach stared back at the C.O. but as soon as the stick poked six inches out of the water, the firing recommenced (a disconcerting experience) and the sea boiled all round them. Willmott brought the periscope down with a rush and they just sat there wondering if they'd been spotted this time. In the strained silence only two things were audible:- the sharp pinging noises outside and the eternal plopping of a submarine's condensation inside.

Eventually the fall of shot faltered and moved away, causing Ken Hudspeth to observe that:-

They must be jolly vigilant if they saw our periscope. We shall soon know whether they did or not.

As no further signs of native irritation were observed they gently slithered away. Thirty minutes later, more musketry was heard in the distance, though nothing had been visible to the Jerries during that time. Five minutes later, firing was again heard denoting further waste of ammo, which lent colour to the view that now (at least), they were shooting at flotsam and might soon realise that they had lost face by their outburst. Les Moulins seems to be a cantankerous locality!

Thankfully there was only another hour of daylight, for they had been down too long for comfort. The effect of the Benzedrine tablets was wearing off and grogginess affected them all.

The third night of crawling up and down enemy beaches was looming and in their tired and vulnerable state it might not be third time lucky and Willmott had to face this glaringly obvious fact. Nowadays the Manual says that one night in three must be devoted to recuperation. At that time it hadn't been written and common sense had to supply the directions. The barometer was falling too and it would have been madness to jeopardise the operation at this stage. 'Steer 348' said Willmott and they turned about and made for home.

They found the gap in the minefield and steered North, with the Westerly swell thwacking them on the beam. As soon as he stood up, the 'unfortunate' on the casing began to 'wish he'd never joined' (an often repeated wartime quip). Great dollops of sea flattened themselves on the casing and against him. He felt like a soused herring. It was only the leather strap that prevented his being washed overboard.

Worse was to follow, when they cleared the lee of the French coast and met the full force of a Westerly gale. Mild attacks of mal-de-mer broke out among those down below and the position of Officer of the Watch was again becoming ever more difficult.

Came the dawn at last, although it brought little relief, except to the Officer of the Watch who was called down from his saturated perch in the biting wind into the fug and comparative cosiness below.

When on the casing, the Officer of the Watch was supposed to be able to communicate with the men beneath his feet by wearing an R.A.F helmet with the headphones and microphone inside. He clamped a plug into a socket on the casing and could then speak to the two control positions down below and vice versa. In practice and in those seas, the socket soon became flooded and shorted, whereupon communication was just a crackle.

Fortunately no shipping of any sort was sighted, so no alteration of course was necessary. They then proceeded on the surface until they made contact, exchanged recognition signals, and rendezvoused with the faithful DARTHEMA which had been patrolling in the northern part of the channel in case X20 required assistance. Finally, they were escorted under their own power to berth at Fort Blockhouse.

Willmott's dry but light hearted naval prose reports with masterly understatement:-

1230 21.1.1944:- St. Catherine's Head (I.O.W.) fine on port bow as hoped for. Rendezvoused with DARTHEMA and Motor Launches. Telephones flooded out and communication with helmsman, controls and casing officer (now restored to his perch) was sporadic and exciting.

Ken's verdict on this quite remarkable and little-known achievement, Operation 'Postage Able', was delivered with typical modesty and equal restraint; Praising the COPP people's who he said were the key people in X20's Winter Operation. He had just provided the taxi. In answer to the writer's question as to any problems, he replied that they had not seen any sign of the enemy on the return trip and arrived back at Gosport in time for dinner. Although in fact a passage crew had been ready aboard the DARTHEMA, but Ken had decided to see the job through to the bitter end.

The time was 1815 on January 21, 1944 and in five months time hundreds and thousands of ships and men would have reason to be grateful to the crew of X20 and especially to those Very Gallant Gentlemen, the two Coppists, Major Logan Scott-Bowden D.S.O. and M.C. of the Royal Engineers, and Sergeant Bruce Ogden-Smith D.C.M. and M.M. of the East Surreys. The two swimmers had already swum ashore from an L.C.N. just two weeks previously, and Willmott had first swum ashore on enemy-held Rhodes, in 1941, to prove that this kind of 'recce' could be done. The information thus obtained in January 1944 proved to be so satisfactory that no similar operation was planned prior to the invasion itself.

In a D-Day context, these two men were the second pair of seals to land on French soil since Dunkirk.

Chapter Nineteen
Operation 'Gambit', The Opening Move on D-Day

'Much the greatest thing we have ever attempted' Winston Churchill
June 1944

X20

The Crew:-
Lt. Paul Clark R.N.
S/Lt. Robin Harbud R.N.V.R
Lt. K. Hudspeth D.S.C. and two bars, R.A.N.V.R.
S/Lt. Bruce Enzer R.N.V.R. M.I.D. (twice)
E.R.A. L. Tilley M.I.D.

X23
Lt. L.G. Lyne D.S.C.
Lt. J. G. M. Both M.I.D., CdeG, R.N.V.R.
Lt. George Honour D.S.C., R.N.V.R.
S/Lt. J. H. Hodges M.I.D., R.N.V.R.
E.R.A. George Vause M.I.D.

'IF THEY COME, THEY'LL COME HERE'. So said Field Marshall Rommel with prescience. He was standing on the beach at Ouistreham, Normandy, in May 1944. And how right he was. He was referring to the Allied Invasion of Europe, and just four weeks later it happened and THEY CAME. Engraved on a plaque on the sitting room wall at home are the following stirring words:- This Vessel(X20), with her sister ship, led the Invasion of Europe by the Liberating Armies on D-Day, 6 June 1944.

The Invasion of Europe provided an opportunity for the midget submarines to write a further page in the distinguished history of the Submarine Service. To X20 (Lieutenant K. Hudspeth R.A.N.V.R.) and X23 (Lieutenant G. Honour R.N.V.R.) fell the honour of leading in the British and Canadian forces on 'Juno' and 'Sword' beaches and a great debt is owed to the young crews and the COPP parties that manned these tiny craft. Further West, the Americans disdained the use of X Craft having said, at a demonstration of beach marking, that such aids were not necessary and might even jeopardise the operation. They were to pay dearly for their lack of confidence in the use of X Craft to spearhead their armies.

Already in April/May of that fateful year of 1944 preparations for the Great Day were far advanced and saturation point for ships and craft in South coast creeks and harbours had, to all intents and purposes, been reached. It was then that the indomitable Ken Hudspeth found himself on the casing of X20 as her C.O. The craft was en route for a big invasion exercise.

This exercise at Slapton Sands near Dartmouth was to involve all three Services and various nationalities. The effect on X20 of the extra buoyancy tanks, which had been fitted to offset the weight of the extra fifth man and all the gear, was as yet unknown.

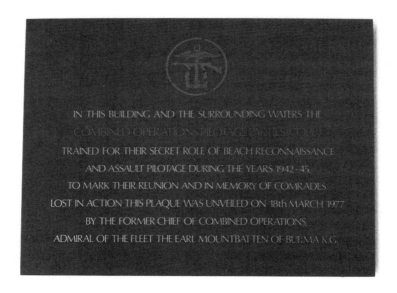

IN THIS BUILDING AND THE SURROUNDING WATERS THE
COMBINED OPERATIONS PILOTAGE PARTIES (COPP)
TRAINED FOR THEIR SECRET ROLE OF BEACH RECONNAISSANCE
AND ASSAULT PILOTAGE DURING THE YEARS 1942-45.
TO MARK THEIR REUNION AND IN MEMORY OF COMRADES
LOST IN ACTION THIS PLAQUE WAS UNVEILED ON 18th MARCH 1977
BY THE FORMER CHIEF OF COMBINED OPERATIONS,
ADMIRAL OF THE FLEET THE EARL MOUNTBATTEN OF BURMA K.G.

Earl Mountbatten unveiling the COPP Memorial plaque in Hayling Island Yacht Club.

Ken Hudspeth:-

We had a kind of test on our run to Portland and Dartmouth. Our attendant trawler allowed us to stray into Portland Race, where at one point, we were rolled almost on our beam ends, with me on top! I don't know whether the tanks helped or hindered but it scared hell out of the crew below. However, we survived with the loss of only our ensign and staff.

Prior to the first beach reconnaissance in January 1944 (Operation 'KJH') a top level and rather unfriendly conference had taken place.

The bevy of brass had disagreed, not as to whether the reconnaissances should happen, and several were planned, but whether a towing trawler be used at all.

Lt. Carl Brunning C.O. of the towing trawler DARTHEMA has this to say about the discussion:-

I doubt if any record was kept of that conference. (He goes on to justify the view of the opposition.) DARTHEMA was, as trawlers go, a fairly big ship having been built for fishing in the Arctic or White Sea. She was considered by some to be far too conspicuous a vessel. If we had encountered any German E-Boats or destroyer patrols, there was a danger that the secrecy would have been blown.

Be that as it may, in April 1944 H.M. Trawler EN AVANT was escorting X20 a few miles off the South coast of England, and was enjoying a surprisingly peaceful passage. Perhaps the German Navy was not so keen now that Britain had mastery of the air. Or maybe the metal foil which was code-named 'Window', (thousands of strips of aluminium foil dropped by the R.A.F. to baffle enemy RADAR) had foiled them again.

The Juno Beech Memorial. The contribution of the British and the X Craft are not mentioned!

To make the exercises more realistic the operation at Slapton Sands was called Operation 'TIGER' and their small part in it Operation 'TROUSERS'. Live ammunition was used. Nowadays there are four monuments erected on the Sands by the Americans, to the loss of their two Landing Ship Tanks and the appalling total of over six hundred casualties, mostly soldiers, on this exercise. It wasn't a very auspicious start to the D-Day run-up.

What had happened was that a flotilla of German E-Boats had surprised the escort to this vast exercise. The escort was one destroyer short and could not be everywhere at once. Consequently, in no time at all, two L.S.T.'s were sinking and hundreds of fully laden G.I.'s were drowning in the sea. The only plus point of the whole wretched business was that the Germans did not seem to have realised the significance of the exercise. They must have thought it was just routine.

After the exercises when the X Craft had purported to signal-in the Armada Lt. George Honour, C.O. of X23 remarked:-

We didn't hang about. Having marked the beaches, we departed. Due to E-Boat attacks at Slapton we dashed back to Portland harbour. Due to bad weather at Seaford, we ran into Newhaven.

George had badly wanted to be involved with a reconnaissance trip on the French side of the Channel, in command of his brand new X Craft. X23 had not come South, after her work-ups with the COPP party in Scotland until April and:-

After a long heart-search, a high-up meeting had decided no more trips before the actual invasion. It was too risky. It might jeopardise the whole thing. Also the nights were too short and anyway they had obtained all the information they wanted from what became OMAHA beach (Vierville and St. Laurent). It was just unfortunate that OMAHA was allotted to the Americans and the British were unable to benefit from all this information which had been so dangerously gained.

We on X23 were very disappointed. Especially as we had trained right up for such trips. However, we were kept busy on the two pre-invasion exercises within a week of each other and also an attack on Portsmouth harbour, to test the defences. This upset the applecart, as we entered the inner harbour without being detected and proved how open the British were to attack by German midgets.

Fortunately these attacks did not materialise, but exactly the same thing had happened at Scapa Flow, on two occasions.

There was a dearth of X Craft at this time. Which was a pity, for they now had a definite role to play; in contrast to the following year when, in the Far East in 1945, Captain Fell of the X Craft Depot Ship BONAVENTURE was urgently seeking roles. He had half a dozen X Craft but no tasks for them. The Americans who were overlords there were not interested.

X22 had been intended by COPP for beach crawling and marking and had buoyancy tanks fitted. Max Shean, the individualistic Aussie who'd commanded her, had not got on too well with the Army Coppists so was given another X Craft and the tanks were removed. Then the tragedy of Pentland Firth, when X22 had been lost with all hands, had robbed the planners of a first class little boat and crew; X20 which was undergoing repairs after a battery explosion in February. X21 was deemed

Captain Fell and some of his officers with visiting officers of the U.S. Navy.

to be an experimental craft and was not launched until April. X24 was busily sinking a merchant ship instead of the floating dock in Bergen. X25 was still working-up on the West coast of Scotland. All the X5-10 class had been lost at SOURCE in Norway and the first of the XE's didn't appear until August, two months after D-Day.

Shortly before the Great Day, the motor car tycoon Lord Nuffield had descended upon the Submarine base at Fort Blockhouse, Gosport, to see the X Craft for himself. Vastly intrigued with this compact box of tricks, their simplicity and their ruggedness, he could only be torn away to view the other 'Weird and Wonderfuls' that had been lined-up for him, after much cajoling and a promise to be allowed to 'drive' one, if Security permitted!

X20 and X23 had not been alongside DOLPHIN quay for long when, on June 2 they departed for their Great Adventure.

This was it. The beginning of their long-awaited part in the Second Front.

Admiral Ramsay had voiced some stirring sentiments in his eve of D-Day speech:- 'The hopes and prayers of the Free World and of the enslaved peoples of Europe will be with us. We cannot fail them'. With their crews keyed-up, the little X Craft slipped discreetly away into the gathering gloom of dusk. The two midgets rendezvoused with their escorting trawlers outside Spithead, X20 'buttoned-up' (made fast the tow) to the faithful DARTHEMA (C.O. Lt. Brunning R.N.V.R.) and X23 to another trawler, H.M.T. GRENADIER (C.O. Acting Lt. A. G. Day R.N.R.). The weather forecast was not encouraging.

The sea was 'moderate', but Moderate on the Beaufort Scale and as applied to big ships, was distinctly immoderate when applied to X Craft with a 24" freeboard. As Carl Brunning remarked:-

Securing the tow under these conditions was a slight fiasco.

We had rehearsed it several times prior to D-Day but not in a rough sea. D minus 3 was choppy, (actually D minus 4 but they didn't know this at the time). The procedure was that X20 moved up near my stern. We then launched a sizable boat with four oarsmen, a coxs'n and hand. The towing cable was taken over the stern of DARTHEMA and the connecting tow-bar was put in the boat. This tow-bar was three to four feet long (actually 6 feet), heavy and had to be slid into an orifice in the snout of the submarine. My boats now got into position but both craft were pitching up and down, probably six to seven feet. They missed getting the tow-bar into the hole every time.

After about fifteen minutes of abortive attempts, Hudspeth crawled out into the bow of X20 in an effort to grab the end of the tow-bar and guide it into the aperture. In which he succeeded but not before he became like a drowned rat. One minute he was up in the air, the next wholly submerged. He had anticipated this and was clad only in shirt and pants.

When the tow was fixed, they came alongside me and I think I fitted out Hudspeth with some dry clothes.

Afterwards Carl Brunning was to remark:-

I had no trouble with X20 apart from dodging floating mines. Hudspeth was a quiet unassuming man and a first class Seaman. (Coming from a man such as he, this was praise indeed.)

Out of curiosity I spent a little time in X20 but it's not my idea of comfort. I preferred the space of the wardroom and duty free gin. One and ninepence a bottle in those days!

George Honour in X23:-

Having secured the tow in which the 'phone cable had already parted we remained on the surface and then made our way under main engine at an average speed of three knots to a position half way across the Channel and sixty miles from the French coast, where we slipped the tow. We were then on our own in mid-Channel. I remember feeling very lonely and thinking that X23 was very very small. Although we managed to keep company with X20 until the dawn came up.

At 0521 we dived and we stayed submerged for seventeen hours and fifty-nine minutes. We did 'guff through' three times, that means we took in fresh air through the 'snort mast' without surfacing for we were over-manned, with five crew and full of extra equipment. There was no room to move and one could not, of course, smoke. All you could do was yarn or sleep fitfully in the increasingly foul atmosphere.

We arrived off SWORD Beach (Ouistreham) British sector at dawn on Sunday, 4th June.

We all had French identities, in case we were captured or just drowned. I had the complete disguise outfit of a French taxi driver. That would put the Hun off the scent if he got hold of our bodies, dead or alive. They would never think we were members of one of H.M. Submarines!

Mealtimes aboard reminded some of them of a midnight feast in the dorm. The E.R.A. handed round great doorsteps of bread and jam, followed by a tin of pineapple chunks, then chocolate biscuits. They cut down on the washing-up by all eating out of the same tin.

They had put a 'running charge' on the batteries, as the long run under water the previous day, had depleted them. It was essential always to have plenty of 'juice' in the batteries in case of an enforced stay on the bottom and the need to use main motors afterwards. This was actually about to happen.

The moment when George Honour of X23 saw La Belle France for the first time, was a magical one. Although it was just a long thin smudge stretching away into nothingness it had assumed the desirability of the Promised Land. This view was the culmination of four long years of indecision, argument, back-biting and finally whole-hearted co-operation. A frisson of anticipation ran through the crew of X23.

The beach at Vierville where X20 carried out Operation 'Postage Able'. It was later alloted to the U.S. Forces and given the name Omaha Beach. The stone ramp may have been added since the war.

Ken Hudspeth's JUNO sector marked, by X20 stretched West from the lovely old Norman grey stone village of Landgrune for another six miles to Ver-sur-Mer. George Honour's SWORD beach marked by X23 reached to the East from Landgrune to the quaint fishing port of Ouistreham on the Orne River estuary.

The Invasion was indeed, as Churchill had said:-

Much the greatest thing we have ever attempted.

On that glorious June day when they had all looked their fill through the periscope at the Germans sunbathing on the beach, at one of them mounted on a shire horse and balancing his little can of milk from the local farmer, at a couple who were taking the platoon's washing to the blanchisseuse and yet others who were drying it on the casements, the tranquillity of this scene suddenly struck them as being bizarre, when they thought what the morrow would bring. The torn and devastated beach, and the bodies too. 'I'm glad I'm not a Tommy', somebody said and abruptly slammed down the periscope.

The day being Sunday, they watched the devout folks wending their way to the little village church on whose spire they had navigated so successfully the day before.

Five miles West of them, X20 was equally fortunate in her navigator, Paul Clark. He had brought his craft directly opposite a point midway between Pointe de Ver lighthouse and village of Courseulles.

It was a strange sensation to be sitting on the bottom almost under the noses of the enemy, playing Uckers, Liar dice, Bertie-Bertie or anything else that whiled away the time. Darkness came at last and with caution they surfaced, filling the boat with marvellous fresh air. Cooking-up an impromptu meal of soup and M. and V. (Meat and Veg.) produced their first hot repast since leaving England, three days before.

After a rapid clearing-away with the aerial hoisted, they stood by to receive the encoded message which would follow the B.B.C. News. It would tell them whether or not the invasion would take place as planned.

When it came, 'For Padfoot. Unwell in Scarborough', they looked at each other in amazement and disbelief. What had gone wrong? Today would have been ideal for the landings and tomorrow promised to be no different but the Invasion had been delayed for twenty-four hours.

Weather forecasting in June 1944 was uniquely difficult, 'the worst June of the century, and long-range forecasting impossible'. On the coast of Britain one hundred miles to the North the weather must have been very much worse than it was on the coast of Normandy. The Navy's luck was out, in this respect.

Disheartened with the turn of events, the crew promptly 'got their heads down' wherever they could find room. Except, of course, for the man on watch. Robin Harbud who was particularly upset, because he'd been baulked of the rather dashing role that he'd wangled for himself, that of sitting alone in an inflatable dinghy on the far side of the bay and superintending the guiding light into the Bernieres Channel.

'Anyone for a run ashore in Courseulles?' he joked half-heartedly the next morning and crooned 'where the girls are so pretty'. There were no takers and they didn't even look round from their tasks at the everlasting Care and Maintenance.

The next stretch of 'bottoming' was sheer hell. It sapped the men's strength just being there. The air got worse. They couldn't stand upright in the 'sardine tin' and any moving about caused knocked heads and elbows, and inevitably, frayed tempers.

It ended eventually, after another seventeen hours of being cooped up and feeling not unlike Jonah in the whale's stomach they surfaced thankfully into the fragrant Summer darkness. Then it was time to listen for the familiar B.B.C. voice to announce 'another message for Padfoot'. This time it was to say the Landings were scheduled to commence at dawn.

The Dawn of D-Day showing the crowded sea with ships of every size and description.

The air tasted like wine. The Invasion was ON.

The atmosphere lifted marvelously, but relief vied with puzzlement, for the sea had got up since morning and the glass was dropping!

'Theirs not to reason why' though and before 0500 they had the green light shining to seaward on the impromptu mast, but the weather conditions were worsening.

Lights, radar beams and Harbud's baby, 'the Bong stick', (a simple iron rod lowered into the water and hit with a hammer which could be picked up by sound detection instruments 12 miles away) combined to guide in the Great Armada which was, even now, ploughing steadily forward over a hundred miles of restless ocean. (Incidentally his Bong stick also attracted a school of sharks)! The great drama was beginning to unfold.

Robin Harbud hoped fervently that the thousands of benighted P.B.I. (Poor Bloody Infantry) now approaching felt less sea-sick than he did. Although the Americans had spurned the repeated British offers of Channel Marking X Craft, they had accepted British pilots. So the information that had been so hardly acquired five months before was not entirely wasted.

The ceaseless and purposeful drone of aircraft overhead, softening-up the targets inland in France, was beginning to peter out. They would not want to bomb their own people on the beaches!

In their unfamiliarity with the strength and funnel effect of Channel tides and how the prevailing wind could build them up, the entire U.S. Army 5th Corps had been swept inexorably more than a mile to the Westward. Opposite a murderously well-defended beach.

They suffered 2,000 casualties on OMAHA beach on D-Day alone. In complete contrast, there were fewer casualties on UTAH beach on the Cotentin peninsula, than there had been at the exercise on Slapton Sands.

Meanwhile Robin was enjoying himself sitting astride the casing and banging away at the bongle at regular intervals. At least it made vomiting more hygienic and didn't add to the perfume down below.

The tempo was increasing now and excitement was mounting. In one of Robin's frequent backward glances, trying to be the first one to see the approaching horde, a sneak wave caught him without a handhold and he was washed overboard. Ken the watchful C.O. had been expecting this and promptly shot out a leg. Which Robin grabbed then hauled himself back aboard. 'Thanks' he gasped. 'Wish those ships would chop-chop'.

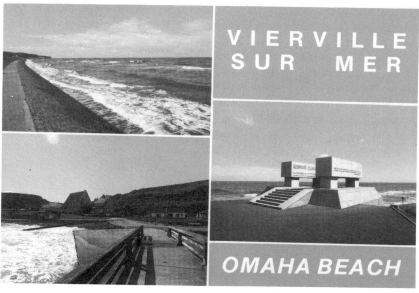

The Omaha Beach memorial.

Shortly afterwards it was Ken's turn to suffer this indignity and he was rescued by Paul Clark's helping hand.

Suddenly there they were!

The landing craft were immediately visible. Clustering round the X Craft and pouring their DD tanks into the water. The swimming tanks then formed a line abreast and proceeded onto the beach. Two sank en route however .

The Americans on OMAHA let down their tanks much further out and only two had reached the beach. The British tank crews all had D.S.E.A. sets and the two tanks that sank lost none of their men, (Unlike the unfortunate Americans).

Due to the bad weather the L.C.T. C.O.'s had decided, unselfishly, to transport their swimming tanks right inshore and crash the underwater obstacles, rather than let them down further out. D.D. Tanks had a six foot high canvas dodger to keep out the whole might of the Channel.

Three miles out the seas were rough and had blanketed the sight and sound of the Allied Navies arriving in orderly lines for as far as one could see.

George Honour was still discounting the vision of his own eyes several years later:-

It was unbelievable. Although I knew they were on our side it was still a frightening sight. One can only imagine what the enemy must have felt, waking up to this awesome spectacle and knowing that they were the targets.

The darker grey silhouettes of the capital ships on the skyline were somehow reassuring. The overall 'eminence grise' was repeated in the bouncing dark grey shapes of the landing craft. They were coming in thick and fast now, almost too fast. For the LOCU Boys had only had time to clear the underwater obstacles to form a narrow path. This small team of brave men were the first people to land on D-Day. Alas, 'Rommel's Asparagus' had been sprouting since the Reconnaissance five months before, and the obstructions were fearsome indeed.

The shore bombardment from our Big Ships was reassuring. Even when the roar of a rocket salvo was so close that it felt to be almost parting their hair. Instinctively they ducked, "I hope they've got their sums right" somebody said. They all laughed as someone made an obscene remark.

An artist's impression of D-Day landings with X Craft showing the light seaward. This was used to guide the invasion to cleared beeches.

The sky was lightening now and revealed a heaving sea, liberally covered with the whole vast concourse of shipping. The Coppists and the seamen were out on the casing, cheering and shouting their heads off. They waved to the seemingly endless lines of helmeted men passing close by, who, probably wet and seasick, took no notice of them at all.

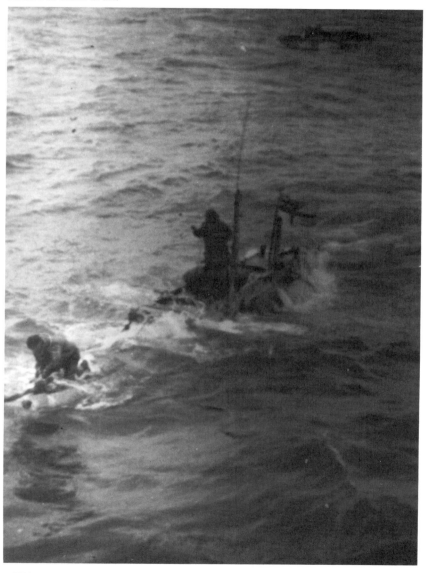

X23 with Commanding Officer Lt. G.B. Honour D.SC. V.RD., R.N.V.R. standing on casing coming alongside H.M.S. LARGS her HQ ship at approx 09.30hrs. on June 6th 1944. She had shared the marking duties with X20 to guide in the invasion fleet.

A Post Office first day cover issued to commemorate the fortieth anniversary of the D-Day landings. Signatures are Ken Hudspeth and George Honour, both X Craft C.O.'s.

So it was with relief that the X Craft's welcoming light beckoned in so many small boats to the safe channel. 'Our own private lighthouse sticking up and how welcome it was too'. (As Robin described it later in DOLPHIN's wardroom). The light was replaced at sunrise with the 'D' flag. George had also been issued with a dolls' house-sized ensign:-

'But I had foreseen problems of identification with friendly forces and had acquired a cruiser's ensign. Which I secured to the beacon mast'.

In fact, as the Director of the Submarine Museum has written:-

With thousands of khaki-clad enthusiasts pouring past them and flocks of so-called friendly aircraft overhead, this was sometimes cited as the most hazardous X Craft Op. of the war.

The bad weather worked to our advantage in one sense, for the Germans thought it was too foul to mount an invasion. Even so and in spite of wind and weather, tidal set and collisions and general mayhem, they had all landed dead on their marks except of course the Americans. X20 and X23 had indeed justified their existence.

Now, with exultation spent, their job done and the surface ships taking over the marking, the crews of the two midgets weighed anchor and proceeded on a reciprocal course, back to their towing trawlers. In George's case, amidst the chaos of shipping, he headed for the depot ship H.M.S. LARGS, only to be told on arrival that he wasn't wanted. Several hours later he found a trawler to tow him home. It was H.M.T. EN AVANT of Slapton Sands fame.

In X20's case it was still only 0900 on June 6, 1944, and the Greatest Armada the world has ever seen, was passing by.

They slipped the tow off the Needles and proceeded into DOLPHIN under their own steam. They were given a rousing and even more liquid than usual reception.

The 'Gods', or at least the 'Clerk of the Weather', had let the Allies down badly. On the other hand, when the South of England threatened to break-off and sink into the sea because of the weight of weaponry and men that were stationed upon it in the weeks leading up to D-Day, it was miraculous that the Germans did not maintain even minimal reconnaissance, and that our arrival on the beaches of Normandy, was totally unexpected!

Field Marshall Rommel, with his prophecy at the begining had guessed WHERE, but even he apparently had no idea WHEN. For on the day of the breaching of his 'impregnable' 'West Wall' he was not even there to see it. He'd returned to Germany for a brief visit to celebrate his wife's Birthday!

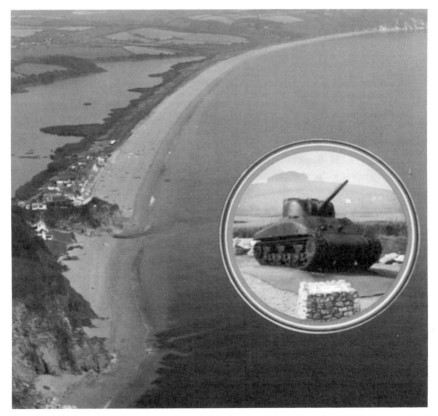

Slapton Sands, South Devon, the site of Operation 'Tiger' in May 1944. It was ideal training ground for the forces who were about to attempt a landing in Europe, as it so much resembled the D-Day invasion beaches in France. The Sherman Mk5 Amphibian tank was salvaged by Mr. Ken Small of the Cove Hotel, Torcross in May 1984 as a memorial to the many hundreds of American Serviceman who lost their lives on exercise Tiger.

Chapter Twenty
Voyage Of Bonaventure In The Spring Of 1945, Departure From The Clyde

The immensely popular Captain Fell became BONAVENTURE's Commanding Officer in January 1944. He describes the uncomfortable arrival of the advance party on Boxing Day twelve months before. Inauspicious it may have been. But then these conditions were commonplace in war-time and the 'Bonny' became a Happy and much-travelled Ship and was in fact continuously in demand for at least ten years. Probably for the next ten years as well, though not much is known about her movements after the War, when she reverted to being a Clan Line steamer. Eventually she was broken-up in Hong Kong in 1962. She owed nobody anything, after ploughing the contrasting oceans of the world for twenty years, from the chilly West coast of Scotland to the warm Pacific.

When she was commissioned in Scott's yard at Greenock she was a Clan Line steamer of 10,600 tons. She was modified with some light A.A. armament and additional mess-decks and cabin accommodation. There were also workshops in nos. 1, 3 and 5 holds.

Wet, cold and hungry after a night of acute discomfort in the unheated train from Chatham, her crew found their new ship a bedlam of noise, dirt and confusion, with the shipbuilders falling over each other in the effort to complete her. To this 'home' on 23 January 1943 they came, to be told by their Captain that their first job was to hazard no guesses about their future employment and to get the ship clean and habitable. (The Advance Party were actually billeted in the local Salvation Army hostel for a few weeks until the ship was completed and before the main ship's company came aboard. Sometimes the Navy was merciful).

In a snowstorm in February of that same year BONAVENTURE steamed down the Clyde, experiencing a hundred teething troubles as she went.

An Able Seaman from Ipswich, Stan Pulham, describes the 'early days' vividly:-

On seeing the BONAVENTURE for the first time, I thought:- This is very strange, a merchant ship manned by the R.N. and I wondered what the large wooden chocks were to be used for on the fore and after well decks. Something secret no doubt, maybe small subs?

Some of us were detailed to clean out the double bottoms with wire brushes. A beastly dirty job which covered us in rusty red dust, crawling about in confined spaces in the bowels of the ship with lighted candles and a few wandering lead lights (she'd only been built the previous year).

Off Rothesay in the Isle of Bute, she anchored in a full gale and was blown ashore during the hours of darkness but refloated next day in the lull that followed.

Eventually we made for Port Bannantyne (Rothesay) and hoisted in the first X Craft, which had just arrived by train at Helensburgh February/March 1943 (probably X5), watched by several gold braided high ups.

When her 'work ups' with the XE Craft were completed 2 years later Able

BONAVENTURE with mysterious crates (X Craft), stowed on her after well deck just before leaving the U.K.

Seaman Alan Kevan had a strange and unique position on BONAVENTURE as he was working in the Captain's office (Operation) and ultimately directly for Captain Fell when he commenced writing the latter's memoirs. He also had a general job at sea operating radar equipment and kept a strictly illegal log of her voyage to the Pacific from which the writer feels privileged to have been allowed to quote:-

21 February 1945

'D' Day for us. After many false alarms we left Rothesay at 1000 on Wednesday 21 February, and having previously spent a few days in Princes Dock, Glasgow, having last minute alterations made to lifting gear and containers prior to joining a convoy en route for the Azores. There were two ships with us as we went down the Clyde to Ailsa Craig. Some more ships joined us there from Northern Ireland and we passed a convoy and escort group searching for a U-Boat which had sunk one of their convoy at 0830. I was on duty during the Middle Watch, when we were joined by eight ships from Liverpool at 1200 so forming a nice little convoy.

22 February

Lost touch with convoy owing to bad visibility. Lt. Smart was Officer of the Watch. Off Milford Haven some more ships joined us. Ship began to roll as we entered the Atlantic proper. About 1800 the weather cleared and I counted twenty-four ships.

I began to feel a little off-colour. Slept most of the day while off watch. Radar not used so I was on Lookout, half hour on, hour and a half off. Had First Watch on bridge, a grand night, moonlight, some more ships joined us. Heard depth charges before turning in.

23 February

Weather grand today but ship rolls a lot. Felt pretty bad during the morning but managed my breakfast OK. Did a spot of work in Radar Workshop. Head down (went to sleep) in afternoon until the Commander, (Lt. Commander Brown) reminded me about Memo on Beards, result I did some typing. One or two of the officers gave up shaving, so Captain Fell and the Commander, for a joke, insisted that they had to grow beards to a certain length and subject to regular inspection. Had Last Dog on watch (i.e. 2nd dog watch 1800 hrs to 2000 hrs). Clocks put back an hour. Counted 30 ships in the convoy (actually 36) 75% of them Tankers (Yankee). Grand weather. Had a long chat with Jock and 'Scratch' the writer, (Captain's secretary, M. Joinson) re-Trinidad women. Jock knows somebody out there, so we will see what we can manage. Our position is West of Bay of Biscay. Turned in at 2130 very tired.

24 February

Weather still grand, quite warm. Morning spent in staff office, afternoon spent in a quiet way off duty.

Had first Dog watch. Nothing much happened. Saw porpoises in water. Played poker with Jock and 'Scratch' until 2300 hrs. I owe 'Scratch' forty cigarettes. He plays his flute quite well now. Went on watch at midnight.

25 February

0300 we left convoy and started to zig-zag to the Azores. No escort or anything. Extra special lookout kept for submarines. I fell asleep on deck and woke up after I had been relieved, did I curse. The clocks have been put back two hours now. Typed Security memo for The Commander re. Harbour Routine. Lt. Tonks (Radar) cursed me for not falling in. Started Radar Set 79B. Had Afternoon Watch. Clocks put back another hour. Played cards with Jock after supper. On watch at 2000 hrs. I picked up the Azores on the 79B Radar at two minutes to eleven, forty-four miles away. Not bad even if I say it myself.

26 February

Up early as we entered Punta Delgada at 0700 hrs, the sound of cable and winches awoke me at 0630. Very quaint looking town, several mountains behind it. Pilot came aboard and we entered harbour.

The houses were all painted bright colours, just like we'd imagined it. We secured alongside the wharf, very clean it was. None of the crew allowed ashore, Paymaster Batey and Sub Lt. Sealy went to buy things for the ship. One or two Portuguese came on board, they were followed wherever they went just in case. We took on oil and water. Batey managed some bananas and pineapples, wine and cabbages. Most of the crew were on deck all day, the Portuguese people amused us so much.

We left again at 1500 bound for Trinidad, due there on Tuesday, 6th March. Got paid today £4.8s.0d. Next pay day 31 March. Weather grand today. Everybody wished they could have got ashore, just to look at some women. I borrowed 'X's '' glasses *and spent most of the day watching people in the Town. Men dived for coins if you tossed them over. Water very clear.*

The Azores

Punta Delgada - San Miguel Island

The harbour had a big breakwater/mole around it. Large merchant ship was in there and a Portuguese destroyer. The square was right opposite us, a large clock tower behind it. The houses were perched on top of cliffs which formed the inside of the harbour.

There was also a seaplane base there. You could see one or two English names on hotels etc. The Standard of Living happened to be quite low, the people seemed to live by fishing and farming. The climate is ideal, only two months of Winter. I should very much like to go there again after the war for a holiday. Played cards with Jock and Scratch.

27 February

I have the Morning Watch, nothing to report. Things very quiet. Weather began to get rough, plenty of rain. Felt off colour again. Slept most of the day. Weather got worse as day progressed. Office flooded out because I left scuttles open. Taffy and Crossman had a 'drip' about it.

28 February

Had Middle (Watch), felt very tired. Nothing happened. Weather began to calm a little, not much though. Radar Instruction during the Forenoon. The Measurement of Echoes. Afternoon on watch, Tonky (Lt. Tonks) gave us a little exercise. Had bath after tea. Batey told me that we wouldn't get ashore in Trinidad, I wonder. Had First on watch. I picked up a ship at 28,000 yards while on watch, Captain had just told me nearest ship was 110 miles. She passed us on our starboard beam at about 1040, distance nine miles. Nobody saw her. Tonky said I should have picked it up beforehand, perhaps so. I took it out to 38,000 yards. No wonder he grumbled at the difference of 10,000 yards. Anybody would think it was a German ship. Thomas and Ryder were on with me and we had a good laugh, Tonky was in his element.

Thursday 1st March

Weather grand today, beginning to get warmer. Had Forenoon on watch, nothing happened. No tropical clothing to fit me, I shouldn't have left it so late. 'Scratch' threatened to run me in because I wouldn't work for him in the afternoon, got off OK. Did dhobeying (laundry) on deck during afternoon, grand weather. Had a chat with Pat and Red before going on watch. Clock put on an hour.

Friday 2nd March

Had Morning Watch, failed to pick up ship spotted by Lookouts at 0730 hrs. Thomas was operating fortunately. Tonky gave us a blast. Did a spot of office work during forenoon and afternoon, had a swim in the (canvas) bath and felt grand. Got my khaki clothing so I was a little cooler. Had First Dog on watch, nothing happened, worked until 2200 for 'X' (Lt. Commander Brown in charge of all X-Craft) on special memo re. Lack of Discipline, had Middle Watch.

Saturday 3rd March

Middle on watch, very quiet, got my head down as per usual, Thomas again nattered, didn't bother me though. Worked in office during forenoon, and afternoon, Tonky and 'X' had a chat about my work, again nothing happened. Usual work at sea.

Tuesday 6th March

We sighted Trinidad about 0700 but it was not until after lunch that we passed through the approaches to the Port of Spain. Clouds hung low over the island and it wasn't a very impressive scene, the weather got better during the day. We anchored about ten miles away from the shore. No shore leave while in Trinidad, worse luck. Slept on deck for the first time.

Wednesday 7th March

M.L.'s brought us fruit etc. (bananas). Mail came aboard, had several letters. Weather grand, had usual dip in the bath on the after well deck. Sing-song on quarterdeck at night led by Taffy. Quite a good time was had by all. It rained a little and my hammock was already slung, too bad! Had a good night's sleep, two XE Craft lowered.

Thursday 8th March

XE Craft began exercises at 0600 hrs. I was up at 0530 hrs to wash down Captain's deck before breakfast, a bit early for me. Navigator laughed like a drain. Trust him. Usual work in the office, all divers down laying limpets, quite a success, both craft not diving properly, need more ballast, density of water the reason. Captain, SMO, Taffy, Paybob all ashore at Port of Spain. A Catalina aircraft used to fly over XE Craft to obtain camouflage ideas for change of waters, i.e. deep and shallow patches make different colours to an aircraft.

The Battery L.T.O. on BONAVENTURE was L/Seaman George Skuse. He remembers the commencement of the voyage and the battery changing that had preceded it:-

When the B.V. left the Clyde for (as we found out later) the Pacific we had on the upper deck forward, two large packing cases and on the after deck, four large packing cases. Yes, you've guessed it they contained XE Craft. The idea of the containers was to prevent the secret coming out. I cannot remember how many batteries there were on an X-Craft (actually 120) but someone, somewhere, had decided that the terminals on the batteries were the wrong size. So we had to lug all of them out of the craft into lorries and the spare ones from the lower battery stowage were exchanged. On the B.V. all the spare XE Craft batteries were stowed right forward, down in the bowels and each one had to be hoisted independently by hand, then carried up on deck and lifted on to the craft. I can tell you that each one was a separate 2v. cell, a good 2ft high and very heavy, It was a rather slow and awkward job. To make the job easier some of them fell over the side!

N.F. Moulsdale was a Gunner on board ML486, one of the previously mentioned M.L.'s:-

H.M.S. BONAVENTURE the parent vessel to the XE Craft arrived in the Gulf of Paria (Trinidad) with strange-looking crates on the deck (the forerunner of containers). I think there were three on either side (No, they were laid fore and aft, one group of four and two more).

It wasn't long before we found what was in the crates, and M.L.'s being the 'maids of all work' that they were, we were very soon involved in exercises with the midgets. Their job was to try and attach limpet mines to the M.L.'s and it was our job to detect them.

We had the honour, on board ML486, of entertaining the crews of the XE Craft after the exercises. Amongst whom were two future V.C's, Lt. Fraser and Leading Seaman Jim Magennis.

The crews of the midget subs were greatly admired among their counterparts in Coastal Forces and indeed had many volunteers from the 'little ships' to the even smaller ships.

Trinidad

Alan Kevan's log:-

Friday 16th March

Left Port of Spain at 0900 hrs for Panama. Our stay in Trinidad was not too bad. Managed two hours ashore at Scotland Bay (U.S.N.) had a very good time, plenty to eat and drink, grand place for a swim. Took on as much fruit as possible before leaving.

At Sea

Sunday night 18th March

Picked up land at 1100 hrs, South American coast.

Monday 19th March

0900 hrs arrived at Cristobal, port for Colon. Picked up our pilot to take us down the canal. I was on bridge all day as we went through the canal. Quite interesting, the Yanks have certainly made a good job of the canal locks. Passed a trooper on way back to Blighty, they said we were going the wrong way, didn't we know it. Reached Balboa, port for Panama City. Stayed there all night to fuel and water, no leave. Berthed alongside. Wish we could have got ashore there, no luck though. Quite a few Yankee officers came aboard to our wardroom, plenty of drink as usual. The Panama Canal didn't make much impression on George Skuse either. (He was still concerned with security):-

''*When we went through the Canal, there were quite a lot of curious eyes but they had no idea what was underneath the crates.*''

Stan Pulham recalls leaving the Canal and entering the Pacific:-

I well remember this as I was mast head 'look out' at the time, and the ocean was like glass. I thought to myself, Easy to spot the wake of a sub's periscope.

I had forgotten the terrific heat below decks; we all had 'prickly heat', sores or pimples around the stomach like pins pricking into you all the time. We had sweat rags to wipe away sweat. We had to take one mepacrine tablet a day to guard against malaria, which turned the skin yellow.

Alan Kevan's log:-

Tuesday 20th March

I entered the Pacific for the first time en route for San Diego, 3,000 miles away, a seven days trip. Weather warmer, air cleaner, hear we are in for rough weather,

I hope not. There was one moment of panic on voyage, a piece of wood, bobbing up and down, mistaken for periscope, so action stations sounded

At Sea

George Skuse mentions the reaction to the mysterious crates:-

Our first port of call after leaving Panama was San Diego. When we came alongside, the shouts were 'Hi Limey, what you got under those crates'? They were told that it was spare parts but that didn't satisfy them because we had guards on them by the orders of the Admiralty. No one was to go ashore in the U.S.A. To make it easier, BONAVENTURE was moved from alongside to an anchorage offshore.

Even an urgent signal from the Captain to Churchill, saying that relations between us and the Americans were being strained got nowhere. So we were glad when we sailed.

Wednesday 28th March

2355 Arrived in San Diego, having moved up the stream we berthed at the docks. The Air Field was just outside, the biggest I have ever seen, more aircraft than that on it. We couldn't get ashore so we moved out into the stream and anchored. We were given the Freedom of the Town and fifty of us invited to Hollywood, not much use, the Skipper couldn't do anything for us. Offices over the warehouses, girls work there. They wanted to come aboard, no dice. They even wrote messages, invitations, on the window with lipstick. We could have had a hell of a time there!

Alan Wilkie echoes these sentiments and also describes this far from unpleasant voyage:-

There was nearly a mutiny at San Diego, after all the offers of hospitality flowed in from Hollywood and elsewhere and shore leave was forbidden.

I went out East as X Craft Spare Crew and must admit to thoroughly enjoying it, having a world tour at the Admiralty's expense!

It was an interesting experience too as we took our turn at watch keeping and working on BONAVENTURE. Middle watch on a starlight night in the Pacific was marvellous and arriving at a fully-lit port after wartime blackout here was a revelation.

Alan Kevan's log:-

Saturday 31st March

0900, slipped and proceeded down stream bound for Pearl Harbour, 2,000 miles away, a six day trip. If only we could have got ashore in San Diego.

Paid today in dollars, twenty-seven of them. Clocks put back an hour.

Friday 6th April

About 1700 we sighted the Hawaiian Islands, we were not impressed, poured with rain, Islands looked just like Scotland. We arrived too late to enter harbour, so did Yankee battlewagon, OHIO. We had to steam up and down all night. No blackout on the islands.

Saturday 7th April

2100 We entered Pearl Harbour, United States Pacific Naval Base. I had two runs ashore here, into Honolulu and to the Rest Camp, Camp Andrews.

However, Honolulu must have been considered safe as security had been

improved since Pearl Harbour. We had swimming at Waikiki beach and two or three days at a rest camp, built on a delightful remote bay for complete relaxation.
They must all have enjoyed it at Honolulu, the first time they had been allowed ashore for four weeks with soaring temperatures making life very difficult down below.

Stan Pulham:-

Yes we had some lovely runs ashore in the Far East. Honolulu I remember a train ride through the pineapple plantations to a U.S. Navy rest camp under the coconut palms.

Alan Wilkie briefly describes what happened from then until V.J. Day:-

Time off at Honolulu, refuelling at Funafuti, Brisbane and the Barrier Reef to 'work up' again. We were based at Whitsunday Island and almost independent of civilisation. For a week or two we anchored off Bundaberg in Queensland to practice cutting old sea-bed cables. This is where we lost two divers in the process. Bruce Enzer and Dave Carey.

Then on to the Philippines, and Borneo from where the operations took place. Finally, when the Pacific war ended, down to Sydney and performances for the Press.

Pearl Harbour

George Skuse:-

Our next stop was Pearl Harbour and we were allowed ashore there, to Honolulu. The craft remained covered up and the armed guards kept watch. The Yanks were very curious, thinking it strange that stores and spare parts should be so heavily guarded. Being one of the ship's company, we didn't know what was going on, all we saw was a lot of coming and going by the Captain and others.

Captain Fell:-

At Pearl Harbour we came under direct control of the United States Navy and proceeded towards the operational area. The blow fell while we were on passage, XE Craft were not wanted and we were sent down to Brisbane to await orders.
However, the ship's company had no inkling of this and BONAVENTURE steamed serenely on.

Alan Kevan's log:-

Wednesday 11th April
At 1300 we slipped and proceeded down stream out into the Pacific, this time on our final trip. Our base is going to be Manus, Admiralty Islands. We are re-fuelling at a place called Funafuti (about 2,000 miles from the East Coast of Australia), just a tiny coral island with nobody there, except an American oiler. Literally just a 'fly drop' on the chart that nobody, not even Captain Fell, had even heard of.

Monday 16th April
At 1300 we crossed the line, with great ceremony.
Wednesday 18th April

At 0800 we arrived at Funafuti in the Ellis Islands. A small U.S. Base. We re-fuelled there and had to wait for sailing orders. Had Bathing over the side.

Stan Pulham:-

While swimming in the sea there, we had a Leading Seaman in a motor cutter with a rifle, to ward off sharks. We also had a canvas swim pool on the after well deck. We didn't get ashore at Funafuti, you could see some palm trees and a few thatched huts, but to me it only seemed to be few feet out of the water. It looked as if a tidal wave would wash right over it. I believe it was there that a sea plane picked up Captain Fell, probably he was searching for XE Craft operations for us. Obviously we were not told what was happening at the time.

The XE Craft had still been boxed at Pearl Harbour but we took the boxes off after leaving, briefly, and then replaced them. No, we saw no signs of wreckage or burned-out hulks while there, I suppose it had been cleared up by then.

Alan Kevan must have been more venturesome, because he noticed some, which must have been there, for nowadays it's been preserved as a tourist attraction. The security-conscious George Skuse is relieved too:-

After our visit to Pearl Harbour, we went towards Australia at last. The crates were removed and XE's 1 to 6 were on full view, but not until after we left Brisbane.

They (the XE Craft people) spent a lot of time exercising off the Barrier Reef and the crews spent a lot of time ashore, learning to live on what they could find.

Meanwhile BONAVENTURE was still at Funafuti.

Ellis Islands
Funafuti

Alan Kevan's log:-

Thursday 19th April
Still in harbour awaiting orders. Bathing over the side.
At one time there were 8,000 troops on this small island including large quantities of equipment. They had air raids on the island. The Yanks are now evacuating it, too bad we couldn't have taken it over.

Friday 20th April
0700 we sailed for Brisbane. Our destination has been changed, we wonder if our mail is all at Manus.
As soon as we put to sea we put our clocks on 24 hrs and so made it 0700 Saturday 21st.

Sunday 22nd April
Weather very rough.

Arrival in Australia

Friday 27th April

We entered Brisbane. Went right up river to 'A' Berth and I went ashore that night. I liked Brisbane, not then, but later on when I found my way round. Everybody on the ship was happy at the thought of a few days in port.

Stan Pulham enjoyed his run ashore too:-

Brisbane was very nice. I made friends there with someone who of course didn't know what the ship was engaged in or carried and of course I couldn't tell anyone, very secret. Later on they sent me some newspaper headlines, 'Brisbane's Mystery Ship'.

We used to enjoy a drink in an Australian Naval Barracks or depot in the city, sitting in a nice garden by the river. Talking about beer I remember in Brisbane and Sydney the pubs only opened in the evenings for one hour between five and six. There was always a crowd of Service men milling around outside, waiting for opening time. The counter was covered with glasses of beer already filled to the brim ready for drinking to save time. You didn't ask for a pint or half pint, it was either a 'middy' or a 'schooner'.

Everybody enjoyed Brisbane and Alan Kevan was no exception:-

'We stayed in Brisbane until the 14th of May. I really had a good time there. I fell in love with the town. It was just the right size and I soon got to know everywhere. The people treated us well. There had not been many British ships in there before us. I played hockey and cricket against the SLINGER, the only other British ship of any size.

I met the Keogh family, especially Marie, she was one of the best girls I have ever known and we had a good time together. Mrs. Keogh made me very welcome and I regarded her house as home. It was very hard saying goodbye to Maria, if I had met her under any other circumstances, I should have fallen in love with her, perhaps I did but nothing could come of it.

V.E. Day was quiet, except for Australian troop disturbances against the Americans, these went on for a few days. 'V.E. plus 1' and I got drunk, really and truly drunk, Marie's brothers, Den and Jim were on leave and we celebrated. I managed to sober up to take Marie out that night. I shall never forget Marie and our first trip into Brisbane, very happy memories. The Captain flew North to Subic (Philippines) to confer with Rear-Admiral Fife (Consubs 7th. Fleet), after going down to Sydney first with 'X' to see Admiral Fraser. Apparently we were not wanted, the Americans said there was nothing for us to do out here. In other words they wanted to do it all themselves. Captain tried to convince Fife of our capabilities, he had an operation in mind in Hong Kong. Meanwhile, we left Brisbane to work-up and wait for an answer.

Alan Kevan's log:-

May 14th
Left Brisbane in afternoon for CID ISLAND and then Townsville.
May 16th
Arrived CID ISLAND, stayed there an hour or so and then went up to Townsville.
May 17th
Arrived Townsville pm. I went ashore. Not a very pleasant place. Very small and

hardly anything to do. Had a couple of drinks or so and met two Australians, good chaps, also a Concert Party who wanted to come aboard and give us a show.

May 18th

We left port and went down to CID HARBOUR.

May 19th

Arrived Cid Harbour in the Whitsunday Islands group. We stayed here for quite a while working-up the craft. I didn't have much to do. The Captain came back, his operation quashed as the 'Hot Intelligence' we had was two months behind the times. Our future was uncertain and the general feeling was that we would go down to Sydney and pay off. Our tails were right down.

To have concluded a successful part in the European war and steam 20,000 miles in order to help the Americans conclude their part in the Pacific war then to be told you were not wanted,, was a blow to anyone's esteem.

Alan Kevan:-

We had one hope, the Americans had a special operation they wanted doing and XE Craft might be the solution. The Captain was quite hopeful. This operation meant new trials to be carried out before we could say whether we could do it.

Meanwhile we landed a party of officers on an island, equipped only with one twenty-four hour pack and a few odds and ends. They stayed there for five days. It was only done to pass the time away. Captain Fell must have been at his wits end. Most of the crew had decided we were paying off and were getting things squared off.

Living rough on Hazelwood Island in the Whitsunday Group. Left to right: Bergius, Briggs, Sheppard, Spree, Butters, Britnell, Coles, Shean. Front row; Kelly, (unknown), Gillard, Rhodes and Perritt.

There was not much of interest in CID HARBOUR, just a group of small islands, uninhabited, I went ashore once or twice for a swim and a walk around. Snakes were plentiful and I killed plenty. Mail was brought quite regularly by a 'Walrus' plane, good show.

The party of officers that had been landed on Hazelwood Island for a Survival Exercise included N.C.O.'s and one of these was that veteran correspondent Chief E.R.A. 'Ginger' Coles. Pass the time away it may have done, but Ginger still relishes the memory of this 'Boy's Own' Paper holiday, especially as it included some vital First Aid which probably saved the life of Jock Bergius (Sub Lieutenant A. K. Bergius R.N.V.R.).

Max Shean had sought permission for all three crews of XE4, ten men, to spend five days living rough on this small uninhabited island in the Whitsunday group, to toughen themselves up. They landed from XE4 by anchoring very close to some rocks and stepping ashore on to 'terra firma'. They had found this flat-calm lagoon by accident and wasted no time in carrying the gear, (such as it was), ashore and setting up camp. They even named their bay after their X Craft, XE4. Is it still called EXCITER Bay?

They were thoroughly enjoying the life, living off the land, but not the sea, they hadn't been able to catch any fish. On the second day, Jock and Ginger were harpooning in the lagoon's two foot of water when Jock was stung by a sting ray.

Fancying a bite for supper, Jock had pressed it downward with his harpoon. Whereupon it had lashed out with its barbed tail, leaving Jock with two nasty holes in his heel.

Ginger dragged him out of the water, there was no-one else about, and applied First Aid in the prescribed manner. He made a tourniquet, then nicked Jock's leg to make the blood flow. He was in great pain and gradually becoming paralysed. Unable to walk, he was half-carried and half-dragged over the sand to where XE4 was lying.

Unfortunately BONAVENTURE was twenty-five miles away, so XE4 had to get steam up and proceeded with all dispatch to B.V.'s welcoming side. By now Jock was in agony. He was helped up and back on board and spent a couple of weeks in the Sick Bay. Equally fortunate (and surprisingly) the Doctor, Surgeon Lieutenant Cody, knew what to do and it was thanks to he and Ginger that Jock emerged from his ordeal, weak but completely recovered.

George Skuse had a sensitive ear for the buzzes (rumours) at this dispiriting time:-

The craft were very good for their size and had everything that the big subs had, only smaller, (they had more in fact, for the big subs didn't have a W. and D.), yet our C. in C. out there (Admiral Sir Bruce Fraser) had no interest in them. He thought they were toys which caused much resentment.

After a lot of running around by the Captain, an American Admiral became very interested. So the BONAVENTURE took the craft to Subic Bay in the Philippines, which was a U.S. Submarine Base. (Subic is, or rather was the main Far Eastern American navy base and was only disbanded in 1992.)

The Admiral, who was a sub expert, thought up some jobs for the craft and plans were laid. So we left Subic, with BONAVENTURE having the distinction of being the only R.N. ship going to sea flying the flag of a U.S. Admiral. His name was Fife and he and his (ninety-strong) staff enjoyed their stay on board.

We had some of the ratings in our mess and they thought our Navy was better than theirs. Of course the rum ration had a lot to do with it! Also they preferred our type of messing to theirs, which was cafeteria.

BONAVENTURE in the Philippines with awnings rigged in the very hot weather to give some protection to the men working down below.

Alan Kevan's log:-

> *June 12th*
> *We hoisted in all craft ready to sail.*
> *June 13th*
> *Sailed for Townsville and arrived pm on the 14th. We had to store ship in twenty four hours but starboard watch got ashore again. I drank quite a lot, met the same two Australians again and also Doris, quite a pleasant girl. I was forty five minutes adrift and got 'one and one' (one day's detention and one day's stoppage of pay). It was worth it.*
> *June 15th*
> *Pm. We left for Hervey Bay, about 150 miles North of Brisbane, getting nearer.*
> *June 17th*
> *We arrived in HERVEY BAY for our trials. These trials were as follows:-*
> *Cable cutting, there was an old cable there, going across to one of the Pacific*

Isles (Fiji). About 1890 it was laid. We had to lift it, cut it, and insulate it. In spite of several difficulties, these trials were successful. Unfortunately we lost Lt. Carey and Lt. Enzer while cutting the cable.

Because there was no obvious reason for their deaths, all diving equipment was checked and all personnel who needed to dive were then ordered over the side. No more problems.

Everybody was pleased at the thought of Operations, including me. I had to type the proposed operational orders for the Captain to take up to Admiral Fife, I took great pleasure in this. We anchored about three miles off the coast. The town of Bundaberg lay eight miles up the Burnett River which was quite near to us. We got no shore leave. The Captain left us for Subic two days before we sailed for Brisbane.

Hervey Bay may be small on the map, but it's a huge area and the place where these ancient cables came ashore/entered the sea is a tiny bay called Mon Repos beach. It is now a Conservation Area, being one of very few Turtle Sanctuaries.

The place still has a rather sad feel about it as if remembering, and regretting the lives of the two brave men it had taken, so many years ago. A memorial is being organised for the Bundaberg History Museum and perhaps even at the beach, to commemorate their deaths.

Back aboard BONAVENTURE again, on June 26th, we sailed for Brisbane.

June 27th

Arrived am. in Brisbane. A gale blowing and it took us nearly two hours to tie up at Cruiser 'A' wharf at Pinhenba, or across the river from Pinhenba, Lytton. About five miles from the town. I went ashore and met Marie and the Keogh family again.

June 28th

Went on four days leave. Marie had, however, arranged to go away, apparently a boyfriend had cropped up. My stay in Brisbane was quite a good one except that Marie and I drifted apart. Her mother was very nice to me and I visited her quite often. I bought her a book for her Birthday. I met a WAAAF, Vera, and I went out for the day with her one Sunday in Lone Pine. My best day in port. My last night in Brisbane, I did not see Marie, she had a date. I went to a dance at the Naval House. A grand place for us sailors. Kath (Marie's sister) and her B.V. friend Dougie were there. The Captain came back, went down to Sydney and rejoined us the day before we left. The operation was on. Great excitement.

Leaving Australia
(for the time being at least)

Alan Kevan's log:-

Sunday July 8th

We left in the morning for Subic via the Admiralty Islands. A long trip through dangerous waters and we were in a hurry (Subic had only been recaptured from the Japs three weeks previously). XE2 and XE6 have been laid off, no crews. The operations at present are as follows:- XE1 and 3 to attack two Japanese cruisers MYOKO (XE1) 10,000 tons and the TAKAO (XE3) 10,000 tons lying in the Straits of Singapore; XE4 to cut cables at Saigon and XE5 to cut cables at Hong Kong. We were to arrive at Subic on July 19th, leave XE5 with MAIDSTONE (the affection-inspiring Submarine Depot Ship) and go down to Brunei Bay in Borneo with the other craft. All craft are due to sail July 27th, 'D' Day being 31st July. This is open to alteration. I was on Radar but got taken off owing to the amount of work for me in the office, all the orders etc. had to be typed by m. Lots of lists to prepare. I am quite happy.

Tuesday 13th.

Arrive MANUS (Admiralty Islands, Part of the Bismarck Archipelago in Australian New Guinea). We fuelled and took on a few stores and water and left again that night, we were in a hurry. Our mail had been directed to Subic but strangely enough we picked some up at Manus. Everyone was surprised, even 'X'. I sleep in the office now at night. Much time being spent by Taffy and I on checking recent photographs of Singapore, looking for possible net defences.

Manus where the old men have giant holes in their ears, where most of the river-bank houses are built on stilts over the water and have thatched walls. Where the numerous children go naked up to the age of about ten (and then only wear a necklace of sharks' teeth) and where they are all completely amphibious, paddling around in dugout canoes, capsizing and laughing. Where the children draw exceptionally well and are advanced for their age in other ways too.

Saturday 14th

We crossed the line again but this time without ceremony at 0710. The weather is not too good, plenty of rain and a strong wind. The wind however is very refreshing. We went to Action Stations during the day for exercise.

Sunday 15th

We went to Emergency stations for exercise again during the forenoon, it poured with rain at the time. I saw the Captain and got my extra pay up to July 21st, about £4.10s.0d. We had reports of Subs and a mysterious force of enemy ships, we maintained a steady lookout. One item of interest - picked up echoes ahead of us but flying towards us. We turned the ship round and steamed back for several miles so we could use our twin four-inch guns on the stern (they could not fire forward). Aircraft turned away so resumed original course.

Friday 20th

6.30 entered Subic Bay on the S.W. tip of Luzon, base of U.S. 7th Fleet. Pouring with rain, atmosphere very heavy. As soon as we anchored out XE Craft, all heads of departments across to MAIDSTONE (8th Submarine Flotilla (we are the 14th)) all Staff people. Lt. Philip now in charge of XE Craft trials. SEANYMPH had explosion in battery compartment, one towing sub down. We have now got STYGIAN (XE3), SPARK (XE1), SPEARHEAD (XE4), SELENE (XE5). All the orders have been typed in draft, new ones will have to be done. Things have slackened off in the office, but it is the calm before the storm. All the crews briefed tomorrow. There is a U.S. show ashore but I have the programme to type. A big battle in the wardroom. Scratch got a black eye, Crocket split his hand, Potter very sore, Cody almost out.

The trip up here was very interesting, we passed quite a few well known places, we saw the South East corner of New Guinea, went round the coast in sight of New Britain. We also went very close to New Guinea and could see fires ashore. We passed through the Bismarck Sea and up to Manus.

There were quite a few ships in Manus, most of them belonging to the Fleet Train, no big warships there. We left the Admiralty Islands and went through a dangerous stretch of water, in range of Jap planes in Caroline Islands. We had our exercises on this trip. We entered the Philippines from the East, South of Leyte. We turned South then past Mindanao and then up the West coast of Negros, Panay and Mindoro to Subic Bay, passing Manila Bay on the voyage.

22nd July

A typhoon hit us and XE6 got washed ashore. Max Shean swam out to his craft (XE4) which had broken loose, Westmacott slipped in record time. All the orders are now completed Admiral Lockwood CONSEVENTHFLEET went out in the rescued XE4.

Captain Fell describes what he saw and felt, when they were hit by a solid wall of wind:-

The wall came at us in screaming fury. The low swell that had been rolling in for the past hour, turned almost instantly into steep tumbling seas where crests were torn off and flung away by the wind. I ran to the bridge and ordered 'Slow ahead both' to ease the strain on the two bar-taut anchor cables.

Visibility was almost nil through the sheets of driving rain but occasionally I glimpsed the situation at sea level. Craft of every description had broken loose or had been cast off and were milling around in chaotic confusion. It was nothing short of a miracle that none of our midgets were damaged.

As suddenly as they had begun, the wind and rain stopped. To our astonishment we saw that XE6, who we imagined must have long since piled up on the rocks astern, had fetched up ten yards from them when the mooring and sinker that she was dragging, had fouled an outcrop of coral.

Alan Kevan's log:-

Tuesday 24th July

Sailed for Brunei Bay at 0700, Admiral Fife on board. His flag at our mast head, two destroyers as escort.

Wednesday 25th

On passage, finished Intelligence for operations.

Thursday 26th

Arrived Brunei Bay at 1000 having lost our way during night. Out craft, trim dives and final briefing. Fraser damaged periscope on PAX (Advance Penetration Exercise). His first Cdr. 'X' didn't know he hadn't done one. 1600 XE1 and 3 with SPARK and STYGIAN, XE3 damaged induction trunk as she slipped, Cdr. E not at all pleased. (No wonder, two major defects acquired just before an operation) Operation 'Struggle'.

Friday 27th

0700 SPEARHEAD sailed with XE4, Operation 'Sabre'. From that date we did nothing in the office except study more recent photos, two lots of special information was lost in air crashes. I had an easy time. Cinema shows every night, pleasant weather, no mail.

Chapter Twenty One
Operation 'Sabre' July 1945

Operational Crew:-
Lt. M. Shean D.S.O., R.A.N.V.R.
S/Lt. B. A. N. Kelly R.N.V.R., M.I.D.
S/Lt. A. K. Bergius D.S.C., R.N.V.R.
S/Lt. K. M. Briggs D.S.C., R.A.N.V.R.
E.R.A. V. Coles D.S.M., M.I.D.

Passage Crew:-
S/Lt. J. Britnell R.N.V.R., M.I.D.
E.R.A. Sheppard (G.E.M.) M.I.D.
P.O, Rhodes (V.D.) M.I.D.
Sto. Butters (P.W.) M.I.D.

Towing Submarine:- SPEARHEAD
C.O. Cdr. R. E. Youngman D.S.C., R.N.R.

In the summer of 1945 with the war drawing towards it's inevitable conclusion it became apparent that the cutting of the Hong Kong to Saigon submarine telephone cables would make it less difficult to drive the Japanese out of Malaya and Hong Kong, as they would then be forced to rely upon wireless communications vulnerable to advanced American decoding techniques.

Captain Fell's strenuous efforts to secure operational tasks for his beloved XE Craft had at last born fruit; in the last few weeks of the war. He had managed to overcome American prejudice against their use and persuaded Admiral Fife of the United States Navy to co-operate with him and the Royal Navy.

Admiral Fife, United States Navy:-

If you can locate and sever some Japanese telephone cables for us so that the Nips have to send their signals by wireless, where they can be the more easily intercepted, you'll be doing us a real service. We want to know what they're up to, so go to it for time is running out. The war'll be over before you can change your mind.

Captain Fell needed no second bidding and the Admiral and he immersed themselves in working out the details of the forthcoming operations. It was arranged that XE1 and XE3 would leave Labuan Island, Borneo, on July 26th; XE4 would depart on the 27th and XE5 a day later.

The first two XE Craft were detailed to cripple the Japanese 'Atago' and 'Nachi' class heavy cruisers, TAKAO and MYOKO in Johore Strait, Singapore; XE4 was to cut the Saigon-Hong Kong and Saigon-Singapore cables where they converged off the entrance to Saigon River and XE5 was to make the same attempt on the

X Craft aboard BONAVENTURE with limpet carriers waiting to be filled. Differing only slightly in shape from the side cargoes, they carried a number of small limpet mines which could be attached by magnets, to various vital parts of the target.

incoming and outgoing cables outside Hong Kong harbour. In the event, only XE4 was completely successful. Or so they thought at the time.

The concept wasn't new but the idea of cutting submarine cables from a small submarine was. All the operational details had to be worked out from scratch and at speed, there was no time to waste. Intelligence reports had supplied the actual line of the cables but they still had to be found; the nature of the seabed was largely unknown and anyway the cables had been laid in the nineteenth century and might have become irretrievably buried.

However, XE4 was equipped with a 'Flatfish' type grapnel towed from a short length of manila rope attached to a chain bridle. She was to cross and recross the known position of the cable, streaming the grapnel until the latter snagged the former. Whereupon the diver would emerge and after inspection would either attempt to free the grapnel from an obstruction and return dissapointed to the craft, or gleefully snip out a section of cable and bear it triumphantly back to the W. and D. and control room.

XE4 being hoisted out of BONAVENTURE with both limpet carriers attached and plainly visible. Before setting out to sever the Hong Kong - Saigon cable.

XE4, christened EXCITER slipped quietly away from BONAVENTURE's protective side at noon on July 27 and was soon 'buttoned-up' in tow by the Submarine SPEARHEAD.

They would have loved to have bathed in the blissfully cool South China Sea (Nan Hai) but someone had spotted a sea snake on the surface. As the bite of this deceptively mild-looking reptile can be fatal within minutes they decided to forego this luxury. Even though the nearest known enemy shipping was 650 miles away. A three-day passage on a flat sea ('Harry Flatters' in naval jargon), brought them to the change-over point about 30 miles S.E. of the entrance to the Saigon River (Dong Nai) and the same distance from the Mekong Delta where the emmission of

water from scores of fresh water tributaries was to cause XE4 some trim problems.
From XE 4's Patrol Report:-

30th July

*0350 Surfaced to change over crews. Sea and swell II. Wind SW force 1.
      Lazy ruffled surface.*

*0400 SPEARHEAD stopped. Rubber dinghy was not used. We closed SPEAR-
HEAD's stern, secured forward on short line and kept going slow astern (to maintain
tension on the line and to prevent it getting round SPEARHEAD's screw). Crew
stepped from submarine to X Craft and vice versa, and change over was completed
in a few minutes.*

*0415 Slipped securing line and got under way in tow. Operational crew on board.
Ran engine to ventilate.*

0440 Dived. Craft in excellent condition.

0750 SPEARHEAD dived. (It was daylight now)

2115 Surfaced (Darkness had now fallen)

*2120 Slipped tow in position 112 degrees Cape St. Jacques lighthouse (Not
      lit)*

Actually the light was never lit and Lt. Max Shean was forced to navigate on
the only prominent landmark distinguishable at night, the Nui Baria range of
mountains behind. The weather was too good to last and as they closed the land it
deteriorated quickly:-

*2235 Wind and sea increased during the night, especially closer inshore,
where the sea was steep and short. The casing was awash the whole time and
binoculars were useless owing to the spray.*

*31st July 0100 Reduced to slow speed from 5 knots, to go below for dry
binoculars. On returning to the casing at the wrong moment, was washed over the
side, surfacing just in time to grab wire jackstay forward of rudder and crawled back
on board.*

Or it would have been a case of 'Sailor you've had it', for nobody down below
had heard a thing and his despairing shouts would have been lost on the wind.

*The sea was very bumpy over the shallow patches. A little later I fell off my perch
on the induction again; and nearly had another quick swim.*

*0348 Dived and bottomed in a position from which operations could be
commenced at first light.*

*0600 Surfaced to ventilate. Streamed grapnel. Three junks sailing quite close,
one headed straight for us so had to dive a little early. Numerous junks were in sight
throughout the day all under sail.*

*0748 Fixed position on NW edge of Formosa Bank and commenced first run,
keeping depth 10ft clear of bottom. Grapnel dragged heavily through coarse sand
of Formosa Bank even with 1 knot tide in our favour.*

Speed over the bottom under those conditions was an unknown quantity, so a fix
had to be taken at the beginning and end of every run.

*0812 Altered course away from bank, that is towards wreck of cable ship U.S.
CABLE (sunk on rock) which was reported to be visible. The wreck was not visible*

though our navigation for once was correct.

0900   Struck rock/wreck, swung to starboard and concluded that we had completed the first run without success. Divers emerging rapidly from their repose in the battery compartment never complained.

1000   Fix indicated that we had again crossed the cable unsuccessfully. Altered course again. Each run was made 5 to 10ft off the bottom to ensure that the grapnel dragged efficiently.

Watched by interested spectators on a destroyer, an XE carries out diving and surfacing manoeuvres. The difficulty of spotting the slender attack periscope can be imagined.

BONAVENTURE had come out from the U.K. equipped ready for every single eventuality, except that of finding cables. Therefore the grapnel had to be made up, like war-time meals, from bits and pieces. It worked very well and several times in the ensuing hour XE4 was brought up 'all standing'. It had either caught on outcrops of coral or become enmired in deep clay. Fortunately, Max was able to free it without the time-wasting procedure of sending out divers, simply by going astern.

Meanwhile a thorough periscope reconnaissance of the beach defences of that part of the coastline revealed the fact that where the cables entered the sea the Japs were manning the big guns. Max gave this rather alarming discovery a constructive use and following this line out to sea commenced streaming their home-made grapnel again.

1012   Took a fix and altered course, starting 3rd run. Now obviously in mud. Suddenly the craft came to a complete standstill and the object gave. Was it or wasn't it the cable.

1027 At little more than slow speed grouped up, we remained anchored. At full speed grouped up she moved off and, believing that we may have just caught the cable and slipped it again, altered course to the reciprocal, to recross the position.

1043 Craft again brought up in the same estimated position. Depth of water 44ft.

1143 Diver (S/Lt. K. M. Briggs R.A.N.V.R.) out. Five minutes later, diver in. Reported that grapnel and chain was deeply buried in a patch of hard clay but no cable.

1155 Continued on 3rd run, course 075 deg.

1205 Craft brought up suddenly. At full speed ahead, she lurched and swung to the tide which appeared to be running at .5 to 1 knot. At full astern grouped up the craft did not move.

Ken Briggs was into the W. and D. like a flash. Well as soon as he could squeeze through the man-hole-sized opening in his cumbersome diving dress. Then it was:- On face piece, Off air and On oxygen. Slam shut the interior hatches, flood up and climb out into the sea.

Eureka! The grapnel had indeed caught the submarine cable. Ken removed the cutter with the pistol grip from its compartment in the casing. This was also to become his lifeline. The gap in the net cutter had previously had to be widened by Ch. E.R.A. Ron Fisher, to take the 1½" diameter cable.

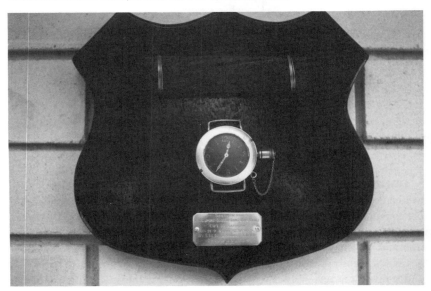

A Section of the Singapore - Saigon - Hong Kong Cable. Cut at Saigon by S/Lt. K. M. Briggs RANVR. Also dispalyed is a divers' watch.

At that depth the sea was cold and opaque as Ken felt his way down the grapnel rope through the sand - clouded water, to where the encrusted cable lay. With Max still hovering 10ft above the bottom, this was more difficult than expected and he had to hang on tight, hauling himself down hand over hand to combat the currents. He said afterwards:-

'The current was a combination of things. Firstly, we were headed into the one knot tidal set to make it easier to maintain trim since the grapnel caught. Likewise way was kept on to ensure the grapnel remained snagged. Thus at the Moment of Cut, we had the combined force of tide and river current, the propeller wash and forward movement of the craft.

'If I hadn't maintained a grip on the cutters, I would have been swept away and been unable to return'.

Ken lost no time in squeezing the trigger on the barrel shaped cutter and releasing the powerful spring loaded blade into the slim cable in two places. The blade emerged from it's housing and bit through the cable cleanly, inexorably and completely just as if there was no resistance to its passage at all. It was a beautifully designed piece of workmanship.

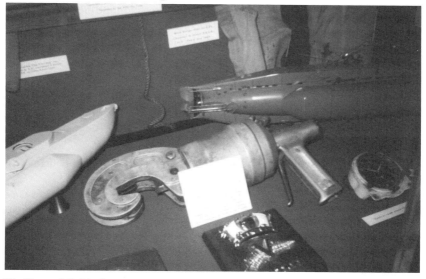

The Net and Cable Cutter. This was operated by Compressed Air. On the right is an X Craft Chronometer.

So it was that a delighted Ken re-entered the W. and D. clutching his 24" length of Saigon-Singapore telegraph cable.

Under way again and very soon the second cable was caught. They felt to be old hands now and S/Lt. Jock Bergius lost no time in emerging, as his partner had done before him.

New orders had been formulated since the Carey and Enzer tragedy six weeks before:- 'Divers to expend the minimum amount of effort when cable-cutting. NOT to remain outside the craft in depths over 33ft for more than 20 mins and over 40ft for more than 10 mins'. The experts had learnt, from bitter experience, a little more about their old enemy Oxygen Pete. In an X Craft context, he was more lethal than the Japs.

So it was prudent of Jock Bergius that, when his cutter failed to work and he returned to the control room for another then spend a little time resting and conserving his energy then he re-emerged, severed the Saigon-Hong Kong cable in two places and returned to the craft.

Max subsequently wrote in his report:-

Sections of both cable cuts are submitted for inspection but not, we trust for retention'.

The authorities didn't retain them for Ken's, at least, is mounted on his sitting room wall in Brisbane together with his diver's watch.

Next it was up stakes, or rather grapnel, and make haste to keep the rendezvous with SPEARHEAD about thirty hours later. (X-Craft carried either an anchor or a grapnel - there wasn't room for both).

Weariness had set in by this time, not to mention reaction and their eyelids were drooping Nobody felt like eating either. It was a different story though, after the tow had been passed by heaving line and the crew exchange completed in a few minutes, for there was a special 'fry-up' awaiting them. Returning to the comparative luxury of the cramped 'S' class submarine was welcome indeed, even the heat seemed less, with adequate air conditioning.

Thereafter they got their collective heads down for the next twelve hours. Until they were awakened and given the news that the first atom bomb had been dropped on Hiroshima. Some optimists even thought that the war would be over by the time they reached Borneo three days later.

It had been a thoroughly successful first operation and Captain Fell gave his unstinting praise:-

It is therefore as well to recall that, until two months ago, not only was such a use for X Craft not envisaged, but no solution had been reached as to how enemy cables were to be cut without considerable risk to surface forces and the certainty of detection.

It is submitted that X Craft crews deserve very high praise for the keenness and efficiency with which they tackled a brand new problem, perfected the necessary technique and put it into successful operation in such a short time.

All of which produced a bar to his D.S.O. for Max Shean, D.S.C.'s for Ken Briggs and Adam Bergius and four Mention in Dispatches for other crew members.

Chapter Twenty Two
Operation 'Foil' July-August 1945

Operation Crew:-
Lt. H. P. Westmacott D.S.O., D.S.C., R.N.
Lt. Beadon Dening M.I.D., R.N.V.R.
E.R.A. Clifford Greenwood M.I.D.
Lt. B. G. Clarke D.S.C., R.N.V.R.
S/Lt. D. V. M. Jarvis D.S.C., R.N.V.R.
1st Passage Crew:-
Under S/Lt. Dawson R.N.V.R.
2nd Passage Crew:-
Under S/Lt. Ken Robinson D.S.C., R.N.V.R.
Towing Submarine:- SELENE
C.O. Lt. Cdr. H. R. B. Newton D.S.C., R.N.

Operation 'Foil' was the second of the two operations mounted with the intention of cutting the two submarine telephone cables between Saigon and Singapore and between Saigon and Hong Kong. Originally thought to have been unsuccessful it was subsequently discovered that XE5 had in fact, so damaged the cable that it became inoperable.

The successful Cable-cutting at Hong Kong was executed in July 1945 by XE5.

The writer is very grateful to Commander P. Westmacott, the C.O. of XE5, who has personally contributed the following account:-

Operations 'Foil' and 'Sabre' were set up with the object of disrupting Japanese communications between Hong Kong and Singapore. Two ocean telegraph cables had been laid westward from Hong Kong, one to Saigon and another direct to Singapore. From Saigon another cable had been laid to Singapore. If these cables could be cut, the Japanese command would have to use radio for all signal traffic which the Americans, having broken the codes, could intercept and read.

XE4 under Lt. M. H. Shean D.S.O., R.A.N.V.R. was assigned to the Saigon operation 'Sabre' and XE5 under myself, to the Hong Kong end, - 'Foil'.

We were based at Subic Bay in the Philippines when the decision to mount the Cable cutting operation was taken. My craft, XE5, along with the members of the operational and passage crews were transferred to H.M.S. MAIDSTONE, while BONAVENTURE sailed to Brunei whence she was to launch XE4 (and XE1 and XE3 to Singapore).

H.M.S. SELENE, under Lt. Cdr. Newton, was detailed to tow us to Hong Kong, a distance of about 600 miles. As with my Bergen operation (X24 the second time), I determined to sail my craft on the outward passage myself, and turn her over to my Passage Crew after the operation was over. That way, I would be 'au fait' with her condition before setting off on the actual mission.

We sailed, in tow behind SELENE, at 1300 in Friday 27th July and dived about an hour later. SELENE increased to her normal cruising speed of around 10 knots. We settled to a good trim at between 110 and 140 feet. The upward pull of the tow was countered with about 5 degrees dive on the planes, and any inclination to yaw was likewise balanced with 5 degrees of rudder. Once set, and settled at an acceptable depth planes and rudder called for no further attention and the crew on watch were free to read, cook, mop, clean, etc.

We found that under way, at the 10 or 12 knots at which SELENE proceeded, we could work the air conditioning plant being driven by the idling propeller. This made a most tremendous difference to our personal comfort, and to the condition of the craft itself, which would otherwise have sweated appallingly.

Working our 6 hours watches, life pursued an agreeable even tenor. Every 6 hours SELENE would reduce to around 5 knots, and we would surface for 10 minutes and run the engine to ventilate the craft. At 2000 we would surface for a couple of hours to charge the battery and ditch gash. The sea was glassy calm and I recall for the whole operation, sunny, hot and humid.

By night, looking forward through the night periscope (only about two inches above the casing), one saw the little spots of phosphorescence stirred up by the vibrating tow ahead flying towards one, as if the watcher at the periscope was in some space craft shooting through space; a glorious sight which I never tired of watching.

XE5 from the deck of towing submarine H.M.S. SELENE just before leaving to cut the Hong Kong Singapore cable.

I now quote from my report of the operation:-
Monday 30th July

0100 *Communications well.*

0120 *Craft lost trim and went slowly down to 240 feet.*
Communications with SELENE broke down. Considered that she had probably dived and that the break in communication was a coincidence. Trim regained. Steady at 130 feet.

0215 *A lonely feeling. Getting suspicious. Started the gyro.*

0220 *Surfaced. No sign of SELENE. Tow hanging down in the water at a steep angle. Estimated that it was about 54 miles, 325 degrees to the slipping position. Slipped the tow and proceeded. Course 325 degrees. Rendezvous with SELENE seemed unlikely. I intended to proceed with the operation, assuming that SELENE would await me at the pre-arranged recovery position.*

0245 *Sighted green flare bearing 070 degrees. Altered course towards. Burnt one flare, Forty minutes later, no more flares having been seen, I resumed my course for Hong Kong.*

It was glassy calm as I recall, and warm. Eventually, however, after the expenditure of several more flares, contact was made at 0503, and a very relieved SELENE ranged up alongside. It seemed best for me to go over and agree a plan. I stripped off my shirt and shorts, turned over XE5 to Beadon Dening and swam across.

In fact what had happened was that the shackle securing the tow to SELENE had come undone and this had plunged to the bottom of the China Sea about 400 feet deep.

We soon decided to pass the spare tow, and postpone the operation by 24 hours in order to get some rest. At 0655, we dived and continued in leisurely fashion towards Hong Kong.

The fact that they had been sufficiently alert to regain trim, so soon after the tow had parted, was recognised in elevated circles as a considerable feat, and they were congratulated.

Lt. Westmacott:-

The fact that we had been able to make a rendezvous by the prodigal use of flares and conclude our arrangements well after sunrise, was indicative of the American mastery of this part of the China Sea.

Next morning at 0750 on Tuesday 31st July, XE5 slipped her tow and set off/dived, to cover the 25 miles in to the locality of our operations adjacent to Lamma Island.

At 1545 we passed the estimated position of the boom defence net across the East Lamma Channel, of which there was now no sign. The movements of various junks satisfied me that the risk of mines was negligible.

At 1850 I bottomed in 4½ fathoms in the West Lamma Channel to await the fall of night before surfacing (at 2245) to charge the battery and rig the grapnel and cutters. At this point I will describe the equipment provided and the method of using it. I will also add some comments on the limitations imposed by physiological conditions.

The principal one of these was the risk of a diver succumbing to Oxygen poisoning. Our diving sets were provided with oxygen in a bottle which was bled into a bag on the diver's chest, whence it was inhaled by the diver and breathed out through a CO_2 absorbent back into the bag and thus recycled. It was capable of sustaining a man for up to five hours per bottle if not working hard. If, however, the diver had to exert himself, and particularly if we had to work below 33 feet, the risk of oxygen poisoning was unacceptable. As we had learned to our cost during our practices off the Australian coast, in which we lost two divers and had two black-outs, one of each from my craft.

The implications of this on our operation were serious. Where the cable left Hong Kong Island (still in Japanese hands) in the East Lamma Passage it fell steeply to the muddy bottom in about 40ft.

There was therefore only a narrow strip about 100 yards wide in which we could search and yet put the diver out to work. Furthermore, submarine telegraph cables were particularly heavily armoured when running into shallow water, which might mean that we would not be able to get the jaw of the cutter over it.

Add to that the possibility of sharks, which we had heard about, and the certainty of stings by Portuguese-men-of-war which we had learnt about, and the diver earned his pay!

Although closer in shore than I cared to be, the night passed without alarm and at 0524 we dived and commenced dragging for the Hong Kong-Singapore cable.

At 0953 the grapnel fouled something and at 1027 the diver, S/Lt. Clark left the craft. The bottom was soft white mud, into which XE5 sank about four feet. The visibility was barely 2 feet. After about 20 minutes, we heard the cutter working and four minutes afterwards Clark re-appeared at the W. and D. hatch and entered hurriedly. It was clear that he was in some distress. We pumped down and opened up. What had happened was that Nobby Clark had caught his finger in the cutter's blade and had badly cut it and fractured the bone. In addition, his body had been stung all over by the barbed tentacles of Portuguese men-of-war.

This was the last time that a diver emerged into tropical waters clad only in a pair of swimming trunks and a breathing set. When the injured Lt. Clark was exchanged for S/Lt. Jarvis we dressed him in a complete diving suit in view of the previous unhappy experience. You can imagine how he sweated.

I got Nobby Clark out of the W. and D. and laid out in the battery compartment. I told him to roll over on his tummy as I was going to stick some morphia in his bum. Intelligence which he received with the remark, 'God! if it isn't one thing it's another'.

We were still stuck fast to whatever it was the grapnel had hooked. Clark told me that he thought it looked like a piece of netting. At 1228 I put the second diver out, (Lt. D. V. M. Jarvis). Unable to free the grapnel, he cut it clear, restowed the cutter and entered the craft. I set course to rendezvous with SELENE.

At 2021 we surfaced and proceeded on main engine; we were in contact with SELENE two hours later; transferred S/Lt. Clark and returned to our search area off Lamma Island.

At 0515 we dived and resumed dragging the grapnel, up and down, up and down. Nothing. We never even found the original 'obstruction', whatever it was. I spent most of the time at about 25 feet, ploughing through the ooze, into which XE5 sank up to half her girth. There was nothing to see in the murky water, and the unfortunate diver was up to his armpits in sticky tenacious mud.

The night too was uneventful. I thought long and hard about the possibility of heading into Hong Kong itself, and seeing if there was any kind of target to which it would be worth attaching the two limpet mines I carried, but I was forced to abandon that idea when I realised that we had only got enough oxygen for the purification of the boat itself until early the following p.m. This did not provide an acceptable margin.

The air inside an X Craft got pretty thick to breathe after six hours, hence the six hourly routine of surfacing on passage. However, on operations we were supplied with three hundred cubic feet of oxygen which would be bled into the craft and fans passed the air in the boat through Protosorb (CO_2 absorbent) canisters to rid it of impurities.

At noon on Friday, 3rd August, after three days of dragging and seventeen passes over the supposed area of the cable having been completely unrewarded, XE5 gave up, and set course for the rendezvous with SELENE.

We were in contact at 2130, and an hour later had passed the tow and exchanged crews with the passage crew under S/Lt. K. St. J. V. Robinson. An uneventful passage back to Subic ensued and XE5 secured alongside H.M.S. MAIDSTONE at 1930 on Sunday, 6th August.

Uneventful? Lt. Westmacott was aboard SELENE at this time and must have had his head down for:-

At 0110 on 5th August aboard XE5, the W. and D. was found to be flooded when we submerged. Blew, M. B. SELENE did not see XE5 surface and at eleven knots, we were dived forcibly! W. and D. was drained down and it was perceived that the heads pump was not seating and this was the cause of the trouble. Stayed at 30ft until 0300 when we surfaced to ventilate and the pump was repaired. Whereupon we dived and carried on with the normal passage routine. (There was no phone cable laid up in the spare tows so they could not inform the towing submarine of their plight).

Although they considered this operation to be unsuccessful; when the British occupied Hong Kong four weeks later, they found the cable to be kaput, useless and the Japs had to increase their wireless signals enormously. Thus enabling Japanese-speaking Americans to intercept and decode the signals much more easily than by telephone. So XE5 must have snagged it, lain upon it or damaged it in some way, and Operation 'Foil' was a success after all. Although Lt. Westmacott's report is dry and understated to the point of casualness, Captain Fell describes it as:-

One of the most daring, dangerous and tenacious operations of the war.

Chapter Twenty Three
Operation 'Struggle' 31st July 1945

XE3 Operation Crew:-
Lt. Ian Fraser V.C., R.N.V.R..
S/Lt. W. J. L. Smith D.S.O., R.N.Z.N.V.R.
E.R.A. C. Reed C.G.M.
L/Seaman J. Magennis V.C.
Passage Crew:-
S/Lt. Frank Ogden M.B.E., R.N.V.R.
E.R.A. Albert Nairn
A/B. Ernest Dee
Stoker 'Spike' Hughes
XE3 Towing Submarine:- STYGIAN
C.O. Lt. G. C. Clarabut D.S.O.,D.S.C., R.N.

XE1 Operational Crew:-
S/Lt. J. E. Smart D.S.O., O Leg.Mer., M.B.E., R.N.V.R.
S/Lt. H. E. Harper D.S.O., R.N.V.R.
E.R.A. H. J. Fishleigh D.S.M.
L/Seaman W. H. A. Pomeroy D.S.M.
XE1 Passage Crew:-
S/Lt. E. H. Munday M.B.E., R.N.V.R.
L/Sto. J. G. Robinson M.I.D.
E.R.A. Robertson
Stoker George Foulkes
XE1 Towing Submarine:- SPARK
C.O. Lt. D. G. Kent

Although the Allies were reasonably sure that the Jap heavy cruisers TAKAO and MYOKO lying in the Johore Strait were aground (as they hadn't been to sea for many months). They knew that they were still capable of shelling the Singapore Causeway and should allied troops decide to re-occupy Singapore Island from the North mayhem and havoc would be caused amongst them from the cruisers' big guns.

Thus, the order went out that they must be silenced. In the event the operation was only partly successful.

Taken from a written account by Lieutenant I. Fraser V.C.

The first part of 'Operation Struggle' began at about noon on July 26th, 1945. Two midget submarines, XE1, towed by the 'S' Class submarine SPARK, and XE3, towed by submarine STYGIAN, left Brunei Bay. Their purpose, to sink two Japanese heavy cruisers, MYOKO and TAKAO which were lying in the Johore Strait on the north side of Singapore Island.

The Far Eastern midget submarine captains. From left to right: Lt. J. E. Smart M. B.E., D. S. O., R. N. V. R., Lt. I. E. Fraser D. S. C., V. C., R. N. R., Lt. H. P. Westmacott D. S. C., Bar to D. S. C., D. S. O., R.N., Lt. M. Shean D. S. O., and Bar, R. A. N. V. R.

At this stage of the war the Japanese were in the retreat. Already British troops had taken Rangoon and were fast moving toward the heavily-defended harbour of Singapore. These two large ships with their eight-inch guns were a potential menace to any forces approaching by land and trying to cross the causeway from the mainland to the island and could also play havoc among any Allied shipping attacking from the seaward. It was imperative that they be put out of action as soon as possible.

The task of sinking MYOKO had been allocated to XE1, under the command of Lieutenant J. E. Smart, while TAKAO was to be the target for XE3, with Lieutenant Fraser in command. His crew, whom he had picked long ago, while they were still at their home base of Rothesay, were Sub. Lieut. (Kiwi) Smith a New Zealander, Engine Room Artificer Charley Reed and Leading Seaman Magennis. The Passage Crew would have the long and arduous task of manning the midget while it was being towed by STYGIAN to the target area.

The passage from Brunei to a spot within striking distance of Singapore took four days and when the time for change over came, (apart from a break in the telephone cable between the two boats), Ogden and his crew handed over XE3 in tip-top condition. This was no mean feat. In those warm tropical waters the inside of the boat must have been like an oven and with a continuous watch being kept for all that time, keeping the correct depth, constantly checking the density of the batteries, maintaining the equipment and with the never-ending mopping-up of condensation. The job of passage crew was by no means a 'soft number'.

At 0600 hrs on the morning of July 30th came the time for change over. Each member of the operational crew had checked the 'escape gear' which had been issued to them for use should their craft be disabled and make it necessary for them to cross enemy territory. Some of the gear afforded them a good deal of amusement.

First and foremost was a square of silk with a Union Jack printed on it, surrounded by various expressions in three or four different languages, like 'I am a friend', 'Please help me to reach British territory', or, 'I am hungry'. Another silk oilskin square, when unfolded, disclosed a map of the Malay peninsula and was marked with the best routes for making an escape, or a quick passage to a pick-up point on the coast. Compasses were disguised as buttons or pen clips, or sewn into the lining of a cap badge; a file had a hacksaw blade for an edge and a rubber cover for inserting, with considerable discomfort, into the rectum; a packet contained 48 hour rations, medical equipment, benzedrine boxes of matches and various other items reckoned to be useful against mosquitoes, leeches and other jungle pests. In addition, each man had a machete, fishing gear and a heavy .45 Colt automatic pistol, which, as Fraser says, 'took me all my time to lift, let alone shoot'.

From a storage space on board STYGIAN a yellow circular aircraft dinghy was manhandled, laid on the casing and inflated by means of a compressed air cylinder. A light 'grass rope' was made fast to the towing bracket on the dinghy, then it was pushed over the side. Fraser and his men slipped into it and with the grass line being payed out from STYGIAN, the dinghy slowly drifted back the 200 yards to XE3.

The change over being accomplished without a hitch, STYGIAN, with XE3 still in tow continued on its way. The passage crew, now being able to stand upright for the first time since leaving Brunei, settled down to the comparative luxury of life in the big submarine for a few days.

D-Day for the operation was July 31st and at 2300 hrs. on the 30th XE3 was slipped from her tow in position 036 degrees from Horsburgh Light. Fraser and his crew were now on their own.

The operation had been made rather easier for them by the fact that the submarine Captain had taken them two and half miles further than first planned, However, they were not going to be lucky all the time. For although Intelligence reports at briefing had implied that the buoys marking the swept channel through the minefield were lit, all except the Horsburgh Light were in darkness.

In the absence of lights and with only the help of some rather dubious land-fixes, the passage was made; as Fraser described it. 'by guess and by God'. At 0217 hrs. the main engine was stopped and they crept silently past the listening post using the electric motor only. After half an hour Fraser fixed his position 129.5 degrees Johore Hill 8.3 miles. XE3 then went ahead on main engine at 4.5 knots on course 280 degrees.

The Captain was still sitting on the casing, when, just after, he sighted what appeared to be a channel buoy. XE3 closed to within fifty yards of the object and made the startling discovery that it was a fishing boat. A hurried alteration of course was made but apparently XE3 had not been seen, which was extremely fortunate. All on board her must have been asleep for XE3 was between the fishing boat and a very bright moon.

Another thrill was experienced an hour and twenty minutes later, when two ships suddenly came into view. They looked like a large tanker and an escorting motor launch. They appeared to be closing at high speed, so Fraser gave the order to dive. They dived, hurriedly, and remained sitting on the sea bottom for twenty minutes. Then they surfaced and noted with horror that the two vessels were still in the vicinity, heading straight towards them and now even closer. Again came the shouted order 'Dive, dive, dive' and down the craft went again.

They were now minus a very important part of their navigation equipment. For when they had made that first hurried dive they had bumped along the bottom rather hard for thirty-six feet and in doing so had damaged the log. This was the piece of equipment registering the speed of the craft and the distance travelled. Their passage towards Singapore Island would now be even more 'by guess and by God'.

Under way once more, on course 360 degrees, the midget carried on towards its destination. Fraser switched on the sounding machine which registered the depth of the sea underneath him. It showed the depth as a blob on a green electronic line, in a way somewhat like a radar screen. He continued on that course until the machine indicated that the Johore Shoal was being crossed, just to the Westward of the buoy. Then, with the depth held at 30ft the craft slowly made her way up the Johore Strait.

By 0600 hrs. Fraser, Smith and Magennis were all feeling the effect of a night without sleep. Reed did not seem to be affected at all so all but he took a benzedrine tablet to keep themselves awake. However, the effect of the tablets did not show immediately and even twenty-five minutes after they had taken them Fraser saw Smith dozing off while at the hydroplane controls. However, Smith had caught such a perfect trim that Fraser was able to keep depth by watching his own depth gauge in the periscope dome and stepping a foot or so forward or aft in order to give it a bow-up or bow-down angle.

At 0700 hrs. Fraser reckoned that the boom would now be about a half-mile ahead and as there was no point in trying to get through it until 0800 hrs. when there would be enough daylight for him to see through the periscope, he decided to rest for an hour. So they stopped and sat on the sea bottom and all but Reed slept for a while.

When they awoke at 0745 hrs. the benzedrine tablets had taken full effect and morale was up 100 per cent.

Before re-starting their passage Fraser had Smith put out the 7lb tins of Protosorb in the fan intake and by turning on a steady flow of oxygen from one of the cylinders in the engine room before the fan was started, the air in the boat could circulate through the Protosorb and get rid of excess carbon dioxide and so replenish the oxygen content.

At 0800 hrs. they got under way and with the fervent hope that Lady Luck would remain with them they set off again towards their target. However, eight minutes later, when a periscope fix was taken. Fraser found that they had three and a half miles still to go before reaching the boom. This was considerably more than he had reckoned, so he had to run the risk of using up the strength left in his batteries by increasing speed, in order to reach the target that day.

His gamble paid off. At 1030 hrs. at a depth of 10ft, in a flat calm sea the XE Craft passed through the boom, which appeared to be a ramshackle affair with a permanently open gate. There was a trawler there too, anchored on the east side of the gate and presumably used for opening and shutting it. This vessel was passed with caution in case of it's being fitted with submarine detection gear. The only other shipping in the vicinity was a small craft which was going in the same direction. Owing to the fact that the water was so calm and oily and the periscope could be raised only partly for a few short periods, very little navigational evidence could be gathered but Fraser was able to write in his final report that all lights and buoys were in position as shown by the Admiralty charts.

At 12.50 TAKAO came into view and a buzz of excitement passed through the crew as Fraser gave them the news. Then course was altered to effect the 'run in to' the attack, to which, during years of training, they had looked forward. This was the great moment. It was eight minutes past two in the afternoon. Fraser had one last look before commencing the 'run in' and received a violent shock. Only about 40ft away was a boat packed with Japanese liberty men on their way ashore. They were so close that Fraser could see the mens' faces quite distinctly and even noticed that one of them was trailing his hand in the water. He could see their lips moving as they chatted.

How they failed to see the periscope sticking out of the water so close to them, would be difficult to explain.

'Flood 'Q', down periscope, quick, thirty feet!' came the order. 'Bloody Hell' said Fraser.

At 30ft the craft flattened out and continued at slow speed. Then, with the sound of the keel scraping on gravel, they touched bottom but kept moving forward slowly and with Reed fighting at the controls to keep her on course, the craft scraped her way over the bank sometimes at a depth of only fifteen feet. Which meant that the upper deck was a bare ten feet below the surface in water as clear as crystal.

Something scraped along the starboard side of the craft. Then with a reverberating crash she hit TAKAO and stopped dead. Surprisingly nobody except those inside the XE Craft heard or felt the jar. Fraser was unable to see anything through the night periscope which would give him any indication of his position in relation to the ship, only her dark shadow on the starboard side. Obviously though they were not underneath the target, for the depth gauge still showed only thirteen feet. Fraser decided that he must have come in at the wrong angle and gave the order to alter course and run down TAKAO's side. The motor hummed into life but the craft did not move. It seemed that somehow they were jammed, either beneath the ship's curved hull or that the slack of the anchor cable was lying across her. However, by means of some powerful motor movements in both directions and ten minutes of severe strain, she finally broke loose and dragged her way out across the shingle bottom to the deeper channel.

Fraser decided that although it would mean a longer drag across the shallow bank he would try to get under the target amidships. This time fortune dealt more kindly with them and somehow with the depth gauge registering only thirteen feet they succeeded in slithering across the bank and down into a hole over which TAKAO was lying. Even so, in the darkness of her shadow, between TAKAO's keel and the casing of the midget there was barely a foot of water. As the small craft came to a standstill Fraser allowed the crew to look through the scuttle and wonder at the thickness of marine growth which had been allowed to accumulate on the ship's bottom.

Artist's impression of L/S. Magennis underneath TAKAO scraping away at the marine growth, to enable him to affix the limpet mines.

Meanwhile the diver, (Magennis) had made himself almost ready to go outside and carry out his allotted task. With his light, rubberised diving dress (they were later to become known as 'Clammy Death'), sitting there in the humid atmosphere of the XE Craft he must have felt like being in his own personal Turkish bath. In spite of the dangers he might have to face, he would be looking forward to getting out into the comparatively cool water around. He strapped on his oxygen breathing apparatus, entered the W. and D. and with the help of Reed shutting the door behind him and working the valves and pumps, he made his way outside. Fraser, watching through the night periscope, saw the outside hatch of the W. and D. start to open.

Memorial (lower plaque) to Leading Seaman to M. Magennis V.C. in Bradford Cathedral. Vice Admiral Godfrey Place stands to the left. Alas the cheerful nuggetty and incorrigible little Irishman had died in 1986.

It could not open fully though, for there was not enough space between TAKAO's bottom and XE3's casing to allow it. Fortunately though, Magennis was not a very big man and without too much trouble he was able to negotiate what space was available. He gave the thumbs up sign, then those inside counted the six limpets as he bumped them out of the container and moved them one by one along the starboard side, three towards the forward end of the ship and three towards the after end. To Fraser, the thirty minutes that Magennis took to scrape away enough barnacles to allow the magnets on the charges to fix themselves to the steel hull, seemed more like thirty days. Every little sound that he made seemed to be magnified a thousand times. Finally, Magennis appeared at the W. and D entrance. Then giving the thumbs up sign again, he jumped in. Fraser saw the hatch shut and the clip go home. Magennis was back, safe and sound. Now at last they could go.

Quickly they started to release the side cargoes. Fraser, Smith and Reed, in order to relish the full pleasure of dropping two tons of high explosive under a Japanese ship all took turns at operating the wheels of the release gear. The port charge dropped away and they heard it bump down the side. Then they had a rest to allow Magennis to drain down the W. and D. and re-enter the craft. Next the starboard limpet carrier had to be jettisoned, but the short delay nearly caused disaster. During the time they were waiting for Magennis the limpet carrier had become flooded making it heavy, so that it would not release itself and slide away. Even though an emergency release method, thought up by the designer of the XE Craft,

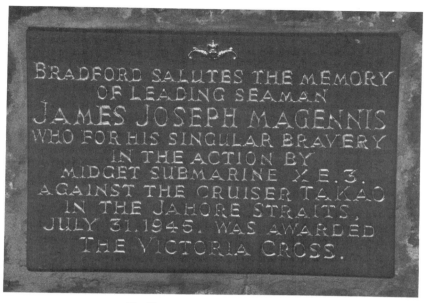

The Plaque in Bradford Cathedral.

was employed the container still refused to budge. Two pins at the top of it were still holding. Somehow the container had to be released. With two tons of dead weight fast to their side the chance of making headway enough to get back to STYGIAN was very remote indeed. Fraser thought that the movement of the craft through the water might shake it loose, but it didn't.

Someone had to go out and release it by hand. In the meantime Magennis had reported that the hard work he had putting in order to fix the limpets, had exhausted him.

Right now though, the main task was to get XE3 out from underneath TAKAO. The cruiser was slowly settling down with the fall of the tide and it would not be long before those few inches of space between her keel and the midget's casing would have been reduced to nothing and XE3 would be pinned beneath her.

Fraser gave the order for the motor to be started at half speed ahead and gave a course of 200 degrees then looked through the night periscope to watch for their progress. The craft did not move. Then came the order 'Full Ahead'. There was still no movement. 'Stop. Full astern group up' Fraser ordered. There was no use in his trying to go astern though as TAKAO's keel was lower than the rear periscope standard. They tried to go ahead again, giving the motors full power but still there was no movement. It looked very much as if XE3 was to be abandoned and left to be ground into the sea bed by her target then blown up with it by her own charges. Fraser began to think that the escape gear which had been issued to them was going to come in useful after all.

They tried pumping water from one ballast tank to another, from fore to aft then *back again, then out and in again. They even partially blew No. 2 main ballast to try to shake the craft loose, but still that black menacing shape floated overhead. Then suddenly, with the motors whirring and the propeller thrusting hard against the water, the craft began to move.*

Slowly she made her way ahead, the flooded limpet carrier dragging like a broken wing on her starboard side.

The black roof above them slid astern and Fraser once again saw the fresh, welcome sunlight streaming through the water. They were free. 'Operation Struggle' had been a most apt name as far as the crew of XE3 were concerned.

Their struggle was not yet over either. That flooded limpet carrier still had to be dumped and it would mean that a diver would have to go out and free it by hand. Magennis was still dressed in his suit and sweating profusely after being out of the cool water for a while and Fraser, seeing that his diver was still suffering from exhaustion decided that he would go out and do the job himself. Magennis seemed quite hurt by the suggestion. He was the diver and work outside should be done by him. Such was this brave, resourceful little Irishman's way of thinking. So, after taking five minutes to get his breath back, he again buckled on his breathing set and went out through the W. and D. This time he was armed with a large spanner which Reed had handed to him and with it he set to work on wrenching the limpet carrier free of its securing bolts. Inside XE3 there was complete silence and the atmosphere among the men was tense. The only sound they heard, apart from the ticking of the boats chronometer was the terrific clanging noises which Magennis made as he hammered away with the spanner. Loud enough, as Fraser put it 'to alarm the whole Japanese Navy', let alone those aboard TAKAO, which was only a few yards away.

After the most anxious five minutes of Fraser's life, he saw the limpet carrier come away. Then Magennis came back to the W. and D. gave the 'thumbs up' sign once more and disappeared inside. They were free of encumbrance, the job they had come to do had been done, so now it was just a matter of getting home again.

However, there was still a long way to travel and more anxious moments to live through before they were again to see the welcome sight of STYGIAN's upperworks outlined on the horizon.

The tidal water in that part of the Strait had come under the influence of the fresh water running into it from the land and as was usual in this sort of situation, the fresh water did not mix before dispersing. Thus a craft which had been trimmed for salt water, when suddenly encountering a patch of less-dense fresh water, would acquire a negative buoyancy and tend to plunge into the depths. This would necessitate a frantic pumping out of ballast tanks to make her lighter, together with the manipulation of the hydroplanes. When a trim was finally caught for fresh water then it was quite likely that the salt water would be met with again and the craft would suddenly be heading towards the surface like a porpoise.

On one of these occasion XE3 did actually break surface for six seconds when they were only a mile away from TAKAO. Luckily they were not seen and made their way to the boom. Another few anxious moments followed when a high-revving motor boat passed immediately overhead with the XE Craft so near the surface that those

inside thought that there really must be a collision. Fraser says of this incident:-
An observer, had he been there, would have seen a complete X Craft crew sitting
with their fingers in their ears, waiting for the bang. Luckily there was no impact,
neither were they seen and the boom was reached and passed at 1949 hrs. without
further incident.

At the boom XE3 altered course and from 2030 to 2100 hrs. and was kept at a
depth of 30ft. Then she surfaced and proceeded on main engine, passing Johore Buoy
a few yards off.

About half a mile away, in the half-light, they sighted a large junk. They also
saw away to starboard, what they thought was XE1 but this eventually turned out
to be a small sailing boat.

At 2330 hrs. a sharp lookout was kept for STYGIAN after she had been called
up by radio every hour and a half. Then, at 2345 hrs. the green light which was their
parent submarine's navigation signal was seen. Both boats then headed out to sea
until 0330 hrs. when the crews were exchanged and the tow was passed. After a job
well done they were now well and truly on their way home.

Lt. Fraser finished his report on the operations as follows:-

I consider that the two greatest contributions to the success of this operation
were the resourcefulness and hard work of the passage crew. After a depressing
start and with a bad trim, (telephone communications had broken down at the outset
and XE4 had only been able to speak to STYGIAN when on the surface using 'Walkie
Talkie' sets), *struggled for two days mending leaks and minor defects and who, on*
turning the craft over to the operational crew, produced a boat without a single
defect of any sort that would impair the fighting efficiency of the craft. Also to the
Commanding Officer and Ship's Company of H.M. Submarine STYGIAN, who fed us
like lords and provided for us in every way.

It was learned afterwards that the charges had exploded at about 9.30 p.m. on
the evening of the attack, totally immobilising TAKAO and thus removing a dire
threat to our advancing forces.

In the meantime Lieutenant Smart and his crew of XE1 were experiencing
difficulties right from the outset of the operation, causing the approach to their target
to be delayed. For some reason they had encountered much more traffic than XE3
and had to continually divert to avoid being seen.

However, there had been no Intelligence as to what time the boom would be shut
and it had been assumed that closing time would be sunset. Smart was in a
predicament. Time was getting on and if he had pressed on with the attack on his
own target MYOKO, he stood the risk of being caught inside the boom with the gate
shut. With the explosion occurring so near, them he and his crew would have been
in great danger. He therefore switched his attention to TAKAO.

In attacking TAKAO he was also running a serious risk. He had no knowledge
of how Fraser was progressing and for although he thought that XE3 was astern of
him Fraser might already have dropped his charges. In which case, the movement
of XE1 in the vicinity might easily set off the disturbance fuse in the dropped
charges, so blowing him and his crew to smithereens. There was also the possibility

ONE OF THE WAR'S MOST DARING EXPLOITS: THE BRITISH

Drawn by our Special Artist, G. H. Davis, from Sketches by and Under the Supervision of Lieut. Ian Fraser, V.C.

SECTION OF AN XE3 CLASS SUBMARINE.

CROSS SECTION LOOKING FORWARD.

THE "XE-3" CLASS OF BRITISH MIDGET SUBMARINES, WHICH CARRY A CREW OF FOUR: THE BOATS HAVE A LENGTH OF 48 FT., THE DIAMETER OF THE PRESSURE HULL BEING 5 FT. 9 INS. A DIESEL ENGINE IS USED FOR SURFACE PROPULSION, WITH AN ELECTRIC MOTOR FOR PROPELLING THE BOAT SUBMERGED. THE EXPLOSIVE CHARGES ARE CARRIED IN CASES ATTACHED TO THE MAIN HULL, PORT AND STARBOARD.

1.—EARLY DAWN, JULY 26, 1945: THE OPERATION CREW OF THE "XE-3," WHICH HAD BEEN TOWED BY THE SUBMARINE "STYGIAN" TO WITHIN 40 MILES OF ITS TARGET, BEING FERRIED IN A RUBBER DINGHY TO THE "XE-3" TO TAKE OVER FROM THE PASSAGE CREW.

2.—LIEUT. FRASER, IN COMMAND, HAVING DELIBERATELY LEFT THE SAFE CHANNEL TO AVOID ENEMY HYDRO-PHONE POSTS, IS NAVIGATING A MINEFIELD. ONCE, SIGHTING A TANKER WITH ARMED ESCORT, HE WAS FORCED TO LIE ON THE BOTTOM FOR HALF AN HOUR. (LATER, HE DISCOVERED THAT THE "XE-3" HAD BEEN ACTUALLY RESTING ON A MINE, WHICH DID NOT EXPLODE !)

3.—10.30 A.M.: LIEUT. FRASER HAD SIGHTED THE TRAWLER GUARDING THE SUBMARINE NETS ACROSS THE JOHORE STRAIT. HE WAS PREPARED TO CUT THE NETS, BUT FOUND THE "GATE" OPEN, AND IS SEEN CREEPING SAFELY THROUGH, PASSING QUITE CLOSE TO THE GUARD-SHIP WITHOUT BEING OBSERVED.

4.—THE "XE-3," PROCEEDING TO ATTACK THE "TAKAO" IN SHALLOW WATER, AND WITH HER OWN KEEL SCRAPING THE SEA-BED. SHE HIT THE CRUISER'S PLATING WITH A BANG JUST BELOW THE FORE TURRET, AND HAD TO REVERSE IN PREPARATION FOR MAKING A SECOND APPROACH.

THE DRAMATIC STORY OF AN ATTACK WHICH SANK THE JAPANESE CRUISER "TAKAO" AT SINGAPORE:

Among the decorations at the Investiture at Buckingham Palace last Tuesday, December 11, were two V.Cs gained during one of the war's most daring exploits— the successful attack by the British midget submarine "XE-3" on the Japanese heavy cruiser "Takao" in the Johore Strait, Singapore, in July of this year. The V.Cs were awarded to the submarine's commander, Lieut. Ian Fraser, R.N.R., and her diver, Leading Seaman James Magennis. The attack was made from a base 480 miles from Singapore, the midget submarine being towed by a larger submarine, the "Stygian," to within 40 miles of its target. From the moment when the crew of the "XE-3" entered their submarine they embarked on a series of hair-raising adventures, including the navigation of enemy minefields, hurried submergings among mines on sighting enemy ships, the negotiation of the net-boom defences within a few feet of the guard-ship, and finally lying beneath the cruiser's

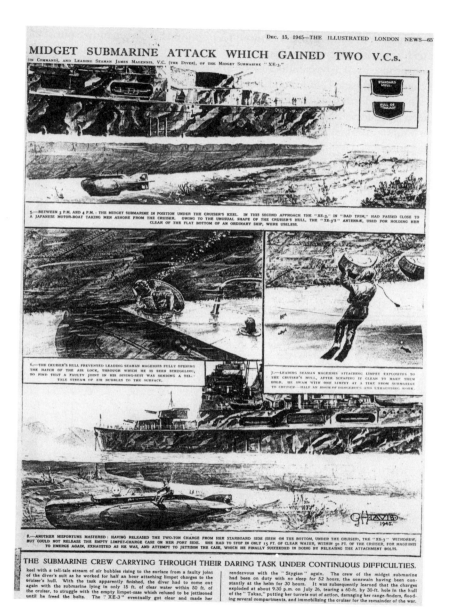

Dec. 15, 1945—THE ILLUSTRATED LONDON NEWS—65

MIDGET SUBMARINE ATTACK WHICH GAINED TWO V.C.s.

(IN COMMAND), AND LEADING SEAMAN JAMES MAGENNIS, V.C. (THE DIVER), OF THE MIDGET SUBMARINE " XE-3."

STANDARD HULL.

HULL OF TAKAO.

5.—BETWEEN 3 P.M. AND 4 P.M.: THE MIDGET SUBMARINE IN POSITION UNDER THE CRUISER'S KEEL. IN THIS SECOND APPROACH THE "XE-3," IN "BAD TRIM," HAD PASSED CLOSE TO A JAPANESE MOTOR-BOAT TAKING MEN ASHORE FROM THE CRUISER. OWING TO THE UNUSUAL SHAPE OF THE CRUISER'S HULL, THE "XE-3'S" ANTENNÆ, USED FOR HOLDING HER CLEAR OF THE FLAT BOTTOM OF AN ORDINARY SHIP, WERE USELESS.

6.—THE CRUISER'S HULL PREVENTED LEADING SEAMAN MAGENNIS FULLY OPENING THE HATCH OF THE AIR LOCK, THROUGH WHICH HE IS SEEN STRUGGLING, TO FIND THAT A FAULTY JOINT IN HIS DIVING-SUIT WAS SENDING A TELL-TALE STREAM OF AIR BUBBLES TO THE SURFACE.

7.—LEADING SEAMAN MAGENNIS ATTACHING LIMPET EXPLOSIVES TO THE CRUISER'S HULL, AFTER SCRAPING IT CLEAN TO MAKE THEM HOLD. HE SWAM WITH ONE LIMPET AT A TIME FROM SUBMARINE TO CRUISER—HALF AN HOUR OF DANGEROUS AND EXHAUSTING WORK.

8.—ANOTHER MISFORTUNE MASTERED: HAVING RELEASED THE TWO-TON CHARGE FROM HER STARBOARD SIDE (SEEN ON THE BOTTOM, UNDER THE CRUISER), THE "XE-3" WITHDREW, BUT COULD NOT RELEASE THE EMPTY LIMPET-CHARGE CASE ON HER PORT SIDE. SHE HAD TO STOP IN ONLY 15 FT. OF CLEAR WATER, WITHIN 50 FT. OF THE CRUISER, FOR MAGENNIS TO EMERGE AGAIN, EXHAUSTED AS HE WAS, AND ATTEMPT TO JETTISON THE CASE, WHICH HE FINALLY SUCCEEDED IN DOING BY RELEASING THE ATTACHMENT BOLTS.

THE SUBMARINE CREW CARRYING THROUGH THEIR DARING TASK UNDER CONTINUOUS DIFFICULTIES.

keel with a tell-tale stream of air bubbles rising to the surface from a faulty joint of the diver's suit as he worked for half an hour attaching limpet charges to the cruiser's hull. With the task apparently finished, the diver had to come out again with the submarine lying in only 15 ft. of clear water within 50 ft. of the cruiser, to struggle with the empty limpet-case which refused to be jettisoned until he freed the bolts. The "XE-3" eventually got clear and made her

rendezvous with the "Stygian" again. The crew of the midget submarine had been on duty with no sleep for 52 hours, the coxswain having been constantly at the helm for 30 hours. It was subsequently learned that the charges exploded at about 9.30 p.m. on July 26, tearing a 60-ft. by 30-ft. hole in the hull of the "Takao," putting her turrets out of action, damaging her range-finders, flooding several compartments, and immobilising the cruiser for the remainder of the war.

that XE3 had foundered and Fraser and his crew taken prisoner. In which case the Japanese would most certainly be keeping a sharp lookout for further attempts by underwater craft to destroy their ship and XE1, could have been blown out of the water by gunfire or depth charges.

In the face of such possibilities Lieut. Smart showed great courage in dropping his charges alongside TAKAO and so adding even more to the damage she sustained.

There was further misfortune to come for XE1 being so delayed, she was unable to keep the rendezvous with her parent submarine and had to wait another twenty-four hours before being picked up.

Wt. 31815/D 8117. 500M Pads. 10/43.

NAVAL MESSAGE.

			INTERCEPT GROUP
...ators Instructions: ...ation of Priority, ...C, NOTWT ...xercise).			
			FROM : STYGIAN
CTF 71.			

Following from FRASER 'My cruiser went upwards – what a bonfire. E.T.A. Victoria Noon 4th. Comment from our waiting position off HORSBURGH LT. Spectacle great. Consider cruiser was well distributed over countryside.

SMART probably responsible 2nd series explosions an hour later but did not make pick up at night. SPARK returning for him tonight.

Book or Table to be used for		Initials of Cypherer or Coder.	Time of Receipt in Cypher or Coding Office.	Date.
...ring or Coding.	Recyphering or Recoding.			

Optimistic signal from H.M.S/m. STYGIAN reporting Lt. Fraser's successful attack on TAKAO, July 31st 1945.

The eagerly awaited sight and sound of the detonations took place punctually and the crew were jubilant, but a short time later aerial reconnaissance showed that

TAKAO was still afloat. (Unless a ship has sunk or capsized, it is very difficult to tell from the air whether she has been damaged or not.)

By an extraordinary coincidence, at precisely the time when Fraser's charges were due to detonate, an aircraft was seen to crash in the hinterland behind Singapore Island. The resultant explosion was visible for miles and, not unnaturally, was thought to be the detonation.

The TAKAO had been damaged but she had not, as Lt. Fraser fondly hoped, been distributed over the countryside.

When the devastating news was received that TAKAO was apparently undamaged, Lt. Fraser and his crew immediately requested to be allowed to go in again and complete the job.

Lt. Fraser was even more 'browned off' when he discovered that, at the time of his attack, there had only been a skeleton crew aboard the TAKAO anyway. Thanks to damage to her stern caused by an American torpedo, the Japanese authorities had already written her off.

This crippling of the TAKAO had not gone entirely unnoticed and in some circles, it was a cause for celebration.

Many years after the war, a Chinese lady married to a European, met Ian Fraser at a function in Liverpool, and she still remembered what it had meant to them and wrote:-

The news that a big Japanese warship, the TAKAO had been sunk in Johore Strait by the British Navy spread secretly and swiftly among us in Japanese-occupied China. We could hardly hide our admiration, mingled with joy and satisfaction at this heroic deed.

I am writing this note to say that your patriotic spirit and the gallant bravery with which you performed this deed, will always be remembered'.

Chapter Twenty Four
Sequel To Operation 'Struggle'

From Alan Kevan's log:-

August 2nd

Received signal from XE3 saying cruiser blown up, everybody in good spirits. XE1 failed her operation, put her charges under Fraser's cruiser.

August 3rd

Received signal from XE4, operation completed successfully.

Friday 4th

XE4 arrived back. Crew congratulated by Admiral, two pieces of cable brought back. Received photos of cruiser still there, great mystery. First doubts that we failed.

Saturday 5th

Fraser back, dumbfounded at photos, conclusion is that her bottom was blown off, she was resting on the bottom fore and aft when they were under. Smart's job frowned upon but we had to wait until his return for conclusive proof. Admiral Fife went down to big sub to break the news there.

Sunday 6th

Smart returned, no cheer or anything, Admiral down on big sub and told him that the cruiser had not gone sky high. Everybody on board pretty browned off.

7th August

All crews interrogated and firmly convinced cruiser must have had its bottom blown out. Fires supposed to have been seen on the cruiser, came from the island (it was actually an aircraft crashing, coincidentally at exactly the same time as Fraser's charge was due to detonate).

Whilst all this was happening and Alan Kevan was tied to the office, the off watch part of the Ship's Company was exploring ashore in Brunei and taking tea with the Sultan under a basket-full of human heads, mainly Japs! (Actually the shrunken heads were kept in the Dyak Longhouse. The natives had reverted to head hunting during the war and these shrivelled and wrinkled trophies were hanging from the rafters.)

S. D. Christie elaborates:-

As for runs ashore, this must be a First when British matelots take tea with the Sultan of Brunei. (Brunei is a country as well as its capital city with, Brunei River and Brunei Bay, of which Labuan is its northern headland, on the N.W. coast of the large Island of Borneo). Just before the end of the war, during the last Midget operations, the B.V. lay at anchor off LABUAN, BORNEO. Three of us went ashore in Brunei, much devastated. We were invited by an Australian Army Sergeant to have tea with the Sultan, who had been put under guard by the Australian 9th Army.

He had been to Oxford but did not understand or speak English, so his interpreter said! Quite amusing. I also bargained with the Dyaks (unsuccessfully) for a Japanese Head.

It was not quite so pleasant being buzzed at anchor by a Japanese plane, a couple of days before cessation of hostilities and frantically trying to spread the fore-well deck awning to conceal the X Craft workshop openings, but I don't think any bombs were dropped on that occasion though.

The Sultan of Brunei and his daughter.

Captain Fell could not resist a sly dig at the Dyaks' head-hunting. He subsequently wrote in his report:-

The Dyaks are very pro-ally, mainly of course because they are again allowed to cut off heads, An open season for Japs having been declared. As three heads is the regulation number to enable a Dyak to marry, there might be a situation amongst the '2 headers' when the supply of Japanese runs out.

S. D. Christie:-

After V.J. Day we went into Sydney. One XE Craft, XE4, went on tour, the others were broken up, decks and workshops were cleared, side charges removed from the after holds and all armoury removed. There was a Power strike on at Sydney at the time and one reason that the craft were cut up and disposed of with such haste, was that the portable generators were needed ashore. The Duke of Gloucester (then the Governor General of Australia) inspected XE4 when she returned from her circular tour of Victoria, before she too was broken up. We on BONAVENTURE took on a contingent of R.E.M.E. and all their equipment, we were in the Fleet Train now, of course, 'lorries, bulldozers, stone crushers and tons of drain pipes etc'.

We also carried rice, furniture, clothing and I can't remember what else. Up to Manus, Hong Kong, Shanghai, Kure (Japan) and the same on return, picking up naval stores to rebuild the Hong Kong Naval base. Sometimes Singapore, Subic Bay, once Ceylon (now Sri Lanka) and India, trooping with Personnel and Stores for the fleet,

V.A.D.S. and civilians, up and down, up and down.

BONAVENTURE was now in Victoria harbour, Labuan, awaiting orders.

Alan Kevan's log:-

9th August

Permission to do 'Struggle' again? (the crippling of the TAKAO and MYOKO), leaving 12th August, D-Day August 17th. This time XE4 and XE3. I did the orders and the big subs were going to do a spot of cable cutting as they were going to lift and cut Singapore-Hong Kong cable themselves!

11th August

At night we had everything ready for the operation and in fine spirits. Our tails right up. News that Japan was willing to surrender came as a surprise. We awaited orders. Just before V.J. Day a W/T operator on board came over to me and said that a new type of bomb had been dropped on Japan and that if they didn't surrender, more would follow.

12th August

Still intended to do operation, craft hauled out. Just as they were in the water, received signal from Fife to cancel operation. Great celebration that night at the thought of peace, had some rum off 'Scratch'. We awaited further orders.

The original crews of XE3 (and 4) had been reasonably keen to 'have another bash' but the relief, when the recall came, must have been overwhelming. There was only a very small chance of them being still alive when peace broke out three days later, for the Japs had been alerted (Captain Fell gave them a zero chance). Even the intrepid 'Ginger' Coles admits:-

We'd had smashing luck on our previous two operations. It was chancing your arm to expect it to remain with us on the third, and I personally was quite glad when the signal came for us to return to the BONAVENTURE.

Alan Kevan:-

14th August

Plans underway to use B/V to take Australian troops down to release prisoners of war, Captain all in favour. Officer came aboard and measured up the space. We reckoned by dropping craft crews and a quarter of ship's company (normally 400), we could take a thousand men down.

This was Operation 'Crocodile' which, like the second Operation 'Struggle', was not destined to take place. Operation 'Crocodile' was designed to cut off and capture the main body of the Japenese forces and separate them from the area where the prisoners and internees were being held and then to effect the release of the prisoners, before the Japs had time to starve or kill them.

Alan's 'log' is drawing to a close now, and he doesn't even mention the fact that it was V.J. Day! Stan Pulham does however:-

On V.J. Day we were anchored in Brunei Bay, Borneo. I don't remember much about any celebrations as such. Being lower deck we didn't have the means to celebrate.

It was different in the cities! Sydney, the only place in Australia to have suffered an attack by Jap midget submarines and then to be host to the British X Craft Depot

Ship carrying all six midgets. Sydney went wild.

Alan Kevan:-

15th August

Received signal to proceed to Subic, Captain told 9th Division and they sent a signal to MacArthur to retain us. Captain Fell must have been at his wits end to remain in the 'battle zone', rather than go home. He loved the Navy. That was at 11 p.m.

16th August

We sailed at 1600 and SPARK and STYGIAN at 0800, no reply being received from Mac.

We put to sea with CROVEAL (the code name for the particular contingent of the U.S. Fleet). Captain expected orders to stay, right up till we left Brunei Bay. Captain spoke to crew and told us he did not know what was to happen to us.

17th August

At sea, calm but raining. Received signal from (Admiral Sir Bruce) Fraser to proceed to Sydney, as soon as possible. I had a chat with 'X' and he said that we still did not know for certain as signals were evasive. However, I think we have had our time. Asked 'X' if he could keep me on office work and he said he would do his best, I hope he can. Commander's proposals sent by air yesterday, I hope they can be accepted.

H.M.S. BONAVENTURE. British Fleet, Hong Kong 1946

19th August

Arrived at Subic. Captain nipped ashore to see Fife about retaining us with the 7th Fleet. Westmacott and XE5 and 6 came alongside and were hoisted in. We should have dropped all our stores with the MAIDSTONE but Captain disobeyed orders. Nothing could be done to keep us up North much to my regret.

20th August

We sailed at 2300hrs., MAIDSTONE apparently having had orders to go to Hong Kong, pinched all our charts. I was on the bridge as we left and Captain very down

in spirits, especially when he said Goodbye to Captain Shadwell of the MAID-STONE. (The two popular Depot Ship Captains had been friends for many years).
21st August
At sea, Captain spoke to crew, he had done all he could to keep the ship up North until all the panic in Australia had ceased, He was sorry but the Fleet train had finally got us. 1st Battle Squadron passed us, signalled 'Well done BONAVEN-TURE'.
26th August
Arrived Manus a.m. I had hoped to see the VENERABLE (aircraft carrier), in harbour with old friend on board, my luck was out, VENGEANCE was there but VENERABLE had sailed North three days before. Here we should have known what job we were going to do, R.A.A.F. Official came aboard but decided we were no use to them and told us to report to V.A. in Sydney. Our last chance had gone. To think we had more work to do with the 7th Fleet than we could have coped with, yet we get hauled back down South to find nothing for us to do. Personally I think Fraser just wanted us out of the American hands. (There was a desparate shortage of ships after 6 years of war and BONAVENTURE was probably the only one of her size in the Far East). *We spliced the main brace, signal dated 17th August. Tonks supplied rum and whisky.*
27th August
0900 We left Manus bound for Sydney. Peace time routine, no blackout, four watches. Since leaving Subic I have been checking up on my future position on board, 'X' has done all he can to keep me on office work and I think it will probably come off, I sincerely hope so.

It seems fitting too, to conclude with the words of Alan's mentor, idol and most humane of all bosses, Captain Fell:-
The evening of August 15, V.J. Day towards sunset, brought the last signal:-'Cease hostilities against Japan.
The finality of those four words left me gasping. I felt utterly empty, drained, without coherent thought. Late that night, while sirens screamed, rockets and tracer flamed and the roar of voices from the Army ashore wafted out to us, I lay on my bunk looking back over the war years and thought how lucky I had been. But for some people it was not the end of everything by any means. For a few it was the commencement of a new life, in this vast, friendly and sunburnt land which they never wanted to leave again. A few more wished they'd taken the opportunity when it arose, and have spent the rest of their lives hankering after the Australian way of life.

George Skuse was regular Navy and he remained on board the post-war BONAVENTURE:-
After the bombs had dropped on Japan and the scrapping of the craft, we joined the Fleet Train running from Australia to Hong Kong and Kure in Japan. On our first visit to Kure, we all went to Hiroshima to see the damage the 'A' bomb had done (it was only two months later). It was terrible, and yet, after all that they had suffered, the Japanese people were very friendly towards us. They were selling ice cream

and souvenirs, but the former was just frozen water, ice from the frig coloured with a few drops of cochineal.

As usual a bit of 'nutty' (bar of chocolate) for the children did the trick.

The Japanese women were already looking smart, just two months after the bomb had been dropped. They had thick make-up on their faces and were pattering round on thick wooden-soled sandals. There were no signs of bodies or victims anywhere. The Americans were in overall command. The second time we went back, a month later, it wasn't quite so good. The Japs were OK but the young newly-enlisted Yanks were being officious and strutting round with rather big heads and guns.

On one trip from Sydney we had on board fifty V.A.D. nurses, going to Hong Kong for the big Navy hospital there. Most of them slept on the deck of the forward welldeck on mattresses (and not much else)!, it was stifling down below. On our way back to Australia, we carried a lot of civilians who had been interned by the Japs. The same sort of people who were in the TV series 'Tenko'. I enjoyed that series, it was very realistic

Alan Kevan finished his log on the 3rd of September:-

Arrived at Sydney for the first time, what a marvellous harbour, I was on the bridge with 'X' and Fell at 0600 and it was pretty cold. The view was magnificent.

Predictably in the euphoria of the first few weeks of Peace, one and all had a marvellous time in Sydney, despite the daft licensing hours. The war was over, there was no black out, no austerity, no rationing, no drabness and there were large numbers of smiling nubile girls, all unbelievably tanned and clean-limbed, and all wearing pretty Summer frocks - in late Winter. In fact there must have been more bigamists created in those first few weeks after V.J. Day, than in any previous period of Australian history. Some of the bigamists became deserters and had to be hauled away from connubial bliss by the Shore Patrol. They were put in the cells aboard BONAVENTURE, along with several other malcontents who had absconded from the ship for one reason or another.

When she finally sailed for the U.K. in 1946, there were some real 'bad hats' aboard. Some were caught stealing from the mess deck lockers and threatened violence. The atmosphere became so tense and unpleasant, and Captain Fell so worried, that he was reputed to sleep with a loaded revolver under his pillow. By the time they reached Singapore, he'd had enough. The worst troublemakers were taken ashore in irons, to await the next ocean-going merchant ship where the opportunities for crime would be strictly limited.

Meanwhile BONAVENTURE, in need of a major refit, went the long way home. She steamed all round Australia, then called at all places to the Suez Canal. Then Malta, Gibraltar and Portsmouth, and Chatham. They 'paid off' at Greenock and she became once more the CLAN DAVIDSON, soon to go out East again in her original cargo-carrying capacity. They had gone out by the Panama Canal and come home by Suez, therefore she had encircled the globe, and, steamed 29,000 miles in six months. As Captain Fell was heard to remark 'her engines must be considered to have been run-in'. The demise of all ships is inglorious, both the 'famous and the infamous', inevitably, but was it really necessary to have the five midget submarines broken up with such unseemly haste, closely followed by the sixth XE4 after they had brought their operations to a successful conclusion, at the eleventh hour? It was only a few years later that the Australians were almost rubbing it in, by raising and painstakingly re-assembling two of the Japanese midgets that had caused the deaths of nineteen sleeping men in Sydney harbour in 1942. I22/27's midget is now restored and displayed for all time in the Sydney Maritime Museum. Like our own X24 outside the Gosport Submarine Museum, but at least she is British!

XE4 in Sydney harbour.

The Graveyard. XE Craft being broken up on Cockatoo Island in Sydney Harbour. September/October 1945.

BONAVENTURE steaming under the famous Sydney Harbour Bridge for the first time.

Captain Fell R.N. talking to Lt. Cdr. Brown R.N. (Cdr. 'X') on board BONAVENTURE In Sydney September 1945.

COMMANDING OFFICER of HMS Bonaventure, midget sub. depot ship, is Captain W. R. Fell, OBE, DSO, RN. "X" craft were very busy during Pacific war, but many operations are still on secret list. Physical examination for midget sub. crews is super-strict.

DRESSED, only in shorts and sandshoes, RN stoker awaits orders to throw starting lever of midget sub. diesel engine. Despite smallness of craft, crews have affection for their ships, and attach special nameplates. Cramped position of crew members is easily seen. Main purpose of midget subs. is to penetrate enemy's minefields and boom defences.

CONTRAST between midget sub. and full-sized craft may be seen in this picture. Midget is passing bows of American submarines moored alongside HMS Bonaventure. Depot ship was built originally for Clan Line, taken over by Royal Navy before completion. In "X" craft, cooking is done in double saucepan exactly like a carpenter's glue pot, but crew have been known to leave spacious depot ship for "gluepot meal" aboard midget sub.! Commanders of "X" craft are the only RN officers to wear a beret with naval badge. Midgets have diesel engines for surface, electric motors for use under water.

From an Australian journal 'PIX' October 1945. The top left picture is of Stoker Gillard in XE4. Although not visible the engine bears the name 'GOZO II'. When X24 was being built, so the story goes, Ginger Coles and Max Shean consulted Cdr. Rendel as to what to call the engine. Rendel thought a minute then said, "There is a small but very important place in Malta called Gozo. You could call your engine that and then if it didn't go, you could always say Go - GOZO - Go"! When the team moved on to XE4, they took the name with them. Max Shean has recently owned a car whose diesel engine is also called GOZO.

Chapter Twenty Five
Deaths Of Lt. D. Carey R.N. And Lt. B.E. Enzer R.N.V.R.

These deaths were due to a combination of factors.

Mon Repos bay was shallow, and the aftermath of a storm had produced a heavy swell; the two men had not dived for several months thus reducing their oxygen tolerance; although Lt. Enzer had been a P.T. Instructor before he joined the Navy nevertheless the two men were ever so slightly out of condition, and they were diving in depths of 40/45 ft which was over the safe limit.

XE3 was lying on the bottom when Dave Carey, the 1st Lieutenant, entered the W. and D., full of beans and confidence, with no premonition of death and determined to prove that he was as good a diver as the rest of them. He was seen by his C.O. who was checking through the night periscope, to emerge in the normal way. When he seemed to falter and left the hatch open Lt. Fraser was horrified to see him give the thumbs down signal instead of the thumbs up, whereupon he drifted away and was lost to view.

Several minutes elapsed before the hatch could be shut from inside the craft (it was always a difficulty task), the compartment drained down and she could surface once more. By then nothing could be seen of the unfortunate diver, and the party in the diving tender on the surface had not known that anything untoward had happened.

The very next day, exactly the same thing happened off XE5 when her 1st Lt. Bruce Enzer, was lost.

When he heard about these two fatalities happening so close together, Captain Fell was so concerned that he ordered every single piece of diving equipment to be checked and re-checked and every diver had to go down again too, to test his nerve.

As it turned out there was nothing wrong with the equipment, or the divers. It was the old adversary, 'Oxygen Pete' (oxygen poisoning) who had made a dreaded re-appearance. Breathing pure oxygen at any depth over 30 ft can produce uncontrollable twitching of the lips, light-headedness and hallucinations. Lieutenants Carey and Enzer had been down to 47 ft and had worked too hard.

S/Lt. Geoff Harding R.N.V.R. was aboard XE5 with Lt. Enzer when the accident happened.

Geoff Harding:-

Yes the loss of my great friend was, and to an extent still is awful. It occurred off the coast of Queensland the day after Dave Carey was lost doing the same thing.

The three of us were experimenting in cutting submarine telephone cables, prior the to proposed attacks on such cables, which were later carried out.

Bruce Enzer and I had, with others, swum ashore through the surf to look for Dave's body the night before and the next night we looked for Bruces.

He and I were getting out of the same craft under water on that day. We dressed, he left the craft first and I was dressed and nearly ready to follow him. As he left the X Craft, I saw him give a thumbs down signal, meaning he was in trouble. Leaving the outer hatch open he appeared to float upwards, apparently unconscious.

"It took us a long time to shut the hatch (it always did) with the mechanism provided, pump out the escape chamber and surface. By the time we got into the water we could find no trace of Bruce. No one on the surface had seen him either and we never saw either of them again.

The subsequent enquiry didn't, so far as I know, really establish what had happened.

Ian Fraser was the C.O. of XE3 and his account of this tragic incident is still more bizarre:-

It occurred to me that this would be a good opportunity to test out the free diving equipment on this cable-cutting job, with the diver wearing the sort of oxygen apparatus plus regenerative fitment that I used to wear in Sheerness baths. Both David Carey and I were well familiar with this gear, and we agreed together to try it out. Of the two of us, David was by far the better diver and, anyway, as commander of the submarine I was not allowed to leave it during the exercise.

'Shall we have a go, then?' I said.

'Rather' said David.

'O.K.', I said, 'Off you go'.

I think they were the last words we exchanged.

David slipped on a pair of overalls and pulled on the breathing apparatus, went through the wet and dry compartment, and then was off with the grapnel. There is a special periscope in a midget submarine which allows the commander to see what is going on around the casing, and through this (night) periscope I saw David go down to have a look at what happened to the grapnel. He swam back and gave me the thumbs-up sign as the manila rope tightened. I watched him go to the stowage compartment and then down towards the cable with the hydraulic cutters, linked to the submarine by tube. I could tell by the pressure in the tube that he used the cutters three or four times to bite a way through the cable. Once more he swam into my view and gave me the thumbs-up sign.

Then he vanished to retrieve the grapnel, and I gave the order to be ready to move. David stowed the grapnel away, slid into the W. and D. and pulled the lid down tightly. I stood by as the valves began to open. Suddenly the lid of the W. and D. flew open, and David re-emerged. Through the periscope I saw him give me the thumbs-down sign. I did not know what was wrong so immediately I gave the order to surface. As we surfaced I saw to my horror David jump over the side and vanish. I was at that moment like a prisoner in my submarine, helpless and hopeless. I could do nothing. I never saw him again. His body was never recovered. He was twenty-one, and my greatest friend.

Captain Fell knew what I was going through after the SIGYN returned to the BONAVENTURE, for my heart was cold inside me, I felt that in some way this tragedy was my fault, that, in fact, I was in some way responsible for the death of David Carey, so he ordered me out the next day to repeat the operation with a different diver. The other XE Craft were ordered out too. In one of them, commanded by Westmacott, Bruce Enzer was the diver. Much like David Carey, he went over with the grapnel and went through the cable-cutting exercise. He was in the wet-and-dry when Westmacott realised something was wrong. He immediately surfaced to where the motorboat was in attendance. Bruce emerged from the wet-and-dry into the sunlight of Cid Harbour still wearing his ''free'' diving equipment. The officer-in-charge of the motorboat drew alongside the submarine and asked him if he was all right. Bruce's answer was to punch him on the jaw and jump overboard. He, too was never found.

Two divers dead in two days. What had gone wrong?

Nothing had gone wrong, except the enthusiasm of the divers. With their apparatus, it was only positively safe for the diver to work at 30 feet. In David Carey's case, he had been down to 47 feet, and he had worked too hard. Using the hydraulic cutters at that depth had put too big a strain on him. Oxygen poisoning set in and we knew what strange effects this could have on a man's mind. The only consolation we could derive from what had happened was that neither David nor Bruce had known what they were doing when they died; and they both died doing a job for which they had volunteered.

Then, not much was known about oxygen poisoning at the time and the system has been largely discontinued for the same reason as X Craft, too dangerous in peace-time.

In the event of any future war, one can only hope that other generations of young people will be as keen to volunteer to be human guinea pigs, as their grandfathers and great-grandfather were before them.

England expects and I'm sure she won't be disappointed. Let's just hope they have 'got the mixture right' by then, if indeed they haven't already, and that we have finally seen the demise of 'Oxygen Pete' and the 'Bends'.

Captain Fell's Tribute to the Passage Crews.

The Passage Crews did their job splendidly.

It is not often realised how big a part these men play in the success of an operation. Towing at high speed (it was sometimes as much as eleven knots) is far from being an easy or even particularly safe job and it is very far from being a comfortable one. It calls for a high degree of alertness, under trying conditions, for several days at a time. In addition it calls for constant attention to the vital routine duties of mopping up moisture, testing and if necessary repairing every item of equipment in the craft.

To a considerable extent, the success of an operation depends upon the condition in which the craft is turned over to the operational crew. In no sense of the word are the X-Craft Passage Crews 'maintenance crews'.

That the craft were turned over to the operational crews in perfect condition, reflects the highest credit on the passage commanding officers and their crews.

Chapter Twenty Six
The Post-War Midgets

The Epilogue is in four parts:-

1) A general description of the post-war period in X Craft, by Chief E.R.A. Bill Reid.
2) Some anecdotes relating to the X Craft concerned.
3) A brief description of the biggest event of this period Operation 'Mainbrace' by Lt. Cdr. Hugh Verry R.N. Retd.
4) A table of events when the war had ended by Commander A.D.C. Lund O.B.E., R.N., until the last X Craft was broken-up.

PART 1

Bill Reid:-

XE7, XE8, XE9 and XE12 had only just been launched when the war ended and, as we have read, XE10 was never completed and XE11 was lost in Loch Striven. Thus these four craft out of the thirty five that were built had the longest life of any, nearly ten years, which again, was quite a tribute to their builders.

They all appear to have been maintained in operational condition from 1945. None of them having been put into "mothballs", though they took turns in undergoing periodic refits. Personnel usually served for a maximum of eighteen months, the object being to train as many men as possible, so as to form a nucleus of experienced operators in the event of any future war.

This unit of The Fifth (Blockhouse) Flotilla operated from Devonport. The craft lay alongside and the crews were billeted in H.M.S. DEFIANCE, the Devonport Electrical and Diving School, consisting of four old ships moored in the Homoaze and a collection of buildings on the Cornish shore of the river.

Up-river from DEFIANCE was H.M.S. GATESHEAD, an auxiliary coal-burning minesweeper reputed to be the last one in the Royal Navy, which served as tender and mother-ship for the midgets when on detached duties, and also acted as towing vessel when required.

Only two of the boats were in full commission at any one time, the others undergoing refits in Portsmouth dockyard, supervised by E.R.A. Charlie Reed who had been awarded the C.G.M. for his part in the TAKAO attack. At approximately nine-month intervals, one of the operational boats would pay off, to be replaced by a boat which had just completed its refit, and which would then proceed to Scotland for deep diving trials.

The size of the crew was increased in peacetime to five for the operational crew and four for the passage crew. In practice, with the exception of the C.O., the two crews frequently exchanged duties, so that the operational crew often became involved in towing, while on daytime exercises from Devonport the crews would operate on alternate days. Operations usually consisted of attempting to penetrate the defence of Plymouth Sound and were more for the benefit of shore-based Asdic personnel than for the boats crews. Occasionally, night operations were carried out, and sometimes we indulged in mock attacks on surface vessels. Although side charges were never carried, the cargo release gear was operated regularly to keep it in good working order. All personnel were required to complete a shallow-water diving course. (I believe C.O.'s were excepted, although my own skipper, Bill Ricketts, insisted on going through with it like the rest of us.)

The diving course started off with classroom lectures, then moved on to a series of simple dives in a tank ashore, in which a number of basic exercises were carried out, usually involving the use of hand-tools such as hacksaws under water. Further training took the diver into the X Craft itself, entering and returning via the W. and D. then finally on a net slung across the Hamoaze at the conjunction of the Tamar and the Tavy using a power-cutter to create a passage through the net for the boat to carry out a simulated attack. The Hamoaze was the only place in home waters where I can personally recall exercises involving nets, (there actually was a small one at Portsmouth) but I believe ops. in the U.S.A., where our boats treated their navy to the benefit of our expertise in 1950 and 1953, involved a great deal of net cutting. I was never fortunate enough to do an overseas trip with X Craft; the only long spell away from Devonport, took XE 12 to Portland for two months in 1951 to carry out trials with the Underwater Detection Establishment.

Other than that, we gave Navy Day exhibitions in Portsmouth, Chatham and Sheerness, and made courtesy calls at the Scilly Isles, Cobh and Dartmouth. The trip to Dartmouth was, I believe, the only voyage carried out under our own power. In every other case, the boat was under tow, either with the GATESHEAD or a parent submarine.

The GATESHEAD carried only two officers, one being her C.O., who also held the position of Senior Officer X Craft (during most of my service S.O.X. was Lt. Cdr. Donald Cameron V.C.), and the other a junior officer who acted as First Lieutenant.

When involved in towing duties, her officer complement was increased by the officers of the X Craft operational crew, who stood normal bridge watches. The three ratings kept bridge watches as lookout.

The worst part of a tow from my point of view was connecting up the cable. Lying full length on the fore-casing, with the boat bouncing about on Plymouth Sound and rain and spray seeping through the collar of my Ursula jacket it was most uncomfortable. However, once clear of port and running submerged life became almost pleasant. Perhaps I should point out that I never experienced tows of very long duration. Life must have been purgatory for Passage Crews during long tows under wartime conditions, and I always felt that their job must have been more exacting than that of the operational crews. (See Captain Fell's tribute to the Passage Crews.)

As I already remarked though, I found life quite pleasant. Once the C.O. was satisfied with the boat's trim we broke into two watches, the E.R.A. and Electrician in one watch and the officer and Stoker in the other. Every six hours we would surface, raise the induction tube and run the engine for about twenty minutes to recharge the air bottles and draw fresh air into the boat; then, once submerged again, the watches would change and the two 'off watch' would take their turn to sleep. A 'hot bunk' routine was worked, with the officer and E.R.A. sharing a mattress which lay from just aft of the hydroplane controls to the engine casing, and the two junior ratings in a much more comfortable position on the battery boards for'ard of the W. and D.

Victualling was adequate, and consisted largely of tins of meat stew, vegetables and soup mixed up together in a carpenter's glue-pot, supplemented by corned beef sandwiches and an inexhaustible supply of coffee and tea. In addition, the E.R.A., in his capacity as Coxswain and senior rating of the boat, would have drawn from stores before departure, sufficient rum to cover the duration of the trip. This could usually be stretched to provide a tot for the officer who, in turn, could usually be persuaded to bring along a half-bottle of brandy, for medicinal purposes only of course.

PART 2
XE7 - The Trip To Southern Ireland
Lt. Martin Wemyss R.N. :-

The trip to Southern Ireland was the only foreign visit we made during my time. Its purpose was more to give us a break from our normal activities (if ever they were normal) than anything else, though I think we and the GATESHEAD were the first R.N. ship to go to Cobh after the war.

The visit started with a formal objection from the I.R.A. to the presence of enemy ships in Irish waters. However, the delegation who brought it liked Scotch whisky and, in a short time, we were all adopted Irishmen and friends for life.

During the course of this visit, we rescued a drunken baker's assistant from drowning and were roundly cursed by his Priest for interfering with the Lord's clear intent that he should die! I lost my valuable cap and was promised a medal from the Irish Humane Society but we heard no more.

Compared with some, that trip was more or less event free. How we survived some of the things that happened to us, or which we perpetrated, I shall never know. We were very young and our seniors were in Portsmouth.

XE7 - Clockwork Mice
Lt. Cdr. H. P. Westmacott D.S.C. and Bar, D.S.O., R.N.:-

About 1949 I was given the task of reviving the X Craft activity, which were required as 'Clockwork Mice' for the development of harbour defences. Three or four X Craft had survived including XE7.

The U.S.N. asked to have an X Craft to examine in Norfolk, Virginia and I was asked to take it over, I agreed, subject to my being in charge of the expedition and planning etc.

We were shipped over to Norfolk in the same ship as our craft, U.S.S. WHITLEY *and had to work under a Vice Admiral i/c of operational research.*

We were there for about eight weeks, playing to an audience of scientists, divers, airships and Harbour Defence craft.

The U.S.N. were very friendly, placing a car at our disposal for business and recreation, in which Wadman and I went up to Washington for a long weekend.

The yanks were entirely amicable. We lived in various wardrooms of U.S. ships. I never realised how many actions U.S. Naval history recorded, in which the U.S. Navy beat an H.M. ship. Mostly tiny little vessels, not worth a mention in the Naval History I was taught!

The Tenders:- these were usually an American P.T. boat with three 2,000 h.p. engines and a top speed of fifty knots. They used to grumble along on one engine at idling speed and every forty minutes or so, declare they had to blow the system through; so they'd start up all three and do a five or ten mile circuit at suitable power, to de-coke the cylinders!

For rest and recreation, we were made honorary members of all the officers clubs around the area, of which there were probably half a dozen. One drank, played the banks off fruit machines, and met the occasional 'grass widow', but I was newly-married then, so as far as I was concerned such encounters were brief and passing. Then we came home.

XE9 also went to America in 1952 and X51 in the mid-fifties, both on similar Promotional Tours. Alas, as we have read, 'They were a damned un- American weapon'.

Lt. Commanding Matthew Todd's contribution is more of a tribute than an anecdote:-

I did indeed have a very happy time in 1949 in XE8, unofficially EXPUNGER, I had an excellent and cheery crew. We had plenty of work (which we quite often did on our own) and the craft was utterly reliable. We did, of course, have the advantage of all being relatively long-term submariners, so the maintenance was pretty straightforward for us. (XE8 was a Broadbent built craft)

Part 3 - Operation 'Mainbrace'

Lt. Commander Hugh Verry was the C.O. of XE8 at this time (1952) and the operation might well be subtitled, 'Bergen the third time':-

MAINBRACE was a huge NATO exercise of which we were a miniscule part. It covered any aspect of naval activity one could imagine, which included our contribution in the Harbour Defence area.

Our objective was to make an initial attack on MAIDSTONE in Bergen, which was defended by a Boom Defence net across the harbour entrance with a 'gate' between two Boom Defence vessels, and the Shore Defence Boat squadron patrolling in the fjord.

We were then to carry out a series of attacks from a base of our choice in the area. For this we selected a small fishing village called Folleso, on the S.W. coast of the island of Askoy (on the East side of Hjeltefjord which runs N.W. from Byfjord to the sea).

In September 1952, XE8 set out from Portland in tow of GATESHEAD, making a 'stop over' at Lerwick before setting off for Bergen. Whilst there we were asked to Dinner with the Provost, an imposing and venerable white-haired gentleman. After dinner, he gave a really expert piano recital of classical pieces, which he then followed up with some virtuoso jazz! It transpired that he had for some years been the pianist in Ambrose's band in London.

Before leaving Lerwick we embarked a team of film cameramen, led by Bill McQuitty, who were making the film 'Above Us the Waves' aboard the GATES-HEAD. They took a lot of 'location' shots during the exercise, which were later used in the film.

We did take them out on XE8 on short trips, to get some shots while we were based at Folleso which, by the way, was most hospitable.

The harbour master came on board GATESHEAD on arrival, and spent some time chatting over a whisky or two. The following morning we received a basket of fresh crabs and a side of Norwegian smoked salmon. All the crabs were eviscerated and prepared aboard GATESHEAD, so I recollect that was our staple diet throughout the stay.

The Attack

The passage to Norway went well and we had arrived before dawn in good conditions with enough sea to mask the radar echo, but after taking over from the Passage Crew, I was able to trim down and run in the last few miles lying flat on the casing. We dived at first light and passed Marsten light into the fjord. This approach took us to Byfjord and Bergen from the South and I planned to go to the West of Lille Sotry, passing through a restricted gap at its northern end back into the main fjord, as this would advance us some way with little likelihood of meeting any patrols.

Unfortunately, very early on the periscope flooded-up and I had no option but to surface, display the 'out of exercise' signal, and let the E.R.A. work on it. He put it right in good time but not before an air patrol had passed over and I had little doubt that the defence now knew which way we were coming.

However, our track to the west of the island would not then have been apparent and indeed, we emerged from the gap to see an SDB busily patrolling to the South in the main fjord. The exit was not without excitement as there was a little less water than the chart showed and it was a tight squeeze. Also we passed round a small islet to find two Norwegians fishing from a dinghy, to our mutual surprise, as I raised the periscope.

The water was by now glassy calm and before long we encountered more of the SDB patrols. The first we eluded but were picked up by the next patrol and after completing the formalities of the A/S exercise, we had to surface and withdraw to our rendezvous with GATESHEAD (who effectively accompanied us everywhere)'.

The Asdic-equipped ML, 3515, which had picked them up, became, soon afterwards, one of the Seaward Defence Boats for whom XE8 had been sunk as a target, off Portland.

In 1976 XE8 was raised from the bottom, to await restoration in Chatham Historic Dockyard. Apart from X24, she is the only one of the wartime midgets to have survived in anything like recognisable form. The peacetime-built X51 is in much better shape and is already preserved at the Imperial War Museum's Outstation at Duxford, Cambridgeshire.

Various Midget Submarines are displayed around the world. A Japanese 'Sydney Harbour' one in Sydney; at least one 'Pearl Harbour' craft remains. There is also one in Japan; one or two 'English Channel' ones somewhere in Germany and no less than eight small submarines of various nationalities are on view to the public around America. There's even a German 'Molch' on display in a leafy harbour in Cape Town! Hugh Verry:-

Later Attacks

For the remainder of the Exercise period, we carried out a series of exercises with the Seaward Defences, culminating in an attack on MAIDSTONE in Bergen harbour. This went well for us and we got up the Byfjord to the net defences without being detected. We then managed to pass through the gate whilst it was opened for an MFV to enter harbour, under cover of the MFV noise. We lined up on MAIDSTONE and after going deep, the good light and clear water made it easy to confirm that we had arrived beneath her. Raising the 'fingers', we spent a few minutes against her bottom.

We then dropped off and withdrew, coming to periscope depth. At this moment, we suffered an unbelievable misfortune in that as I raised the periscope for the first time, it came up directly against the bottom of an untenanted mooring buoy! The tip was in fact bent over, and I was completely blind. In the exercise environment, safety clearly required that we surface and leave the exercise without knowing if we could have withdrawn as successfully as we had entered.

We then started the passage back to Portland, with XE8 in tow of GATESHEAD.

When we left Bergen, we went down the leads between the islands to Stavanger, before turning into the North Sea. Nowadays there is a causeway across one of the leads where we navigated, but it does have a small gate in it.

It was a very scenic passage and most enjoyable, until we noticed a disagreeable and increasingly strong odour. Consulting the chart showed that we were approaching a fish manure factory and that we still had some way to go before passing it. At its peak, the smell was overpowering but I suppose the locals had become immune.

On the way back, we were instructed to divert to the Thames and spend a few days in London. The trip from Stavanger to the Thames estuary took about three and a half days and we arrived in thick fog, and anchored for the night somewhere off Canvey Island.

The next day GATESHEAD went to a buoy just off the Tower, after having had the bascules of Tower bridge raised for her.

For us, the trip up the river was calm, but we were towed on the surface and the shallow water effect meant that the stern dropped to an extent that it put half the ensign staff (brass) below the surface. It took a very long time to get that properly clean again.

The three most memorable events during the visit were:-

1) Lt. Cdr. Tony Troup (later Vice Admiral Sir Anthony Troup K.C.B. D.S.C. and bar R.N.), Senior Officer X Craft, and I paid a call on the Lord Mayor in the Mansion House and I still have a photograph of us, with the Lord mayor in his regalia.

2) XE8 went up river to make a call on the Captain of PRESIDENT alongside the Embankment. This had its excitements, as we went up on the flood tide, returning on the ebb. The force of the tide was such that we passed under the bridges at a most exhilarating speed, and when I turned to come up alongside PRESIDENT against the tide, XE8's best efforts at full ahead group up, were barely able to make any headway at all. We got there in the end.

3) In those days there used to be a weekly Radio programme called 'In Town Tonight', which featured personalities or unusual visitors in London that week. I was invited to take part in this and was interviewed about X Craft and XE8.

There cannot have been many visitors to 'In Town Tonight' who had arrived in London off a submarine, of any sort.

Part 4 - A Potted History Of The Later XCraft

By Lt. Donald Cameron V.C., R.N.R. who was Senior Officer and C.O. of GATESHEAD 1950-52

XE7 EXUBERANT
Launched February 1945
Late in 1946, Degaussing Tests at Southsea (Clarence Pier).
Sept. 1947, Hydrogen Content trials at Barrow.
At DOLPHIN, Dec. 1947.
1950. To Norfolk Virginia, U.S.A.
1953, Broken up.

XE8 EXPUNGER
Launched April 1945
1946, U/water exercises at Devonport followed by DG tests at Southsea.
At DOLPHIN Dec. 1947.
Rail to Faslane in 1949 (see launching).
July 1949, Hydrogen Content Trials at Barrow.
1950-52, Harbour penetration Exercises, Plymouth Sound and Dartmouth.
1952, NATO Exercises off N. coast of France, Cherbourg and in to Bergen, Op. 'Mainbrace'. (Involved in film 'Above Us the Waves'.)
1960. Sunk as bottom target for S.D.B. off Portland.
1976. Raised and taken to Duxford I.W.M.
1987 Transferred to Chatham Historic Dockyard to await restoration.
Posterity lives!

XE9 UNEXPECTED

Launched March 1945
April 1945. Noise Trials at Loch Goil.
At DOLPHIN Dec. 1947.
Feb. 1949. Hydrogen Content Trials at Barrow.
1950-51. Caledonian Canal en route for Op. 'Castanet' in Moray Firth.
Forth and Clyde Canal to Grangemouth and Rosyth.
1952. To Norfolk, Virginia, U.S.A.
1953. Involved in film 'Seagulls over Sorrento' in Portland.
1953. Broken up.

XE12 EXCITABLE
Launched April 1945 went straight into reserve.
1952. Courtesy visit to Cobh, Southern Ireland, Scilly Isles And Dartmouth.
Gave Navy Day exhibitions at Portsmouth, Chatham and Sheerness.
Broken up 1953.

X51 STICKLEBACK
Launched July 1954
1955 By rail to Faslane, trials in the Clyde then by rail to Portland .
1956-7. Exercises 'Bent Pin 1 and 2', Net Penetration Trials at Rosyth.
Courtesy calls to Exeter and Dartmouth.
1957-8. Sold to Swedish Navy as SPIGER. Returned to I.W.M. at Duxford in 1976
and beautifully restored.
(Should be re-christened Sore Point because it ought to have gone to DOLPHIN
along with the remains of X7.)

X52 SHRIMP
Launched September 1954
By Rail to Faslane, trials in the Clyde, then by rail to Portsmouth where she
was put into reserve in the dockyard.
Traversed the canals of W. Riding of Yorkshire on a promotional tour.
Broken up in 1966 at Faslane.

X53 SPRAT
Launched January 1955
By Rail to Faslane, trials in the Clyde, then by rail to Portsmouth also to go
into reserve in the dockyard.
Broken up in 1966 at Faslane

X54 MINNOW
Launched May 1955. Lt R. Compton-Hall M.B.E; R.N. (Now Cdr Compton-Hall
Director of Submarine Museum).
By Rail to Faslane for Acceptance trials. Returned to Barrow where trial

Shrouded
Tail unit fitted. Returned to Clyde for comparison trials (very little difference).
By Rail to Portsmouth and thence by sea to Portland.
Cdr. D. Lund was relieved as C.O. by Lt. Richard Compton-Hall.
After X54's launch X Craft Unit adopted by Perkins Diesels. Three days of
junketing in Portland followed.
Broken up in 1956.

From The Director Of The Royal Navy Submarine Museum

Commander R. Compton-Hall R.N.:-

X Craft were not concerned with their appearance. They kept a low profile, in both senses of the word, and were flat, long and narrow, with bits sticking-out and were frankly unattractive. Looks are not everything. The Midgets, and the Chariots, when properly employed, were quite possibly the most effective and least expensive underwater craft devised in any modern Navy. Although cost-effectiveness was not a term coined until after their premature demise. They can now be recognised as outstandingly good examples of this much-sought-after principle. It is significant that X Craft survivors adapted quickly to command and responsible positions when the opportunity arose, in the post-war naval and civilian worlds. There were probably two principal reasons at the end, for disbanding the Royal Navy's X craft Unit at this point, when the equivalents in other navies had long since crossed the Rubicon.

One, undoubtedly resulted from Whitehall's directive to sacrifice a specific number of submarine hulls, in the usual well-known interests of economy. Whitehall unwisely, failed to specify the size of the sacrificial hulls and so, it was reasonably rumoured, Flag Officer Submarines flung four X Craft to the fire, bows foremost.

There may have been a longer underlying reason for their sudden disappearance. Midget submarine exercises and evaluations tended to be frankly hairy, happily hairy, but hairy none the less. The sort of training they were bound to undertake in order to maintain realistic wartime efficiency in peacetime, was liable to attract the type of publicity that Naval officers concerned with P.R. have always tried, more in hope than in anger, to avoid.

Nevertheless as we have seen, the use of midgets for oceanographic purposes is increasing all the time and, once again, they are being made 'all over the place'.

If the crew of XE8 had got ashore at Cherbourg when they were in Bergen on the third occasion, perhaps the locals would have sent them on their way with a rousing:- 'Vive Les Nains!' (Long Live the Midgets.)

In Praise of XE's by Lt. Cdr. Matthew Todd

Providing the discomfort could be borne, the XE Class were splendid sea boats and unbeatable. XE8 ran like a clock. The only defects we had in a year were the usual minor ones.

To save a great deal of charging, I could pull off a whole day of ping-running and never use the main motor. The Gardner engine took a 6ft head of water over the exhaust well in its stride'.

It was a crying shame that more jobs could not have been found for these cheap, simple and robust little submarines, and that they had not been allowed to justify their existence a lot more than they were.

One has only to think of the imaginative use made of their 'sneak craft' by the Italians early in the War before (and after), they changed sides!

With respect to that great Leader of men, and Coiner of Phrases, Mr Churchill, if he had been less concerned with the 'weaker naval power' (which Submarines were supposed to denote) and given more thought to 'Stealth' and 'Imagination' and Unconventional Warfare, these craft might have beaten the Italians at their own game. It wasn't until the devastating blow to us, of the lengthy loss of the QUEEN ELIZABETH and VALIANT by Italian frogmen, that the change of heart occurred. Thereafter Mr Churchill's support for both types of Sneak Craft, was wholehearted and strong.

But we won the War didn't we? and if there had been many more midget submarine and human torpedo operations perhaps there would not have been so many men happily walking around today'.

BIBLIOGRAPHY

Fell, Captain. 'The Sea our Shield'.
Fell, Captain. Article in Blackwoods Magazine 1948, 'H.M.S. BONAVENTURE'.
Hastings, Max. 'Overlord' published by Book Club Associates in conjuction with Michael Joseph, 1984.
Morgan, Guy. 'Only Ghosts can Live' published by Crosby Lockwood & Son Ltd 1945.
Peillard, Leonce. 'Sink the TIRPITZ' published by Jonathan Cape 1968.
Strutton and Pearson. 'The Secret Invaders' published by Evans Brothers Ltd 1950.
Warren and Benson. 'Above us the Waves' published by George G. Harrap & Co. Ltd.
Brown, David. 'TIRPITZ'.
Fraser, Ian. 'Frogmen V.C.' published by Harper Collins Ltd.

Tributes To Commander H.L. Rendel R.N.

Guy Rendell (his son) :-

Rabbit Rendel, so-called because he was of short stature and reputed to be able to get down a conning tower hatch quicker than anyone else, was a World War I submariner who had been First Lieutenant of K1, when she was sunk in 1917. On escaping from this notorious steam-driven contraption, he had suffered ever afterwards from his severe dose of chlorine poisoning. Not only his lungs had been affected, but also his eyesight from prolonged squinting through the unocular periscope. He was invalided out of the Navy in 1920.

Despite these handicaps he was recalled in 1938 just before the outbreak of World War II, and performed immensely valuable work with the early prototype X Craft, and was soon back in the Submarine Service.

Before that happened, he had also served on submarines:- D1, B6, B11, B9, K1, F3, E25 and E46. The last two were at the Dardanelles and one, at least, had been stuck in the anti-submarine nets, so he'd had first hand experience of these kind of problems.

Between the wars, he worked as a director of a small engineering firm, in Warrington, Lancs. Thus he had an added background of industry and the 'ways' of North Country people, which he found a great asset. He also had innumerable friends in the R.N. Hence his 'corner cutting'.

The writer wishes she had met Commander Rendell when he was at Broadbent's for he was a charming and much loved man, and not only for his 'Contacts' and the corners he was thus able to cut, but she was away at the war herself at the time. Robert Barclay's tribute was also spontaneous and un-sought:-

He was marvellous, very nice, very helpful and an absolute entré to anywhere in the Admiralty to sort out problems, technical, contractual and procedural. He was a 1914/1918 Submariner himself so we spoke the same language.

His son, Guy's anecdotes of their relationship and his boyhood, are legion but the writer's favourite story concerns a certain Lady at the Hamble base. Guy Rendall:-

In the early days at Bursledon, a local lady of means and social standing, invited the R.N. officers at the X Craft base, to drinks:- 'I don't know what you are all doing, so hush-hush but I'll find out' she voiced.

The next day my father and the local Admiralty Provost Marshall called on her and read her the Official Secrets Act in the drawing room. Needless to say, she went off the R.N. a bit after this.

Guy concludes with a tribute to the writer's father:-

My father had the highest regard for Broadbent's and your father in particular, who was so kind to him when my brother was killed in action in 1944. Father certainly had no difficulty liaising with Broadbent's.

He also had a high regard for Mr Barclay at Markham's and Bill Hallitt, the 'M.D'. of Broadbent's was a tower of strength.

Father and I always thought that due recognition was never really given to the 'Manufacturing firms', nor to my father for that matter. There was some political factor that seemed to get in the way.

Perhaps this tribute will go some way towards redressing the balance, despite the fact that both fathers, Guy's, and the writer's have now joined that Great Coxswain in the Sky.

The Midget Submarine
Technical Information

Specification of X Craft

	Beam	Length
X3	5ft 6 ins	44ft
X4	,, ,,	45ft
X5-10	5ft 9 ins	51ft
XT1-4	,, ,,	51ft
XT5-6	,, ,,	53ft
XE's	,, ,,	53ft

Side Cargoes or Charges

Each charge is 30ft long, together they weigh 5½ tons in air and each carries 3,570lb i.e. 2 tons of Amatex. The charge is neutrally buoyant while being carried. Cylindrical buoyancy chambers connected by pipes are flooded on release, so that the charge readily bottoms. Flooding arrangements include an air trap, to prevent bubbles rising to surface and alerting the enemy. Two more large faired buoyancy tanks are bolted to the charge at each end but do not flood.

Speed on Towing

The average speed on being towed through the water submerged was 9 knots. The greatest speed achieved was 13 knots from a 'T' class submarine. At 11 knots, the diameter of tow rope is reduced from 5½" to 4½", and the X Craft tends to dive forcibly!

Towing

X Craft tow better submerged at about 40ft beneath the point of tow. X Craft on surface must not exceed 7 knots. In bad weather 4 knots. Even at full buoyancy craft tends to be towed under at speeds of 8 knots or more.

With a submerged X Craft under tow and in perfect trim, there is always a tendency for the tow to pull her up to the surface. So auxiliary ballast is pumped in. Great care must be taken if there is a danger of tow parting, for craft will then carry on to the bottom unless remedial action is taken.

If out of trim craft will be liable to porpoise between the surface and 100ft with increasing violence.

Rapid variations in speed must be avoided like the plague (increases less so) and may force X Craft to surface. In a rough sea, this will strain the tow and 'shake liver and lights' out of the crew.

Under no circumstances must submerged X Craft be towed over patches of water with less than 15 fathoms. If she touches the bottom, side charges may be loosened or ripped off. Damage to X Craft through failure on part of a submarine C.O. to comply with this rule, can only logically be followed by his 'hara-kiri'.

Limpet Charges

Up to 14 can be carried by X Craft, two stowed in the casing and six each side in carriers (which differed in shape only slightly from the side cargoes).

The limpets that Fraser and Magennis used on Op. 'Struggle', were roughly triangular in shape and had two large handles fitted to the main case. A combined counter-mining and anti-removal switch was also fitted. Dimensions were approximately 3 ft x 1 ft x 2 ft.

Flooding-up the Wet and Dry compartment

The diver squatted in solitary confinement on the heads (W.C.) in the W. and D. while the compartment was being flooded, (from an internal tank, to avoid upsetting the trim). Icy water gradually rose up past him until it reached the top of the compartment. At this point, water being incompressible, the pump exerted all its energy on each and every compressible portion of the diver's body. It also flattened his breathing bag and left him temporarily gasping for breath. This phenomenon was known, without affection, as The Squeeze.

Assuming that the diver survived The Squeeze, he was then free to equalise pressure inside and out by means of a valve, open the upper hatch and go about his business.

The reverse procedure was in force when the diver returned to the W. and D. and then the control room. Except that in one X Craft in particular it took 10 to 15 minutes to shut the lid, and some juggling with valves was found to be necessary.

Anti-submarine and anti-torpedo nets

These were like curtains, made from either thick wire oblong mesh or interlocking steel wire grommets and suspended from buoys. Approaching a harbour, the Captain searched for the give-away buoys through the main periscope, which had a lens the size of a thumbnail. The Anti Submarine nets were obviously of a larger mesh than the Anti Torpedo nets.

Tow Ropes

The original tow ropes were manila. The new innovatory nylon ones, although they had been used with gliders for a year or two, could only be rushed to half of the six X Craft, before they all left for Op. 'Source' in 1943.

The special manila tow ropes were about 600ft long with a breaking strain of 11 tons. A single core rubber sheathed phone wire was laid-up in the centre of each of 3 strands, which comprised the tow rope (circumference 5½ inches).

Main tows were made up to suit each submarine and the particular X Craft in tow. The spare set, which was carried on the submarine, was interchangeable but carried no telephone cable.

When the tow parted on Op. 'Foil' en route for Hong Kong, it was the spare set which was in use, due to the hurried departure. Had they had time to fit the proper set, it would not have happened. Unusually, it all ended happily.

The nylon tow ropes were again 600ft long and 5½ inches in circumference with 3 telephone wires laid-up inside. Minus the 'phone cable, they cost £700 It was a lot of money in those days. A phosphor bronze thimble in the tow rope eye had a built-in junction box for the phone wire with 6ft 'tail' leading away.

Nylon will give stretch of 35% before breaking. The breaking strain is 25 tons. In theory, the 'Unistretch' 'phone cable gave almost 100% stretch with a breaking strain of 500lb. In practice the 'phone cable's insulation contracted under strain and gripped the wire. Which is why it broke down so often on operations.

The Cutter

This was in shape and size rather like a large electric drill, but instead of the chuck a hook had been rigged called the anvil, against which the cutter blade bore. The body of the cutter was in fact a hydraulic cylinder which drove a piston, I guess about 3 inches in diameter, by hydraulic pressure through a hose from inside the craft. The pressure on the hardened steel blade driven forward by the piston was of the order of 5 or 6 tons. A pistol trigger grip controlled the operation of the cutter, which came slowly forward to bite into anything between it and the anvil, and bite it did, most impressively. When not required for use it was stowed in a locker in the casing. There was about 40 feet of hose so that a diver could work with it all round, over and under the craft.

The Grapnel

Various designs had been tried, but the one used was a diamond shaped plate of steel, about half an inch thick, with flukes welded on to each side and called a Flatfish type. The plate was about 2 foot long, and 18 inches wide. The flukes stood up about 10 inches from the plate. The grapnel was secured by a length of wire and chain to the towing release slip in the bows of the craft. A bridle was rigged around the craft amidships so that when not actually dragging on the bottom the grapnel hung beneath the craft by about four feet. This arrangement permitted the craft to manoeuvre satisfactorily with the grapnel in use.

It was reassuring to know that the grapnel could be released from inside the craft if need be:- there was no appeal in the idea that one might hook firmly onto something and be unable to surface.

Oxygen Poisoning

This was liable to attack any diver who was breathing pure oxygen, should he go deeper than the safe depth of 33 ft. It could be worse in some ways than 'the bends' for it caused twitching of the lips, convulsions of the rest of the body, hallucinations then coma and if the diver were not brought to the surface very quickly, death. However, unlike 'the bends', provided the diver surfaced quickly enough, it had no great lasting effects. After coming out of the water and breathing air again he would regain consciousness and after perhaps a short sleep followed by a terrific headache, he would be back to his normal self.

Sometimes the man was affected mentally in that he would be scared of diving, but this was rare.

Normally all it did was to teach him to be more careful in future and to treat 'Oxygen Pete' with more respect.

Oxygen 'Pete'

'Pete' was the brain-child of one of the ratings in the Experimental Diving Unit who were the 'guinea pigs' in experiments with oxygen diving at Siebe Gorman's factory at Tolworth in 1942. The rating composed a poem, warning divers who went down into 'The Pot' (a wet and dry compression tank) to take heed when feeling the first twitching of the lips and to rush up the ladder and switch themselves on to "air". Otherwise they were in grave danger of being severely mauled by a demon who lurked there. Unfortunately the poem was only chalked on to a blackboard and was subsequently rubbed off. The only lines which can be remembered at present are the last two:-

> For down at a depth of seventy feet
> Lives a guy by the name of Oxygen Pete

Trim

A state of buoyancy as near neutral as possible, with the craft floating level fore and aft.

Positive buoyancy - light trim.

Negative buoyancy - heavy trim.

When an object floats on the surface, it is said to have positive buoyancy. If it sinks to the bottom, it is said to have negative buoyancy. If it floats beneath the surface it is said to have neutral buoyancy.

In a submarine, enough water should be carried in the ballast tanks to give the craft a neutral buoyancy:- i.e. it should be able to float beneath the surface of the water with its depth regulated by the use of the hydroplanes.

A submarine in this state of buoyancy is said to have a 'Perfect Trim'. To be able to reach this state of perfection, requires adroit manipulation of the pumps and vents. If the craft tends to rise in the water of its own accord the Trim is too light and the valves on the ballast tanks should be opened letting more outside water enter and so making the craft heavier. If the craft is trimmed down too heavy, water must be pumped out of the tanks so making it lighter.

The submarine should be on an even keel and floating level in the water. If she tends to be lower in the water at the stern, water must be pumped from the stern ballast tanks to the forward ones and vice-versa.

Although a submarine with a good Trim may normally be taken to different depths by the use of main motors and hydroplanes only, there are times when more speed is required in diving, to escape detection and attack by surface forces. On occasions like this, more water is allowed to enter the ballast tanks, so increasing the weight of the craft and making it descend quicker.

The term 'crash dive' beloved of of film people and novelists, is virtually unknown in Submarines and certainly in X Craft, it isn't in the Manual! Trim was caught and maintained by a joy stick controlled pump and shown on the inclinometer gauge with a bubble.

The catching of a perfect or near perfect Trim is a difficult enough process on a large submarine but aboard an X Craft, with its smaller tanks and smaller quantities of water to be moved from one place to another, the margin of error is consequently much smaller. Where on a big submarine the Trim must be correct to the nearest cupful, in an X Craft it would be to the nearest thimbleful!

Credits

The List of Credits is virtually endless but those who have put pen to paper more than ten times, on the writer's behalf, are in the Top Ten. Those who have sent her maps, logs, albums of photos, difficult to obtain information and memorabilia are in the next Top Ten.

Eternal gratitude is felt towards:-

Gus Britton :- Former Signaller, Royal navy. Chief Archivist at the R.N. Submarine Museum, Gosport.

Sid Woollcott D.S.M. Former Petty Officer (Charioteer) Technical Advisor. ALSO

Peter Broadbent (former Chairman of Broadbents) Brian Cross, VARBEL II and Paul of X25, Stan Pulham, George Skuse, John Bowman, Robert Barclay, Ken Briggs, Alan Wilkie, Ken Hudspeth, Geoff Crowe, Vernon 'Ginger' Coles, Jim McCaughan, Jim Skelton, Ivor Jarvis, Alan Kevan, Guy Rendell, Dave Perkins, Jessie Wilson, Louis Sheppard, Bill Reid, Frank Flintoft, Marjorie Warwick, Pat Westmacott, Carl Brunning, S. D. Christie, Dennis Easom, Stan Johnson, Dick Kendall, Joyce Macdougall, Peter Philip, John Ruse, Max Shean, Kenneth Scott, Jo Terry Lloyd, Hugh Verry, Eli 'Tubby' Whittaker, John Norton.

Robert Aitken, Fred Ainslie, Frank Butler, David Brown, Colin Burrow, David Brock, Terry Bishop, Ian Clifton, Ian Fraser, Barbara Howgego, George Honour, Peter Kern, Jack Laird, John Lorimer, Hazel Lloyd-Jones, Bill Pomeroy, Angela Radford, Logan Scott-Bowden, Guy Todd, John Tufnell, Matthew Todd, J. C. Varley,

Doris Wright, Bill West-Firth, Geoff Harding and Bill Morrison, Bill Buckley.

Bill Carlow, H. E. G. Booth, Corrie Ford, James 'Tubby' Fishleigh, Jack Fletcher, Alex Ferrier, Eddie Goddard, J. C. Hardie, Keith Hornby-Priestnall, Squire Jones, John Lindop, 'Mitch' Matthews, N. F. Moulsdale, A. D. Mackay, Gordon Newman, Alan Pawson, Tom Pocock, Godfrey Place, Arthur Rubery, Tony Renouf, Tom Robinson, Sheard Sykes, H. Urmston, Jas. Williams, Martin Wemyss, Arnold Wilson, Tom Willmott, W. M. Waterhouse, R. V. Wallingford, Roy Broome and R. R. McCurrach, John Fraser and Mr. Harrison.

Not forgetting the Naval Artist John Makin, the two illustrators:- Norman Tacey and John Makin; Roger the Photographer; Chris the Map-maker and my highly-commended and long-suffering typist, Eileen Stallard.

Also:- The equally long-suffering neighbours in Lymington, Mr and Mrs A. Prior.

Plus; the B.B.C.; Gardner Diesel; Perkins Engines; the Imperial War Museum (at both premises); the National Maritime Museum, the Public Record Office, the Hayling Island Yacht Club (COPP memorial), Commander Compton-Hall M.B.E. R.N. and the staff of the R.N. Submarine Museum, especially Margaret Bidmead.

Decorations
This one small branch of the Senior Service received:-
4 Victoria Crosses
8 Distinguished Service Orders
15 Distinguished Service crosses
2 Conspicuous Gallantry Medals
4 Distinguished Service medals
26 Mentions in Dispatches

This list does not include the decorations awarded to the Human Torpedo men (charioteers) who were part of the same flotilla.

In Memoriam For Those X-Craft Men Who Have No Known Grave But The Sea.

Albert J. Brammer	Leading Stoker *Rolled of the casing*	Sept. 1944
David Carey	Lt. R. N. *Diving Accident*	July 1945
Bruce Enzer	Lt. R. N. V. R. *Diving Accident*	July 1945
A. H. Harte	Ordinary Seaman *Lost on Operation Source*	Sept. 1943
H. Henty-Creer	Lt. R. N. V. R. *Lost on Operation Source*	Sept. 1943
G. H. Hollett	Stoker *Lost on Operation Source*	Sept. 1943
P. J. Hunt	S/Lt. R. N. V. R. *Fell Overboard*	April 1944
E. Kearon	S/Lt. R. N. V. R. *Lost on Operation Source*	Sept. 1943
Cyril Ludbrooke	E. R. A. *Lost on X22*	Feb. 1944
David H. Locke	S/Lt. R. N. V. R. *Lost on whlst net cutting*	May 1943
A. D. Malcolm	S/Lt. R. N. V. R. *Lost on Operation Source*	Sept. 1943
W. S. Marsden	Lt. R. N. A. V. R. *Lost on X22*	Feb. 1944
B. M. McFarlane	Lt. R. A. N. *Lost on X22*	Feb. 1944
Ralph Mortiboys	E. R. A. *Lost on Operation Source*	Sept. 1943

Tom J. Nelson	S/Lt. R. N. V. R.	Sept. 1943
	Lost on Operation Source	
John Pretty	Able Seaman	Feb. 1944
	Lost on X22	
D. N. Purdy	S/Lt. R. N. Z. N. V. R.	Sept. 1944
	Lost on Operation Heckle	
I. Morgan Thomas	S/Lt. R. N. V. R.	Dec. 1942
	Lost off X4	
W. M. Whitley	E. R. A.	Sept. 1943
	Lost on Operation Source	

Only Four Casualties Have A Known Grave

Rothesay Cemetery

J. J. Carroll	Able Seaman	March 1945
	Lost on XE11	
E. W. Higgins	Stoker	March 1945
	Lost on XE11	
Aubrey Staples	Lt. S. A. N. F. (V.)	March 1945
	Lost on XE11	

Tromso Cemetery

| L. B. Whittam | Lt. R. N. V. R. | Sept. 1943 |
| | *Lost on Operation Source* | |

GLOSSARY

Afternoon Watch	The 24 hours of each day in an R.N. ship are divided into five 'watches' of four hours each and two 'dog watches' of two hours each. The Afternoon Watch is from 12 noon to 4 pm. The two dog watches are to obviate being on the same watches every day.
ANX	Advanced Navigation Exercises
APX	Advanced Penetration Exercises
A/S Nets	Anti - Submarine Nets. Made of steel wire rope about ½" in diameter with a rectangular mesh 2' 6" x 2' hung on a jackstay attached to a line of spherical buoys. They hung usually from the surface to the sea bottom.
A/T Nets	Anti - Torpedo Nets. Made of rigid steel wire ring grommets interlaced with one another and hung from buoys in the same way as the A/S Nets. Being of a much heavier construction, they were only 50ft. in depth. The buoys would not support a greater depth. They were sometimes laid around the ship in 2 or 3 lines, hung at various depths some on wire hanging from the buoys so that each line of nets overlapped the next one.
Asdics	Echo - sounding apparatus for the detection of submarines and other objects under the water (nowadays known as 'Sonar').
B.D.V.	Boom Defence Vessel. Small vessel specially equipped for the laying and lifting up of A/S and A/T Nets.
Baffles	Floating pontoons used as moorings.

Bath	Canvas swimming pool rigged on upper deck of large ships in the tropics and used aboard BONAVENTURE.
Bird Bath	Term used in submarines to describe a temporary bowl-shaped canvas receptacle rigged in the control room during rough weather to catch water washed over the bridge and down the conning tower.
Blow	Expel water from ballast tanks by means of compressed air to bring the submarine to the surface.
Buttoned Up	Made fast the tow.
C.O.	Commanding Officer or 'Captain'.
Cdr. (E.)	Engineer Commander.
Cdr. (X.)	Commander in overall charge of X-Craft on BONAVENTURE.
Chariots	Human Torpedoes powered by electric motors and controlled by two men (Charioteers) sitting astride. They were fitted with warheads, which were detached and secured by magnets to the bottoms of enemy ships in harbour and exploded by means of time fuses.
Clynometer	A spirit level showing the angle of the boat in the water.
CQR	A type of lightweight quick release anchor. Its initials represent the word Se-cu-re.
Compensating Tanks	Auxiliary ballast tanks which were used to catch a trim by pumping water into or out of the boat to obtain the correct buoyancy or used to keep the craft level by pumping water from the

forward tanks to the after tanks or vice-versa. Or to compensate for loss of weight caused by the use of fuel oil, firing torpedoes etc.

Consubs — American equivalent of British Admiral.

C/W Candidate — A Commission or Warrant Rating recommended to be trained as an officer.

D.S.E.A. — Davis Submarine Escape Apparatus. These breathing sets were carried in all submarines for escape purposes.

Deadlight — A steel hinged cover which is shut and clamped down over a scuttle, to protect the glass and prevent light from the ship from showing outside.

Degaussing — Reversing the magnetic field of a ship to avoid magnetic mines and torpedoes.

Denute — Density

Dhobeying — Washing - from Indian word 'dhobey', to launder.

Dit — Sailor's yarn anecdote joke etc. From the French, 'il dit' he says.

Ditty Box — A small wooden box once issued to sailors in which to keep small personal belongings, letters etc. 'Dittybox' was also the name of a popular naval magazine containing 'dits'.

Drip — To complain (slang).

Drip Tin — Metal tray used in the engine room to catch drips of oil from machinery. Also used to describe a man who was always grumbling.

E.A.	Electrical Artificer.
E.R.A.	Engine Room Artificer.
'E' Boats.	Fast German patrol boats, equivalent to our M.T.B.s
'First'	First Watch - 2000 hrs. to midnight.
'First Dog'	First Dog Watch - 1600hrs. to 1800hrs.
'Forenoon'	Forenoon Watch - 0800hrs to 12 noon.
Freeboard	The height above the waterline to the highest continuous watertight deck.
Fuel Compensation and Induction Valves.	Valves shut to prevent water flowing into the boat when induction trunk and fuel compensating pumps are not in use.
Gash	Rubbish or Spare.
Grass Line	A light buoyant rope.
Group Down	Run electric motors at slow speed.
Guff	Take in fresh air or fill breathing bag of D.S.E.A. set with oxygen.
H.M.T.	His Majesty's Trawler.
HHX	Loch Corrie
HHZ	Loch Cairnbawn
'Heads'	Name for the toilet on H.M. ships. In an X-Craft it was cramped, comfortless and complicated, and was emptied against the outside water pressure by means of a hand pump.

Hydroplanes	Rudders moving up or down to control upward or downward direction of craft.
ITX	Initial Training Exercise.
Induction Trunk	A rigid pipe which could be raised when the X-Craft was on or just below the surface to allow air to be sucked on to the main engines. It was lowered when the X-Craft was submerged.
Kingston Valves	These valves on the ballast tank vent, opened and shut to allow water to flow into the tank or to keep it out.
Kriegsmarine	The German Navy.
'Last Dog'	Last dog watch - 1800hrs. to 2000hrs.
LOCKU (boys)	Landing Craft Obstruction Clearance Unit
M.E.	Main Engine
M.L.s	Motor launches. Fast patrol vessels about 70ft long.
M.T.B.s	Motor Torpedo Boats
MAIDSTONE (H.M.S.)	Submarine Depot Ship
Main Motor Grouped Up	Travelling at high speed with batteries in parallel.
Main Vents	Valves on ballast tanks opened to allow air to escape when tanks are being flooded.
MALAYA (H.M.S.)	World War 1 battleship
'Middle'	Middle watch - midnight to 0400hrs.

'Morning'	The morning watch - 0400hrs. to 0800hrs.
Nissen huts	long semi-circular huts made of galvanized corrugated iron, used extensively in Service establishments.
Oiler	Small oil tanker used for re-fuelling ships in harbour.
1 and 1	One and One. A form of punishment for a minor offence. One day's stoppage of pay and one of leave.
Pay Bob	The Paymaster.
Ping running	Acting as target for anti-submarine vessels on exercise, testing their Asdic gear and training operators. When the target was located the Asdic set gave a 'ping' sound.
Pooped	When a large wave rolls up from astern and overwhelms the submarine.
Pusser	Derived from 'Purser'. Keeping strictly to the rules, doing everything by the book.
Q Tank	Emergency ballast tank usually kept full of water when boat is submerged. In emergency, when the submarine needs to be brought to the surface quickly, the water is blown out of it by compressed air, so making the S/m. lighter.
R.P.O.	Regulating Petty Officer.
R.N.Z.N.V.R.	Royal New Zealand Naval Volunteer Reserve.
S Boats	Submarines of the 'S' Class whose names all began with an S e.g. SAFARI, STORM, STYGIAN, SELENE etc.

S/12	Twelfth Submarine Flotilla
S/m	Submarine
S.T.	Seaman Torpedoman
S.U.E.	Signal Underwater Exploding
'Scratch'	A writer, usually the Captain's Secretary. Also the shortening of the nickname. 'Second Scratcher', given to the Second Coxswain in a submarine.
Scuttle	A porthole
Side Cargo	Crescent shaped explosive charges weighing almost 2 tons each, carried one on each side of an X-Craft.
T.s and Super T.s	Large submarines of the 'T' Class e.g. TRUGULENT, TRIBUNE etc.
'That'	A naval expression used during W.W. 2 as a mythical criteria for some great (or small) amount distance height, depth or other dimension being quoted (and exaggerated). 'How far did you have to walk to take her home?' 'Oh, further than that!'
The Line	The Equator - the crossing of it sometimes celebrated by a comic ceremony.
Tickler	Cigarettes made of duty free issue tobacco, mostly hand-rolled by the smoker himself.
Tropal suit	Waterproof suit padded with 'tropal', worn by X-Craft divers and Charioteers underneath the diving suit, to keep them warm.

Ursula suit

Light waterproof suit comprising jacket and trousers.

U/w

Underwater.

Vent

Allow water to flow into ballast tank.

Vent inboard

Allow air replaced in the ballast tank by water, to flow into the boat instead of into surrounding water outside and so betraying presence of the submarine.

W. and D.

Wet and Dry chamber. A water tight compartment in an X-Craft which the diver could enter when submerged. The compartment was then flooded in order to equalise the water pressure on both sides, so that the escape hatch could be opened, allowing the diver to leave the craft to cut nets etc. The toilet in an X-Craft was also located in the W. and D.

Walrus

Small flying boat used by the Navy. Commonly referred to as 'The Pusser's Spitfire'.

Wiped

Unofficial name for de-gaussed. (See under de-gaussed).

Wire Springs

Wire ropes used when mooring a vessel alongside to prevent its movement ahead or astern.

X-Craft

Midget Submarines. No names were given to them at their conception, only a number preceded by the letter 'X'.

Index of Names